PRAISE FOR *EXIT WOUNDS*:

"Modan's storytelling is likewise rich with subtle detail and nuance. The inevitable themes of politics, religion, and identity are addressed only obliquely; those looking for a grand statement on contemporary Israel are likely to be disappointed. Modan's tack instead is to concentrate on the mundanities of life as experienced by Israelis, life beyond the familiar images of young soldiers, peace activists, and the continual threat of violence."
—Matt Madden, *Bookforum*

"Modan is a deft and subtle storyteller, and her meditation on Israeli identity and the possibilities of love and trust (between father and son, woman and man) are finely wrought. Her loose, expressive drawing is both tremendously evocative and precise-always enhancing the plot. The stellar combination makes this one of the major graphic novels of 2007. Starred Review."
—*Publishers Weekly*

"A gritty, stunning graphic novel set in modern-day Tel Aviv, where terror and love brush against each other every day."
—Dan Kois, *New York Magazine*

"[An] excellent, searching examination of modern Israeli life."
—Craig Taylor, *The Guardian* (UK)

"The combination of styles is enthralling; the story is a mysterious journey that feels weighted with genuine regret and hope, and the whole makes for a beguiling introduction (to American readers, at least) to an artist at the peak of the form."
—Eric M. Hanson, *Minneapolis Star-Tribune*

"Deft artwork and the theme of loss partially regained make this one of the most poignant books of the year."
—R.C. Baker, *Village Voice*

"It's hard to imagine that Modan's book is fiction. Everything about the Israeli cartoonist's work rings authentic...It's my favorite graphic novel of 2007."
—Randy Myers, *San Jose Mercury News*

"Perfectly melding the personal and the political, *Exit Wounds* creates a sense of a life lived in a time of war but never quite dominated by it."
—Sam Adams, *Philadelphia City Paper*

"A frank examination of human life during wartime."
—Brian Heater, *NY Press*

"Produced in lavish full colour, *Exit Wounds* is an enormously attractive book, and Modan's striking talent for scenic arrangement, her distinctive jolie laide humans and her snappy grasp of dialogue give an absolutely cogent picture of the weirdness of life in contemporary Israel."
—Tim Martin, *The Independent* (UK)

"A novel that—in its classically clean visual lines and sharp, unsentimental portrayal of young love amid political turmoil—feels like a dream fusion of Hergé, Truffaut and Coetzee."
—Ian McGillis, *Montreal Gazette*

"The narrative keeps taking surprising but believable turns, and Modan avoids both melodramatic confrontations and tidy resolutions."

—Cliff Froelich, *St Louis Dispatch*

"Modan's artwork...is expressive and eye-popping throughout. When words fail-or rather, when Modan resists igniting the narrative's political spark-her depictions of cafes, graveyards, and street scenes create a vivid portrait of a culture that's still alien in the eyes of the Western world."

—Nick Green, *Washington City Paper*

"Comic artist Rutu Modan doesn't mean to humanize the Israeli-Palestinian conflict, it just comes naturally...Modan manages to subtly illuminate the existential confusion that hangs heavy over life in a war zone."

—Rebecca Weiner, *Heeb Magazine*

"*Exit Wounds* is the real thing. Modan brings you a world entire. The final panel of this tender and strange story offers an image half-hopeful, suspended in air. A wonderful book, and beautifully published to boot."

—Sam Leith, *Daily Telegraph* (UK)

"A rare triple threat of a book. *Exit Wounds* boasts superior, *ligne-claire*-style (clear line) drawings harnessed to some top-notch writing...then wrapped in a high-veracity narrative steeped in letter-perfect socio-political/psychological detail."

—Gilbert Bouchard, *Edmonton Journal*

"Warm, funny and touching, *Exit Wounds* is specific enough in its look at modern Israeli life to seem unique, but universal enough in its characters and themes to be easily recognizable. It's one of the best books you'll read this year."

—Chris Mautner, *Harrisburg Patriot News*

"It's immensely readable, beautifully coloured, and richly detailed, but Modan's real triumph is her treatment of the characters."

—Shawn Conner, *Vancouver Courier*

"Modan's art, like her writing, is technically sparse but emotionally rich."

—Rachel Leibrock, *Sacramento Bee*

"Deftly combining realistic family portraits, a compelling mystery and a vivid sense of life in modern Israel, *Exit Wounds* is as plausible as it is unpredictable-and it's impossible to put down."

—Erik Pedersen, *E! Online*

"An excellent storyteller, Modan balances plot and characterization well. Meanwhile, her art is intricate enough to fully evoke physical setting and cultural context."

—Francisca Goldsmith, *Booklist*

exit wounds rutu modan

Israel Lottery Council
for the Arts

Entire contents © copyright 2007, 2008, 2010 by Rutu Modan. All rights reserved. {Except the poem on page 28 by Sara Teasdale.} No part of this book (except small portions for review purposes) may be reproduced in any form without written permission from Rutu Modan or Drawn & Quarterly. Drawn & Quarterly; Post Office Box 48056, Montreal, Quebec, Canada H2V 4S8. www.drawnandquarterly.com; First hardcover printing: June 2007. First softcover edition: October 2008. Second printing: May 2010. Printed in China. 10 9 8 7 6 5 4 3 2; Library and Archives Canada Cataloguing in Publication; Modan, Rutu; Exit wounds / Rutu Modan. ISBN 978-1-897299-06-7; I. Title. NC1729.M63A64 2007 741.5'95694 C2006-905526-2; Distributed in the USA and abroad by Farrar, Straus and Giroux; 18 West 18th Street, New York, NY 10011; Orders: 888.330.8477. Distributed in Canada by Raincoast Books; 9050 Shaughnessy Street, Vancouver, BC V6P 6E5; Orders: 800.663.5714; Orders: 0208 8040400. Story advisor: Yirmi Pinkus. Acknowledgements: I would like to thank Yirmi Pinkus, for his eye-opening comments, ingenious solutions and advice; and Batia Kolton, who, in her nonchalant way, helped me more than I can say. There would be no book without either of you. Thanks to Chris Oliveros for convincing me that I was capable of creating this book. Thanks to my younger sister, Dana Modan, for guiding me through the writing process and to Noah Stollman for translating, editing, and giving me a title. Thanks to Rachel Marani of the Israel Cultural Excellence Foundation for her attentive support and to Thomas Gabison for his good words and intentions. For support and friendship: thanks to Itzik Renert, Mira Friedmann, Moran Palmoni and Lilian Bareto, Alona Palmoni, Orit Bergman, Orit Mazor and Yotam Burnstein, Meirav and Amnon Salomon-Dekel, Ephrat Beloosesky, Tamar and Zeev Bergman, and Zvia Cagan. Thanks to Tom Devlin for the design and for being so nice; to Shachar Kober—such a faithful assistant; to the real Koby Franco for his name; and to David Ofek—whose documentary *No 17.* inspired this story. Most of all, thank you to my patient husband Ofer Bergman.

exit wounds rutu modan
translation by noah stollman

drawn & quarterly
montréal

To Yirmi and Ofer.

chapter one
father figure

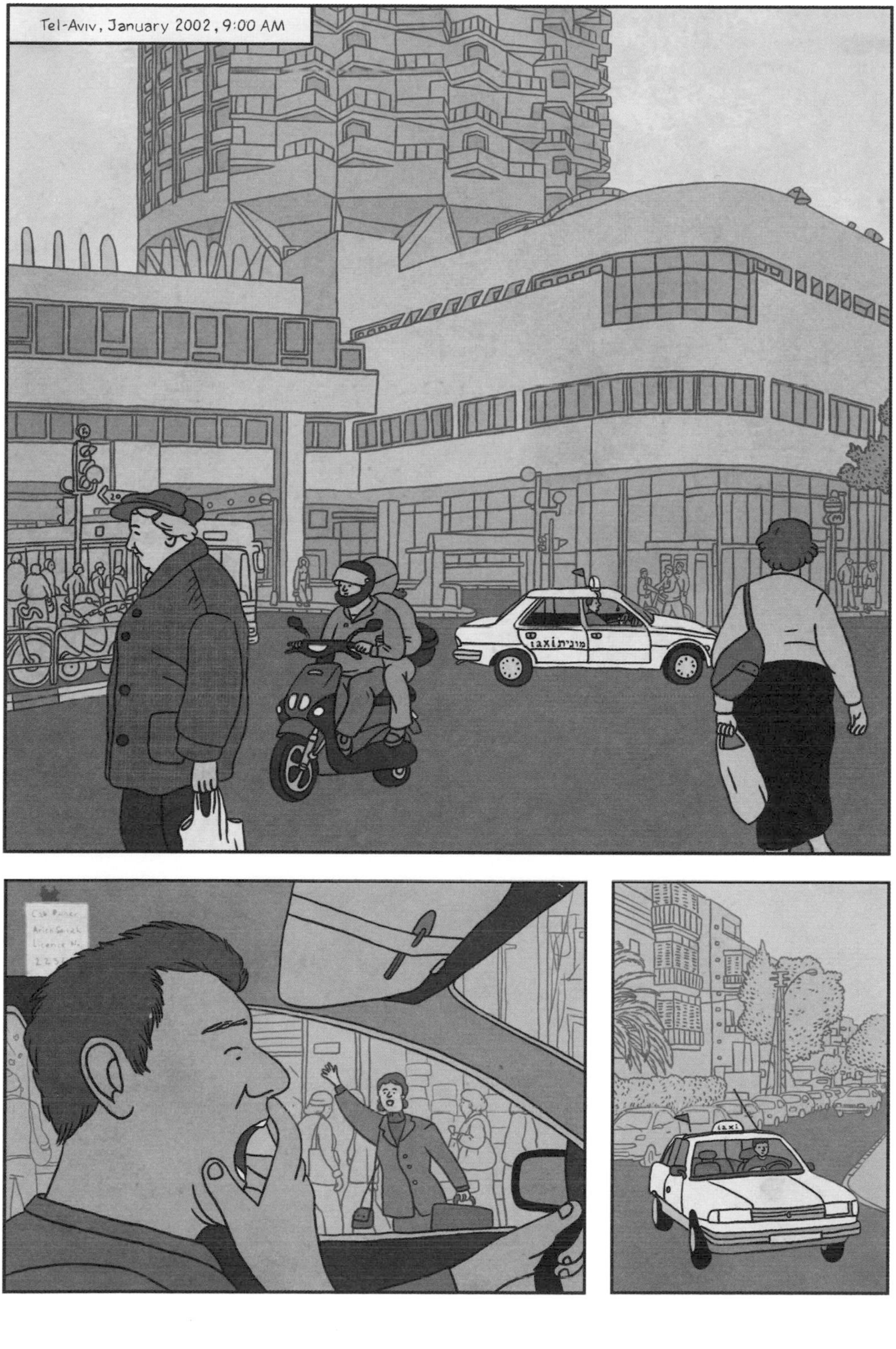
Tel-Aviv, January 2002, 9:00 AM

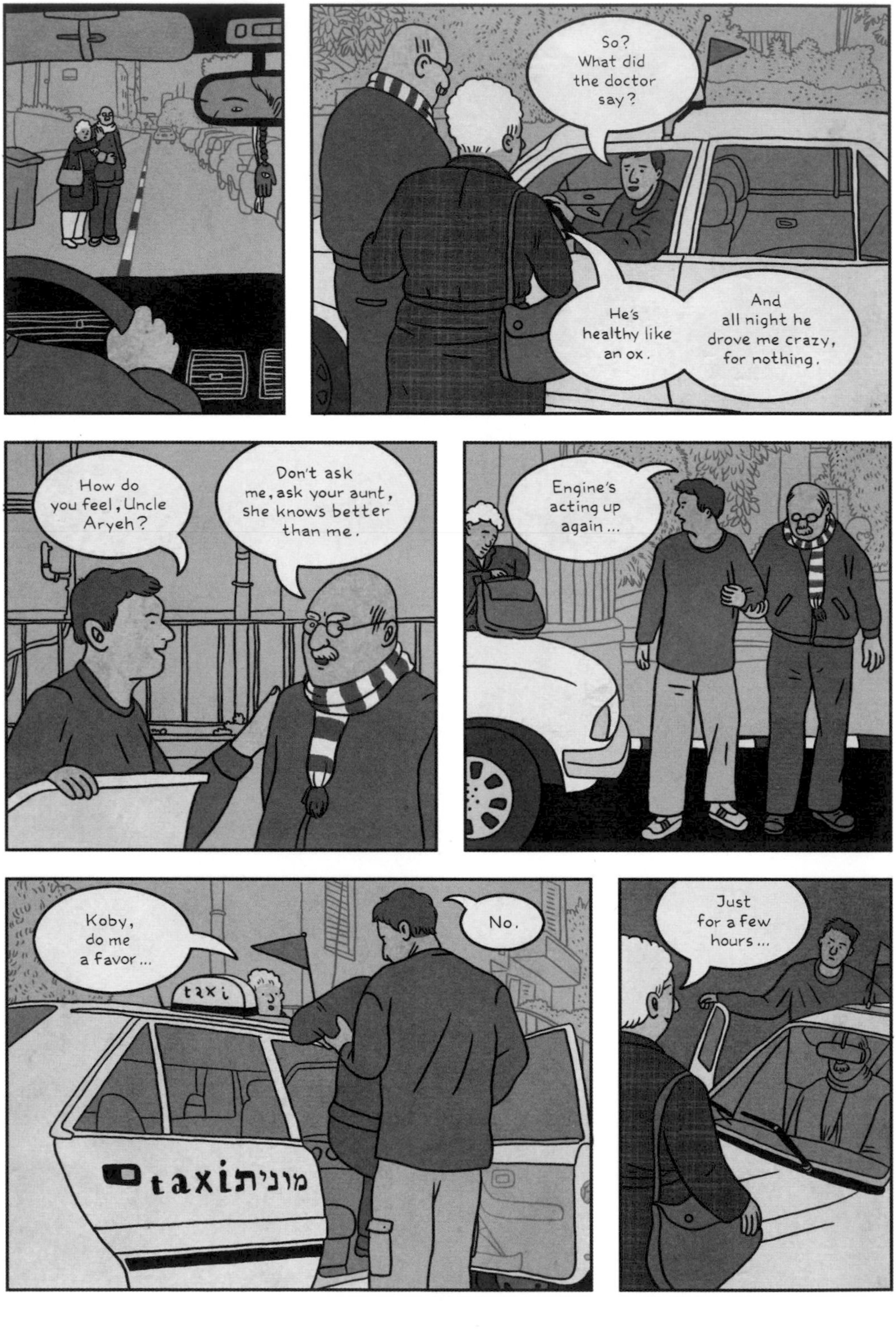
So? What did the doctor say?
He's healthy like an ox.
And all night he drove me crazy, for nothing.
How do you feel, Uncle Aryeh?
Don't ask me, ask your aunt, she knows better than me.
Engine's acting up again...
Koby, do me a favor...
No.
taxi
taxi מונית
Just for a few hours...

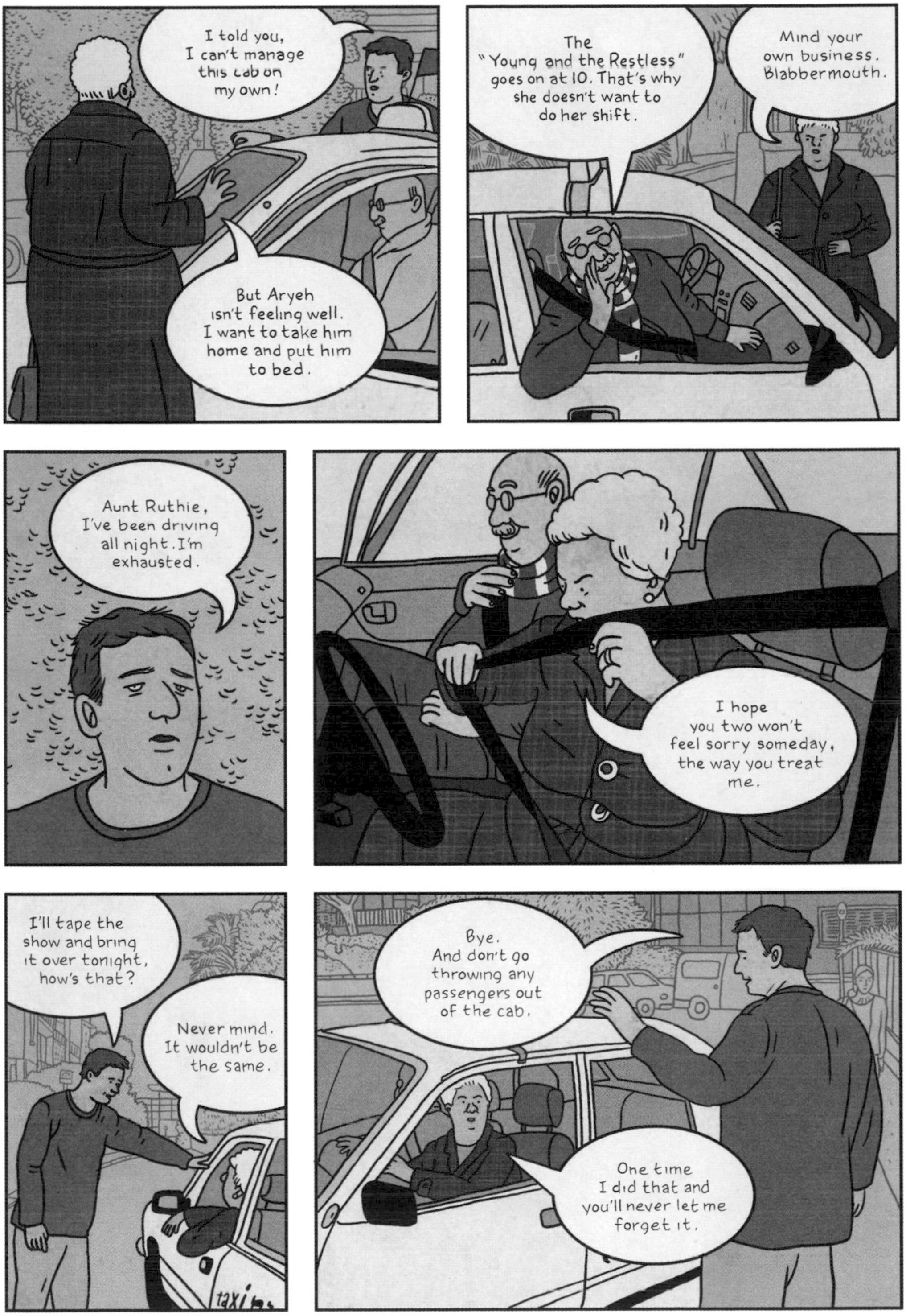
I told you, I can't manage this cab on my own!
But Aryeh isn't feeling well. I want to take him home and put him to bed.
The "Young and the Restless" goes on at 10. That's why she doesn't want to do her shift.
Mind your own business. Blabbermouth.
Aunt Ruthie, I've been driving all night. I'm exhausted.
I hope you two won't feel sorry someday, the way you treat me.
I'll tape the show and bring it over tonight, how's that?
Never mind. It wouldn't be the same.
taxi
Bye. And don't go throwing any passengers out of the cab.
One time I did that and you'll never let me forget it.

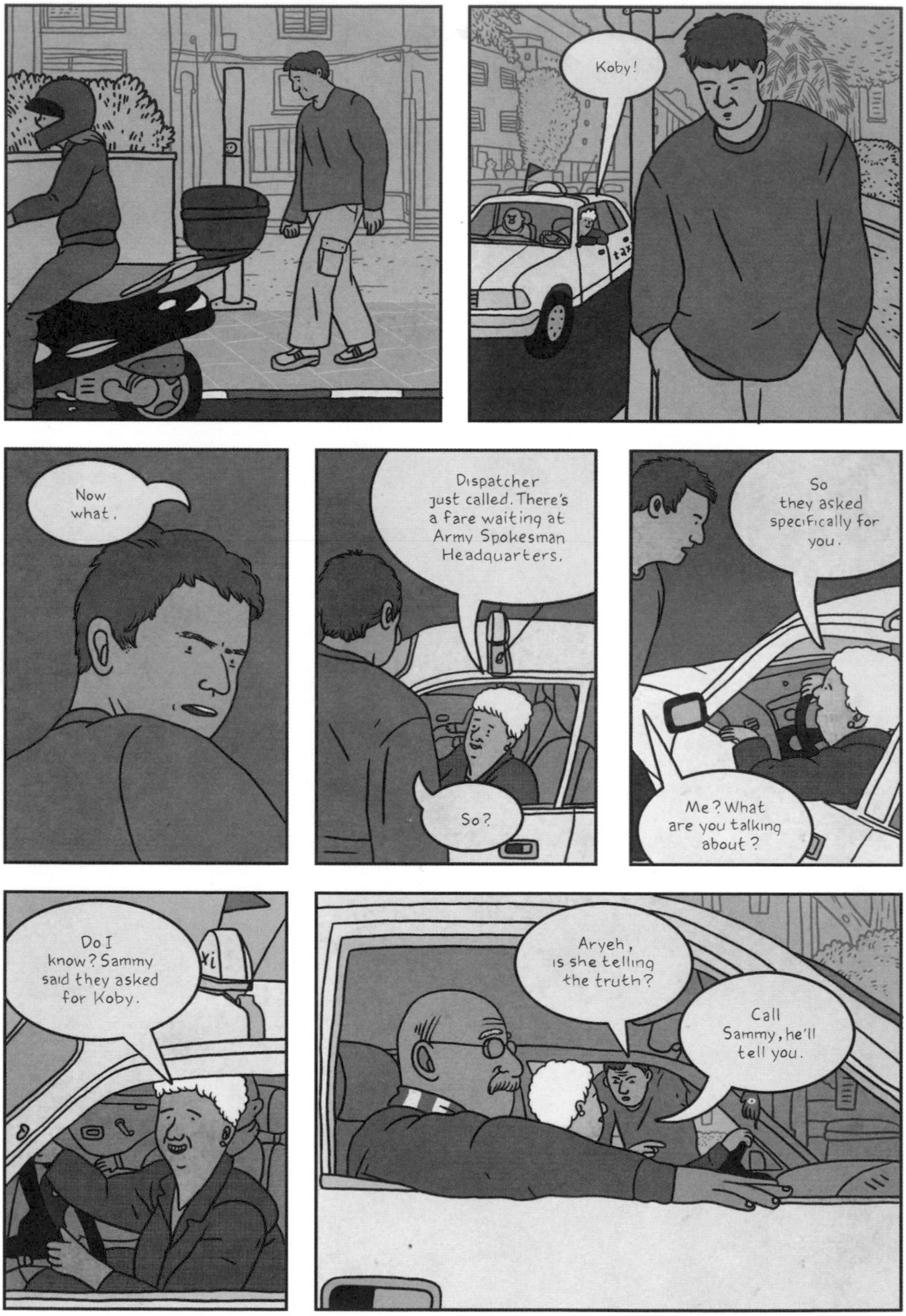
Koby!
Now what.
Dispatcher just called. There's a fare waiting at Army Spokesman Headquarters.
So?
So they asked specifically for you.
Me? What are you talking about?
Do I know? Sammy said they asked for Koby.
Aryeh, is she telling the truth?
Call Sammy, he'll tell you.

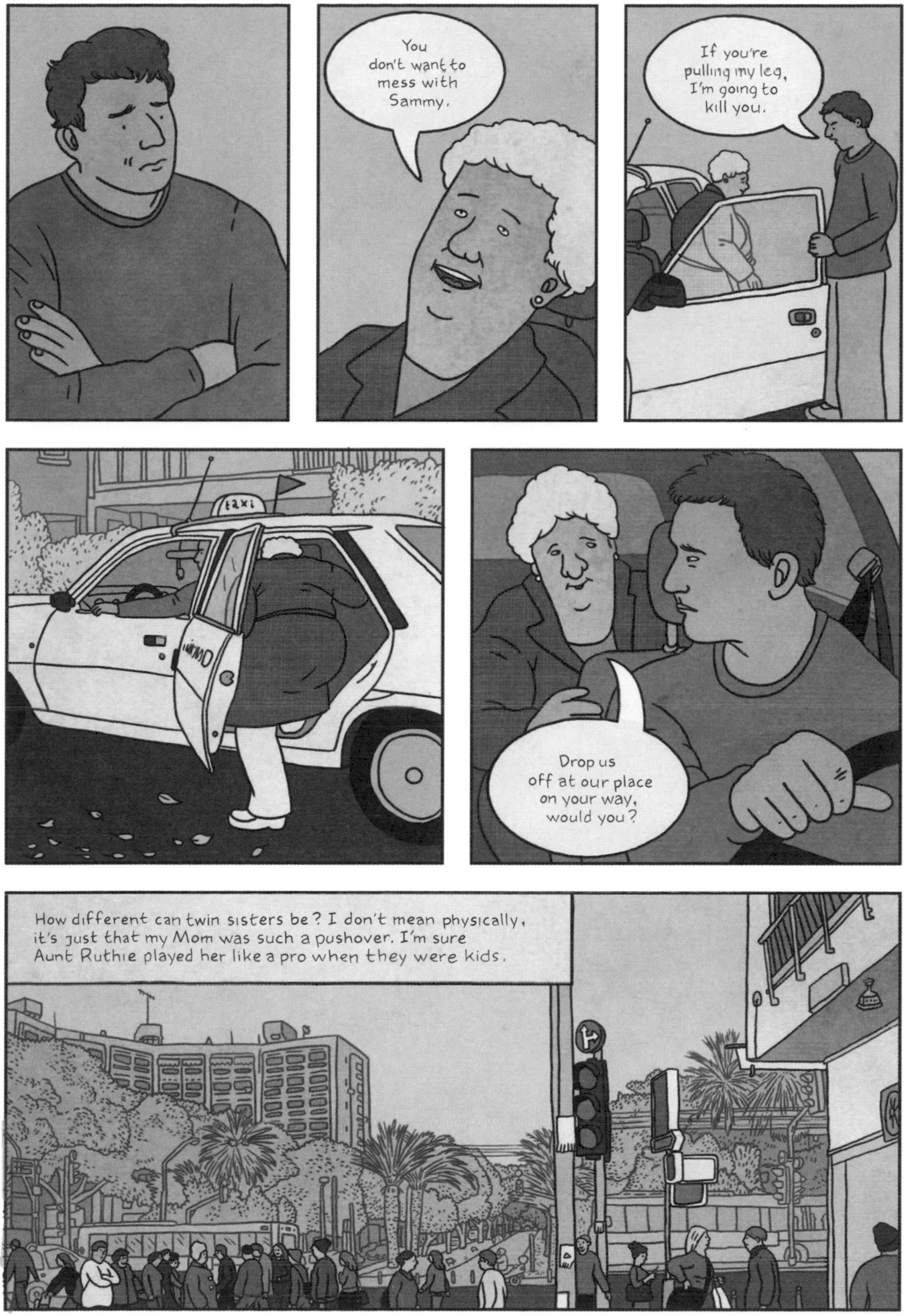
You don't want to mess with Sammy.
If you're pulling my leg, I'm going to kill you.
Drop us off at our place on your way, would you?
How different can twin sisters be? I don't mean physically, it's just that my Mom was such a pushover. I'm sure Aunt Ruthie played her like a pro when they were kids.

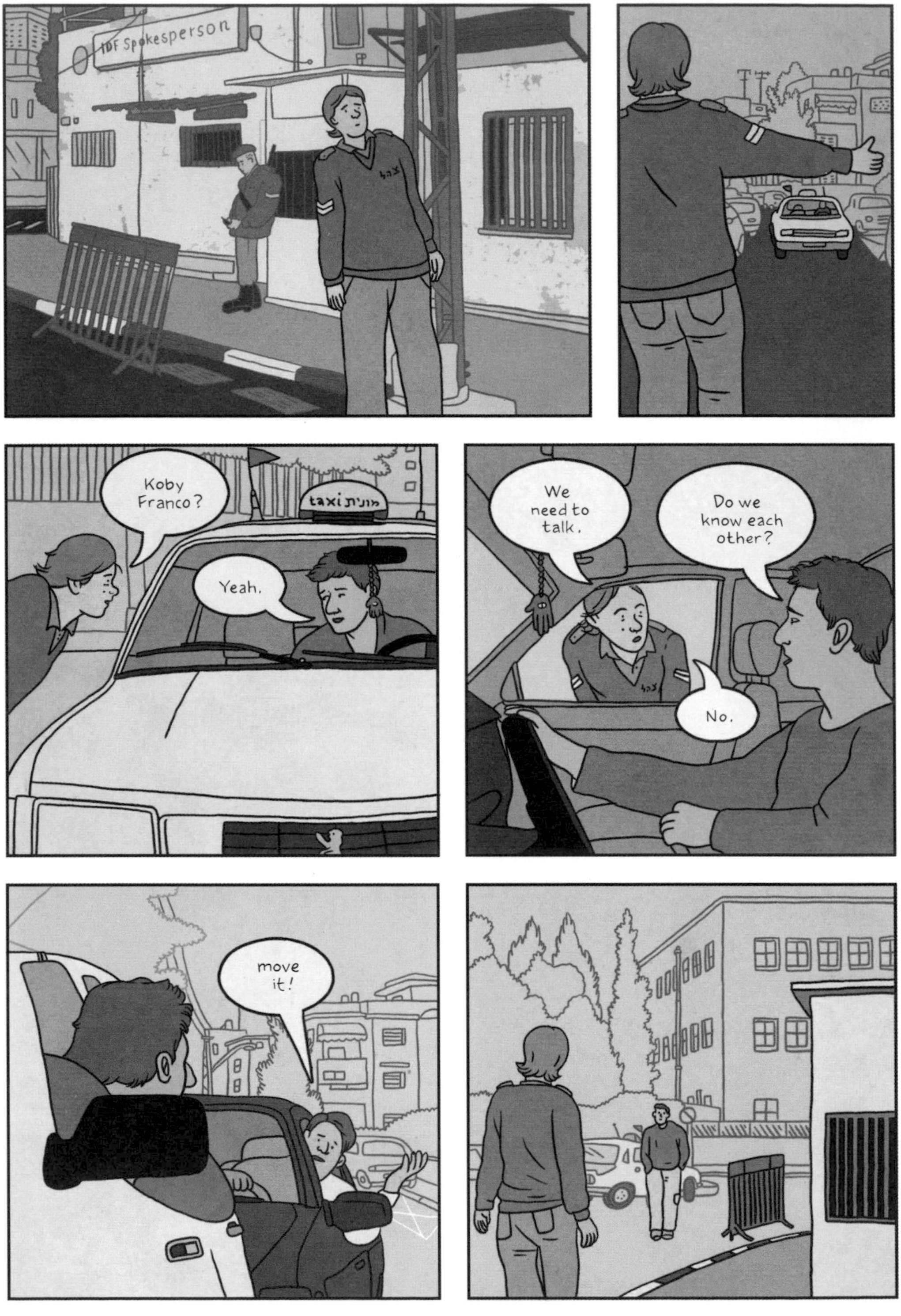
IDF Spokesperson
Koby Franco?
Yeah.
taxi מונית
We need to talk.
Do we know each other?
No.
move it!

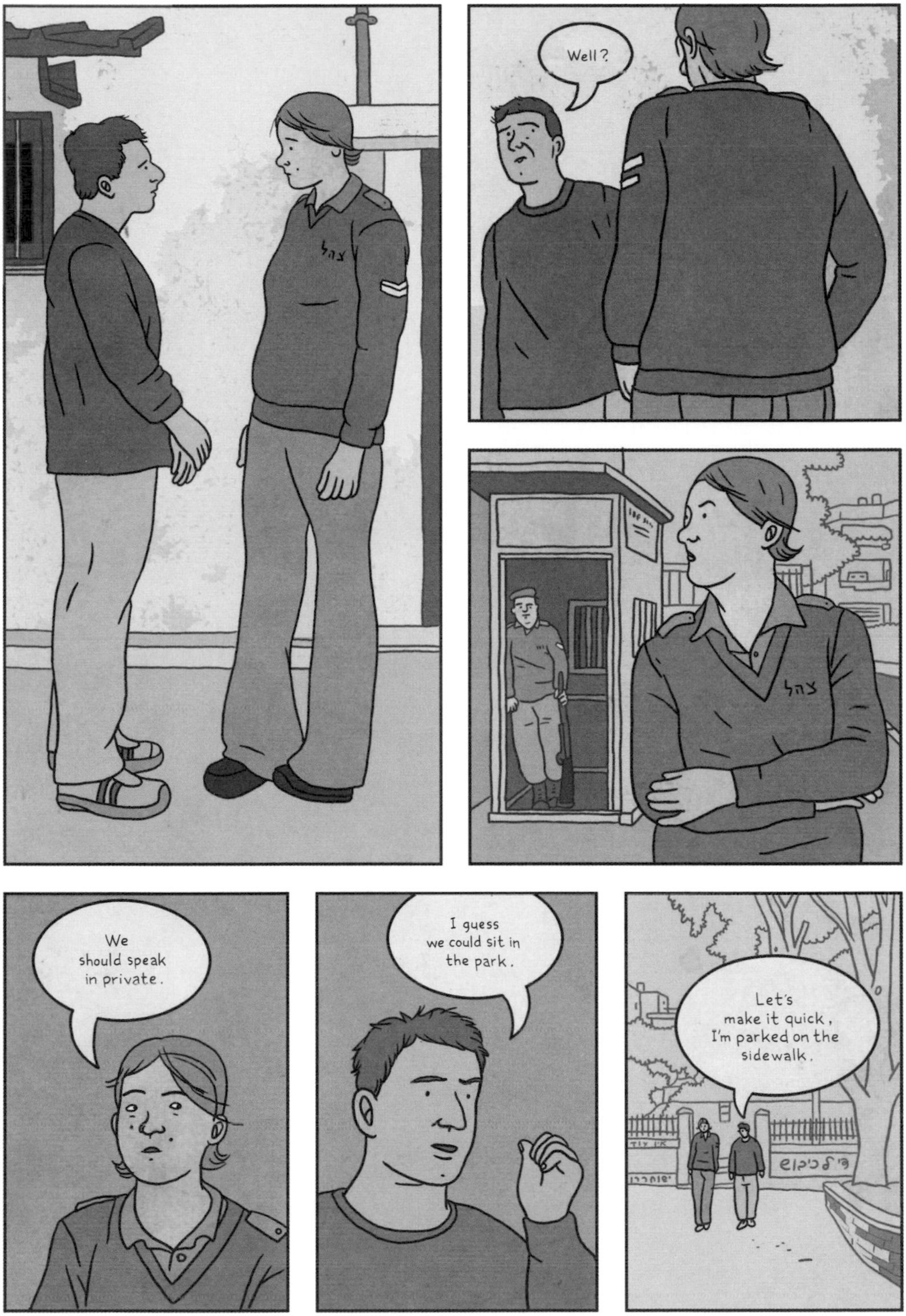
Well?
We should speak in private.
I guess we could sit in the park.
Let's make it quick, I'm parked on the sidewalk.

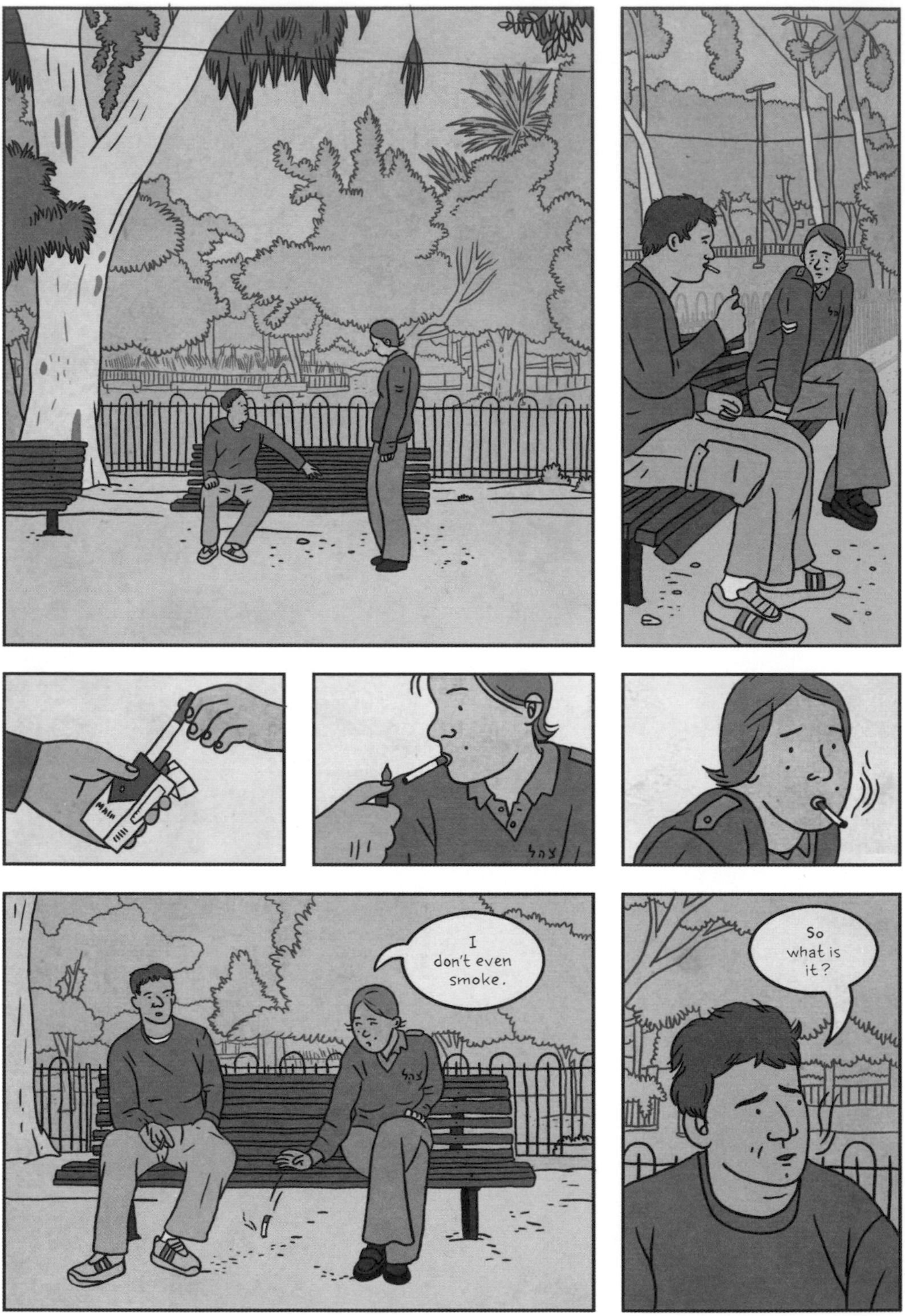
I don't even smoke.
So what is it?

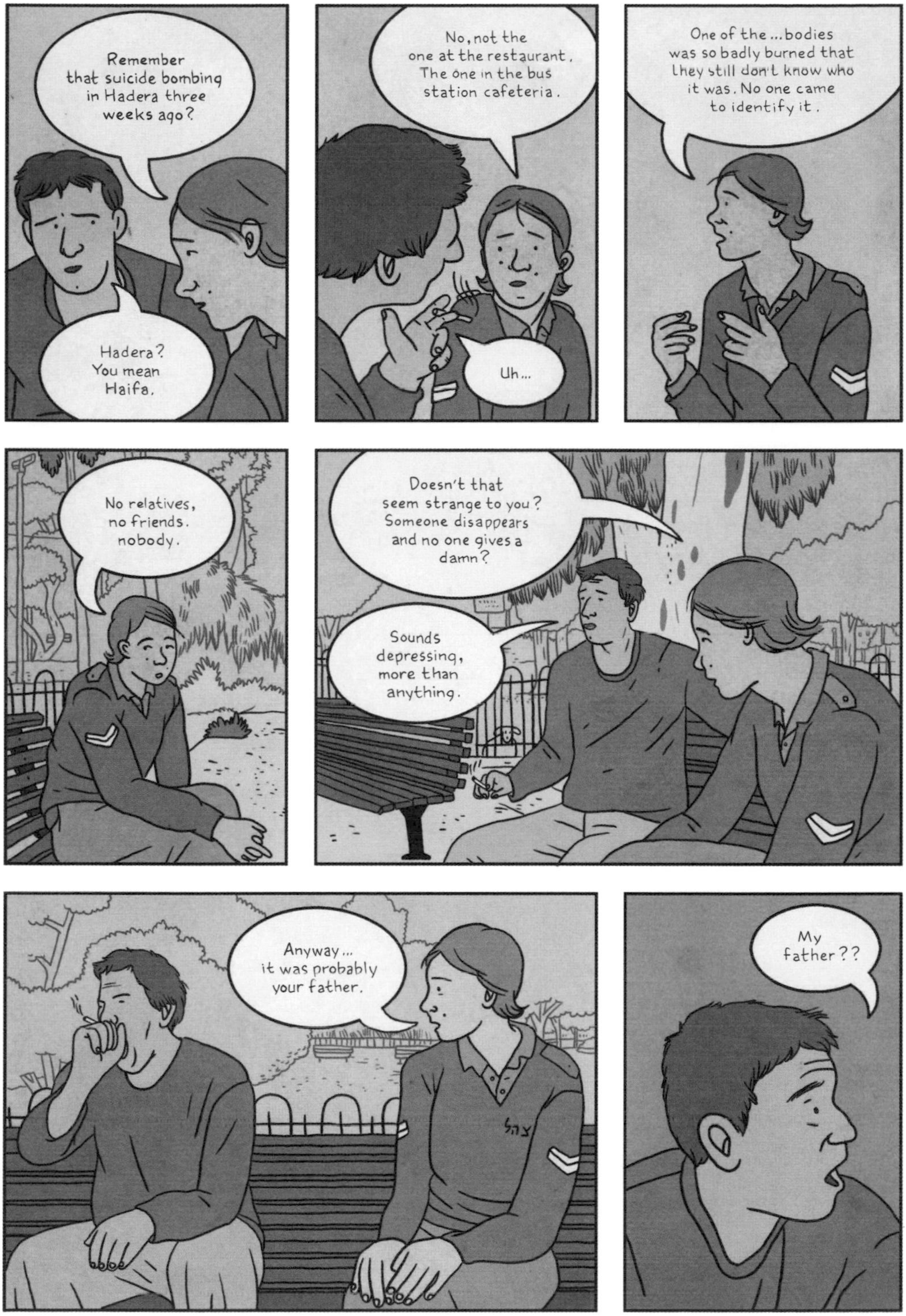
Remember that suicide bombing in Hadera three weeks ago?
Hadera? You mean Haifa.
No, not the one at the restaurant. The one in the bus station cafeteria.
Uh...
One of the ... bodies was so badly burned that they still don't know who it was. No one came to identify it.
No relatives, no friends. nobody.
Doesn't that seem strange to you? Someone disappears and no one gives a damn?
Sounds depressing, more than anything.
Anyway... it was probably your father.
My father??

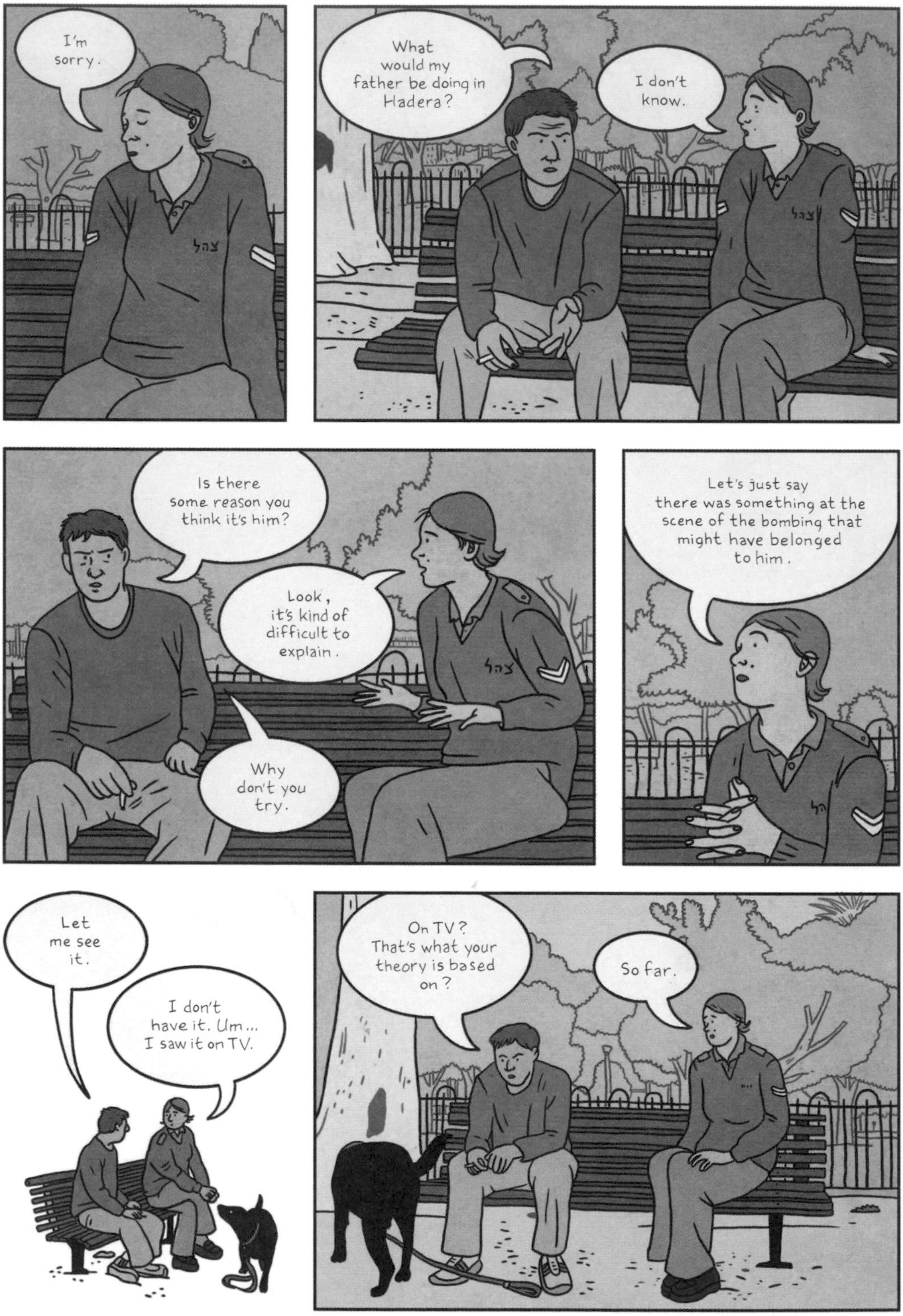
I'm sorry.
What would my father be doing in Hadera?
I don't know.
Is there some reason you think it's him?
Look, it's kind of difficult to explain.
Why don't you try.
Let's just say there was something at the scene of the bombing that might have belonged to him.
Let me see it.
I don't have it. Um... I saw it on TV.
On TV? That's what your theory is based on?
So far.

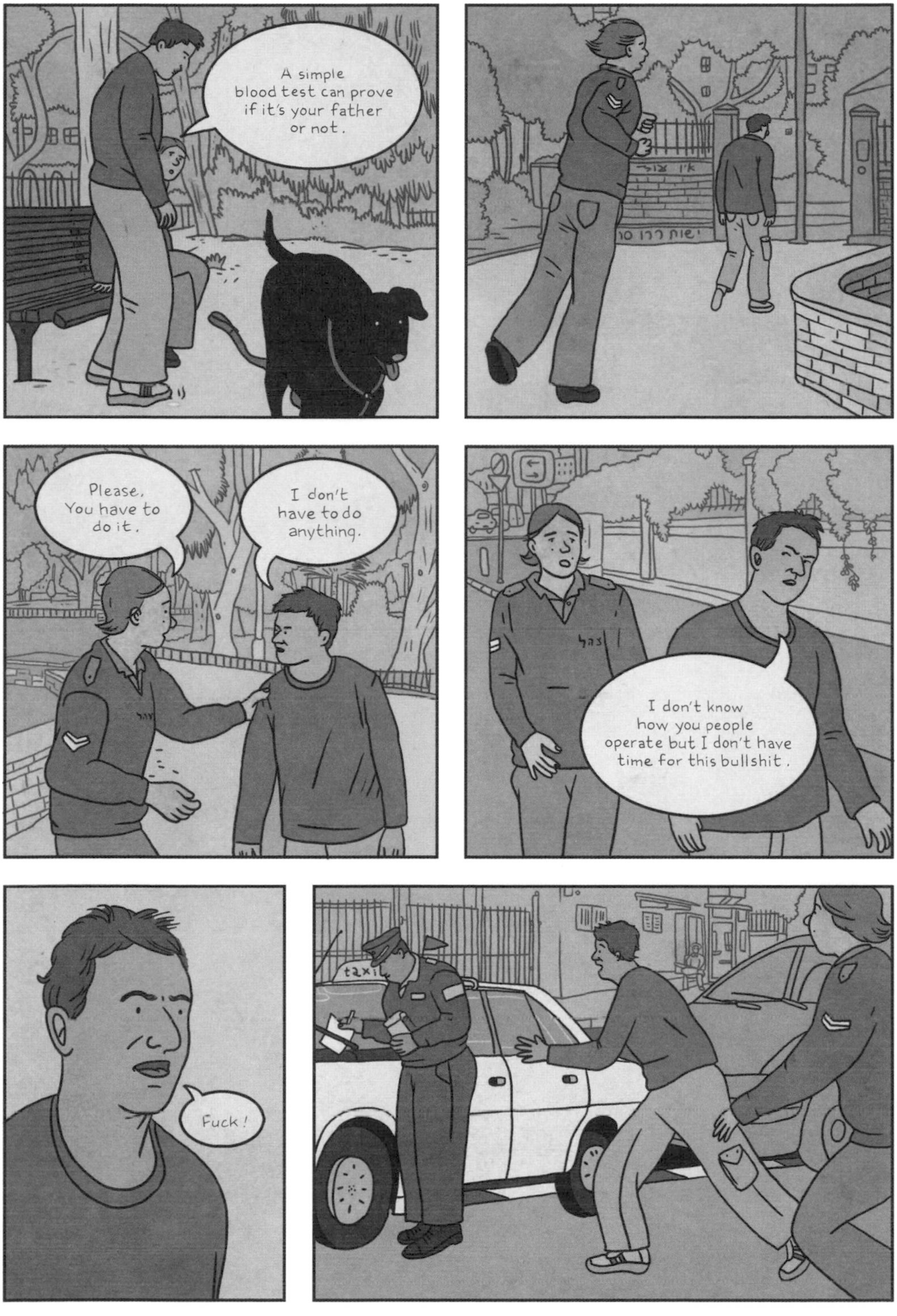
A simple blood test can prove if it's your father or not.
Please. You have to do it.
I don't have to do anything.
I don't know how you people operate but I don't have time for this bullshit.
Fuck!
taxi

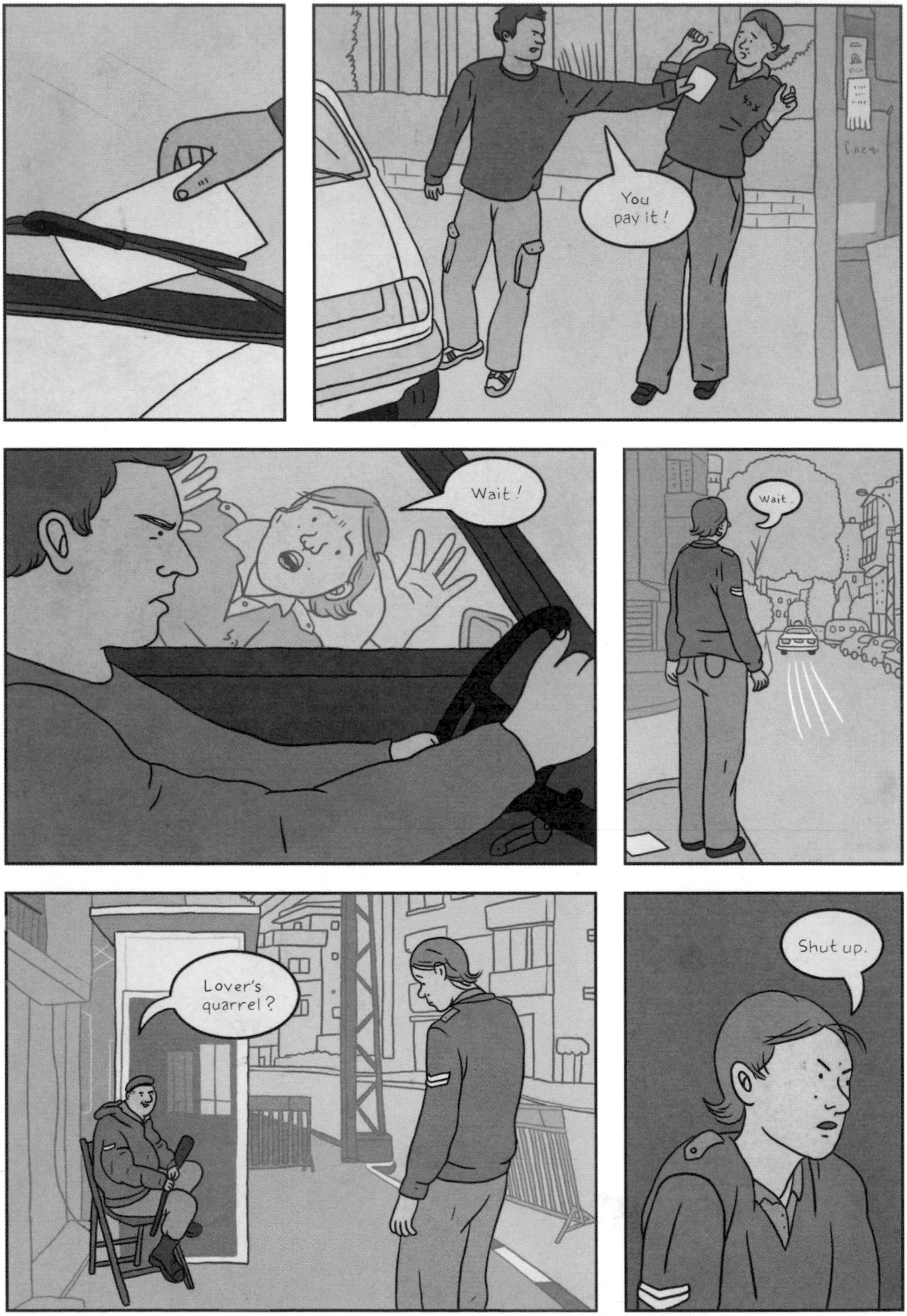
You pay it!
Wait!
Wait.
Lover's quarrel?
Shut up.

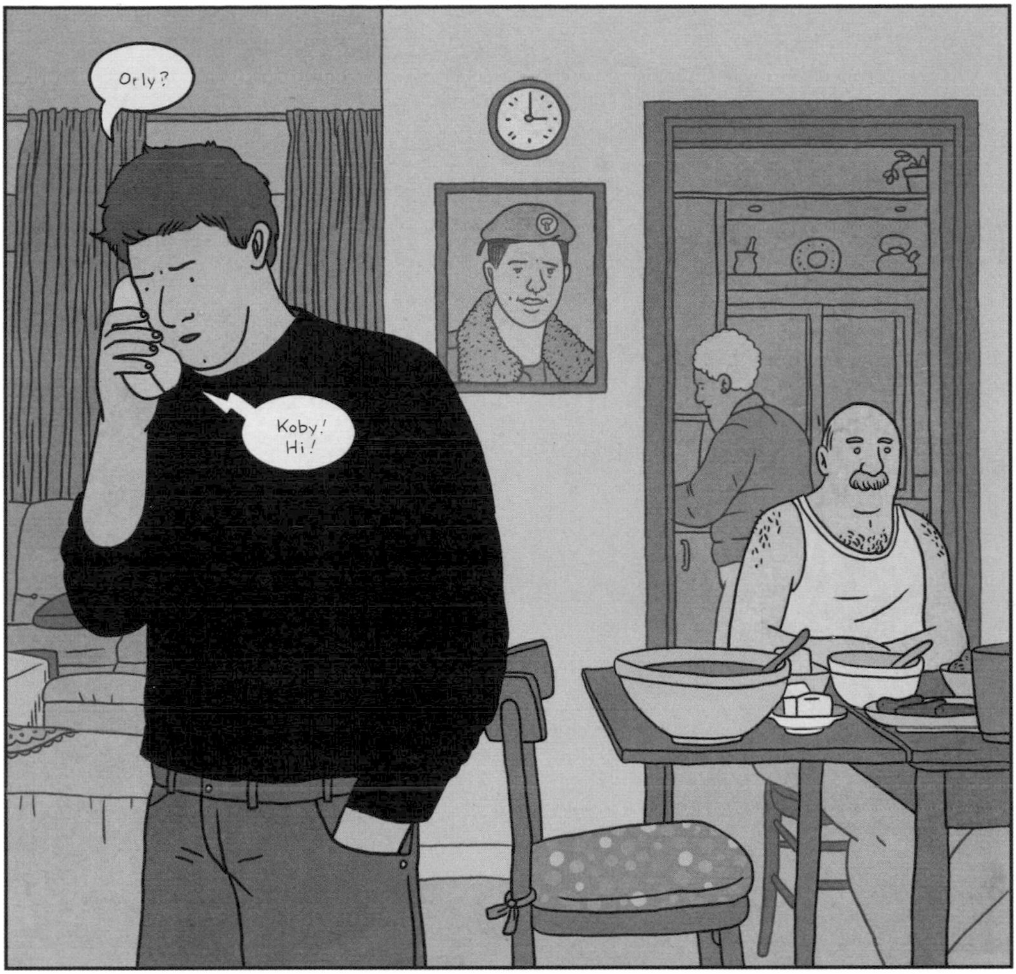
Orly?
Koby! Hi!

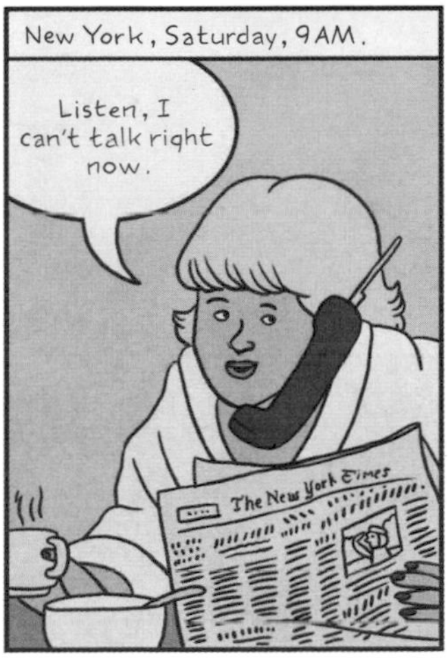
New York, Saturday, 9AM.
Listen, I can't talk right now.
The New York Times

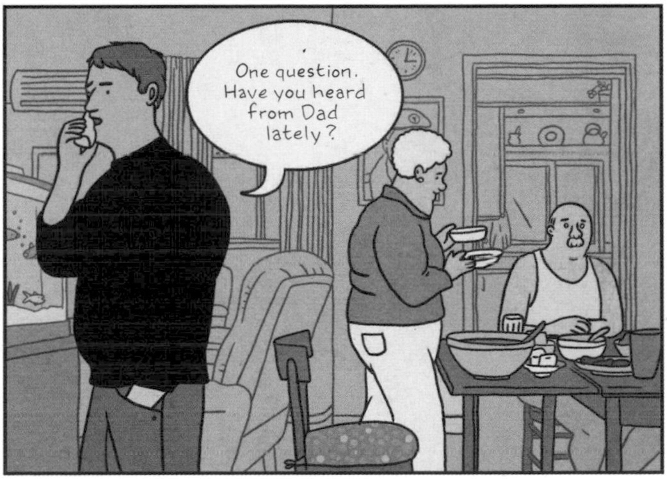
One question. Have you heard from Dad lately?

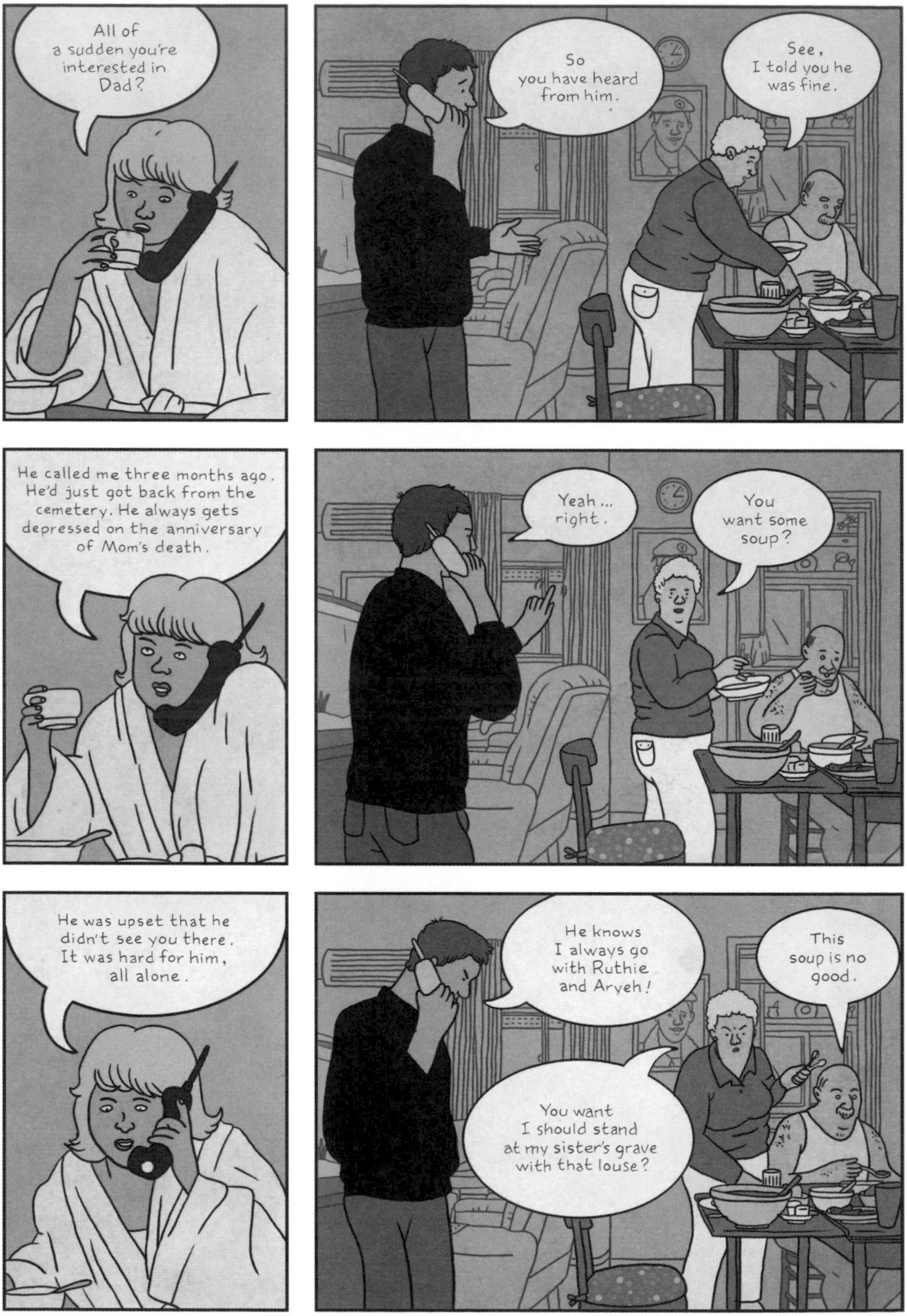
All of a sudden you're interested in Dad?
So you have heard from him.
See, I told you he was fine.
He called me three months ago. He'd just got back from the cemetery. He always gets depressed on the anniversary of Mom's death.
Yeah ... right.
You want some soup?
He was upset that he didn't see you there. It was hard for him, all alone.
He knows I always go with Ruthie and Aryeh!
This soup is no good.
You want I should stand at my sister's grave with that louse?

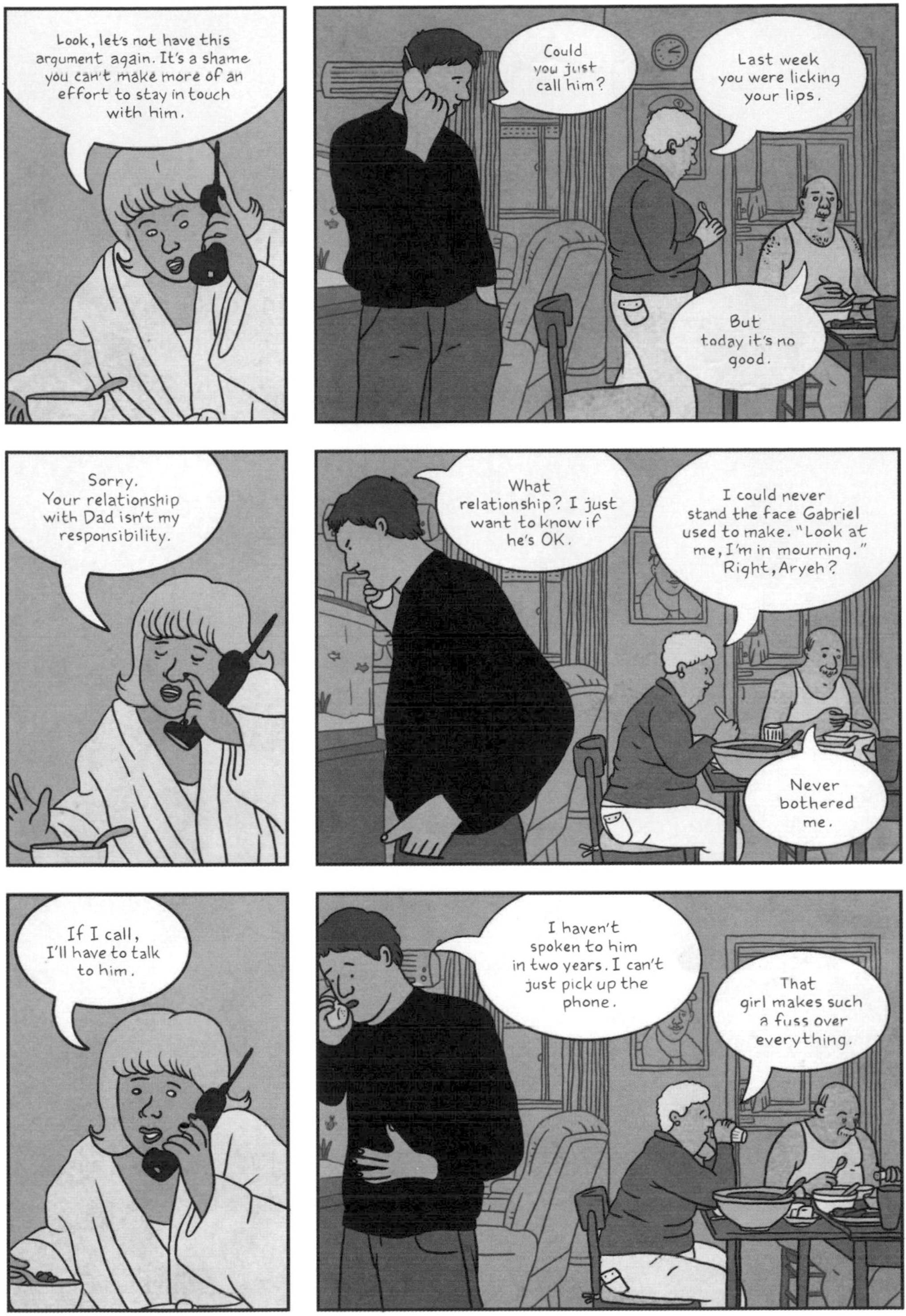
Look, let's not have this argument again. It's a shame you can't make more of an effort to stay in touch with him.
Could you just call him?
Last week you were licking your lips.
But today it's no good.
Sorry. Your relationship with Dad isn't my responsibility.
What relationship? I just want to know if he's OK.
I could never stand the face Gabriel used to make. "Look at me, I'm in mourning." Right, Aryeh?
Never bothered me.
If I call, I'll have to talk to him.
I haven't spoken to him in two years. I can't just pick up the phone.
That girl makes such a fuss over everything.

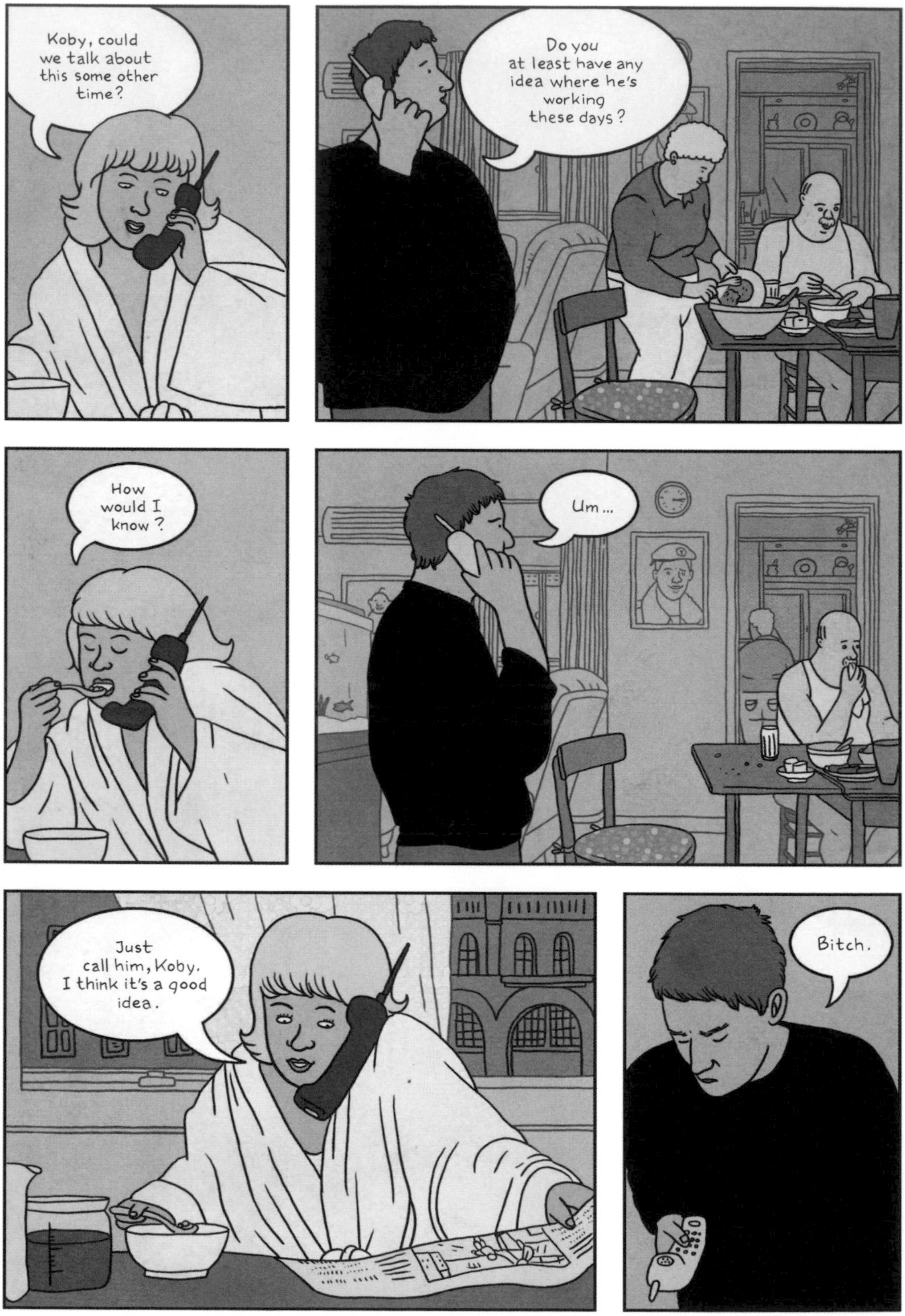
Koby, could we talk about this some other time?
Do you at least have any idea where he's working these days?
How would I know?
Um...
Just call him, Koby. I think it's a good idea.
Bitch.

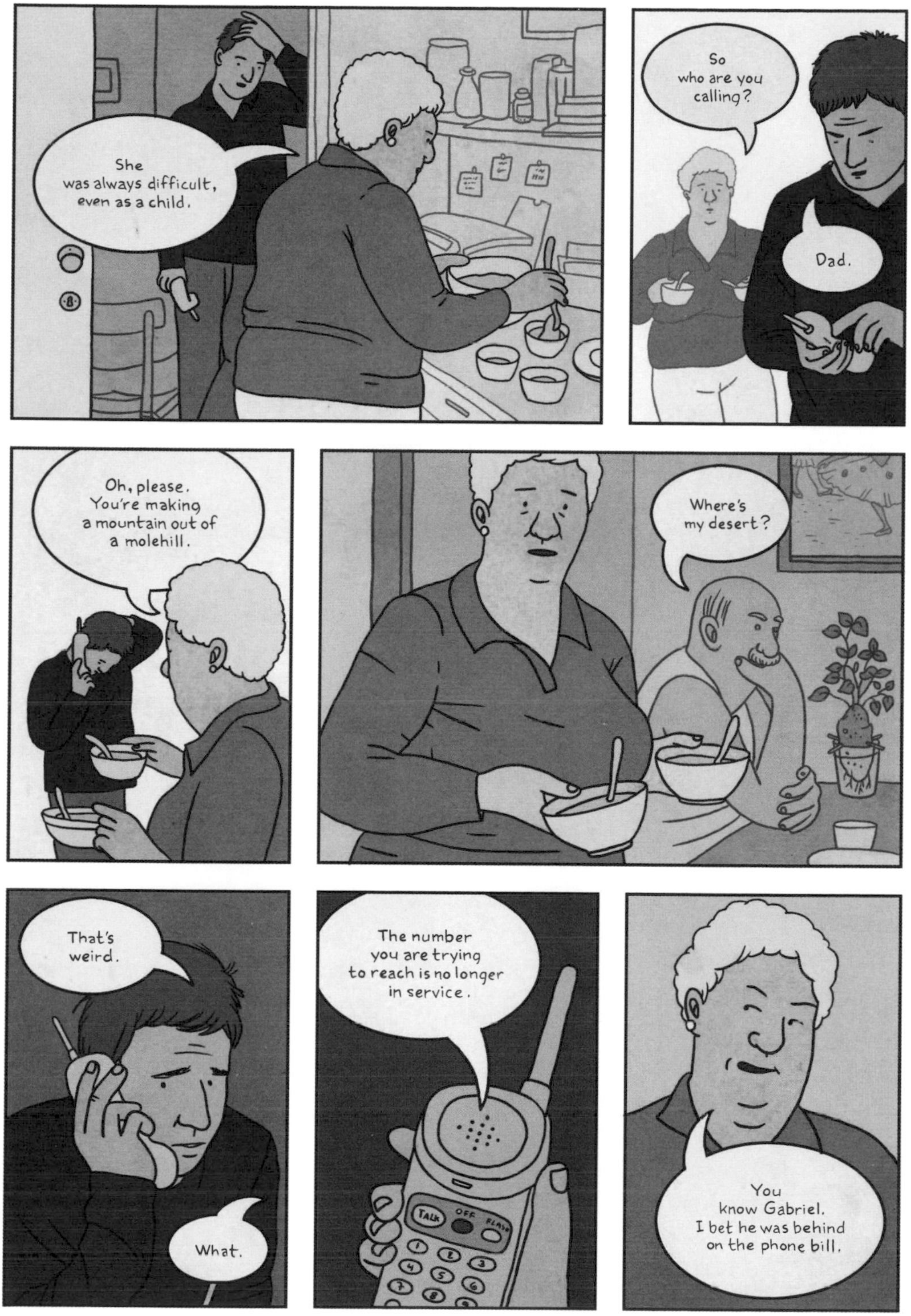
She was always difficult, even as a child.
So who are you calling?
Dad.
Oh, please. You're making a mountain out of a molehill.
Where's my desert?
That's weird.
What.
The number you are trying to reach is no longer in service.
TALK
OFF
FLASH
You know Gabriel. I bet he was behind on the phone bill.

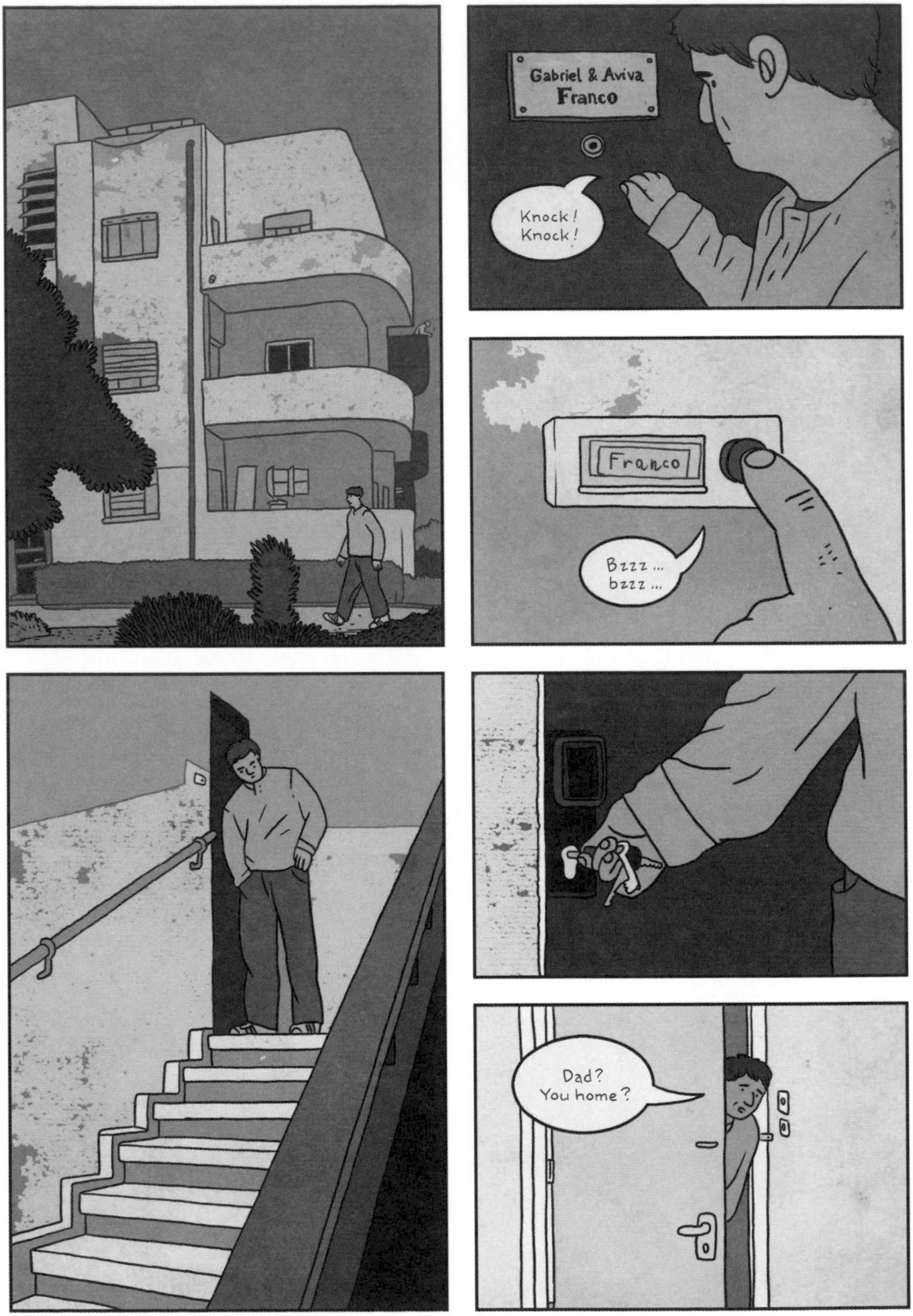
Gabriel & Aviva
Franco
Knock! Knock!
Franco
Bzzz... bzzz...
Dad? You home?

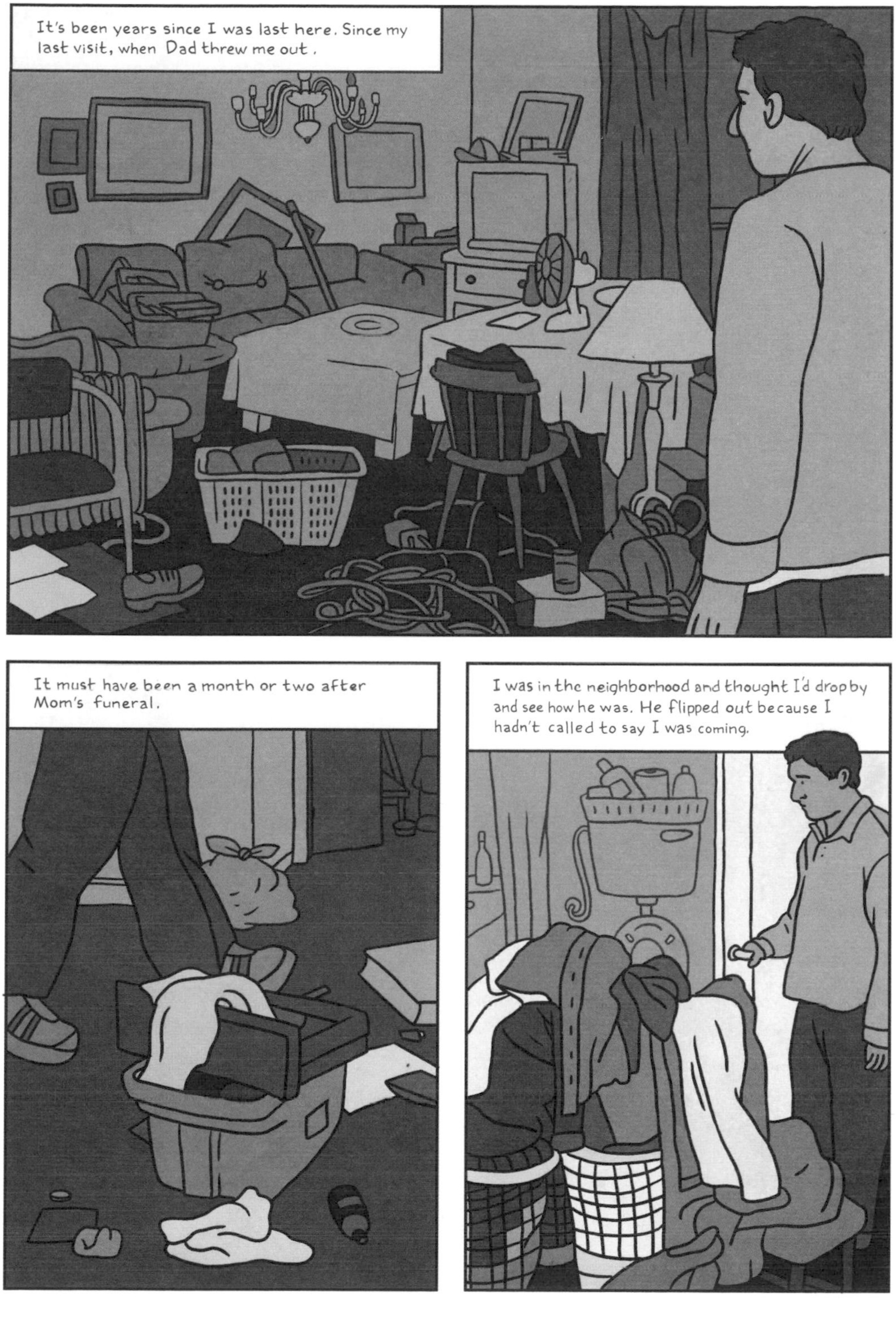
It's been years since I was last here. Since my last visit, when Dad threw me out.
It must have been a month or two after Mom's funeral.
I was in the neighborhood and thought I'd drop by and see how he was. He flipped out because I hadn't called to say I was coming.

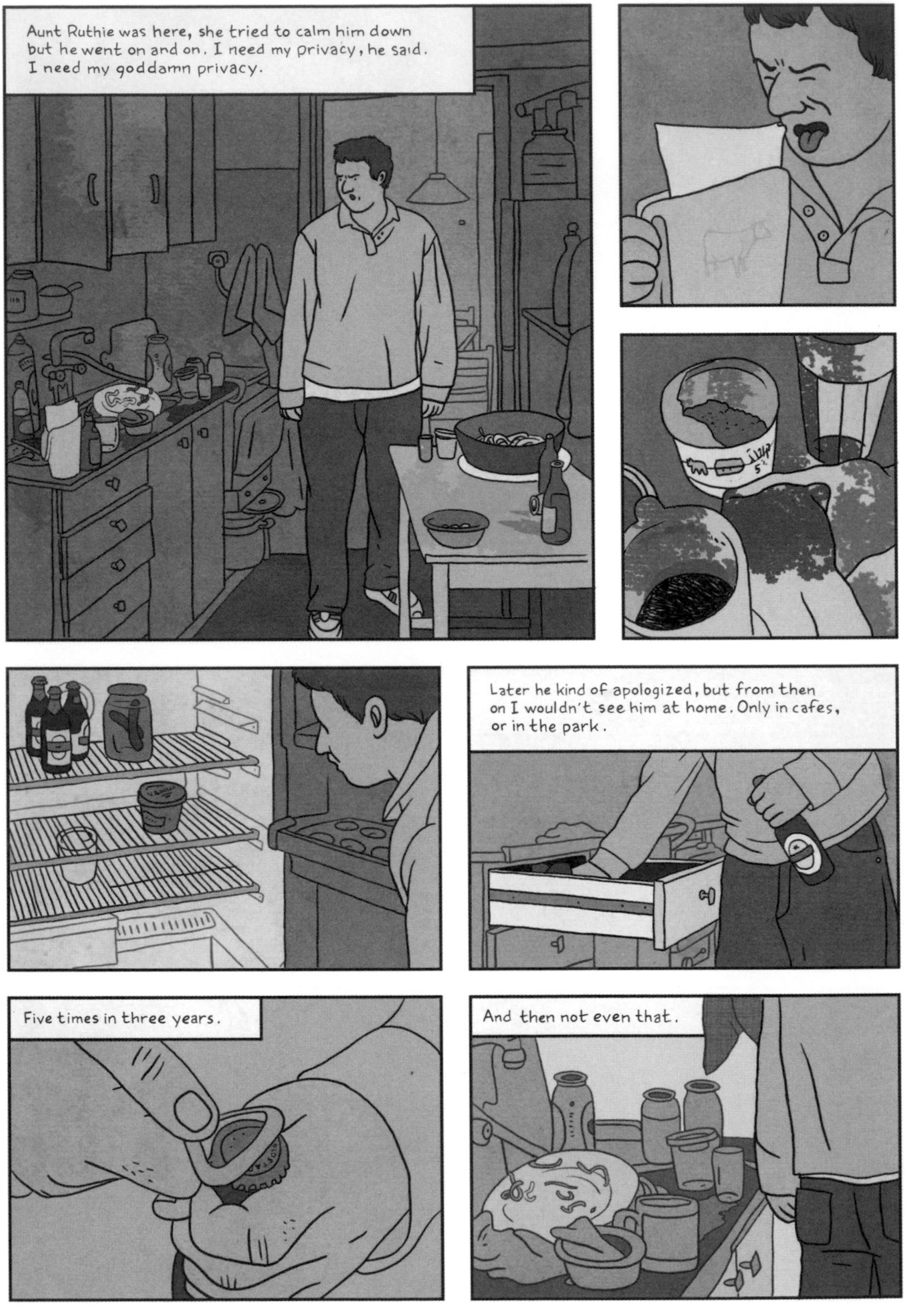
Aunt Ruthie was here, she tried to calm him down but he went on and on. I need my privacy, he said. I need my goddamn privacy.
Later he kind of apologized, but from then on I wouldn't see him at home. Only in cafes, or in the park.
Five times in three years.
And then not even that.

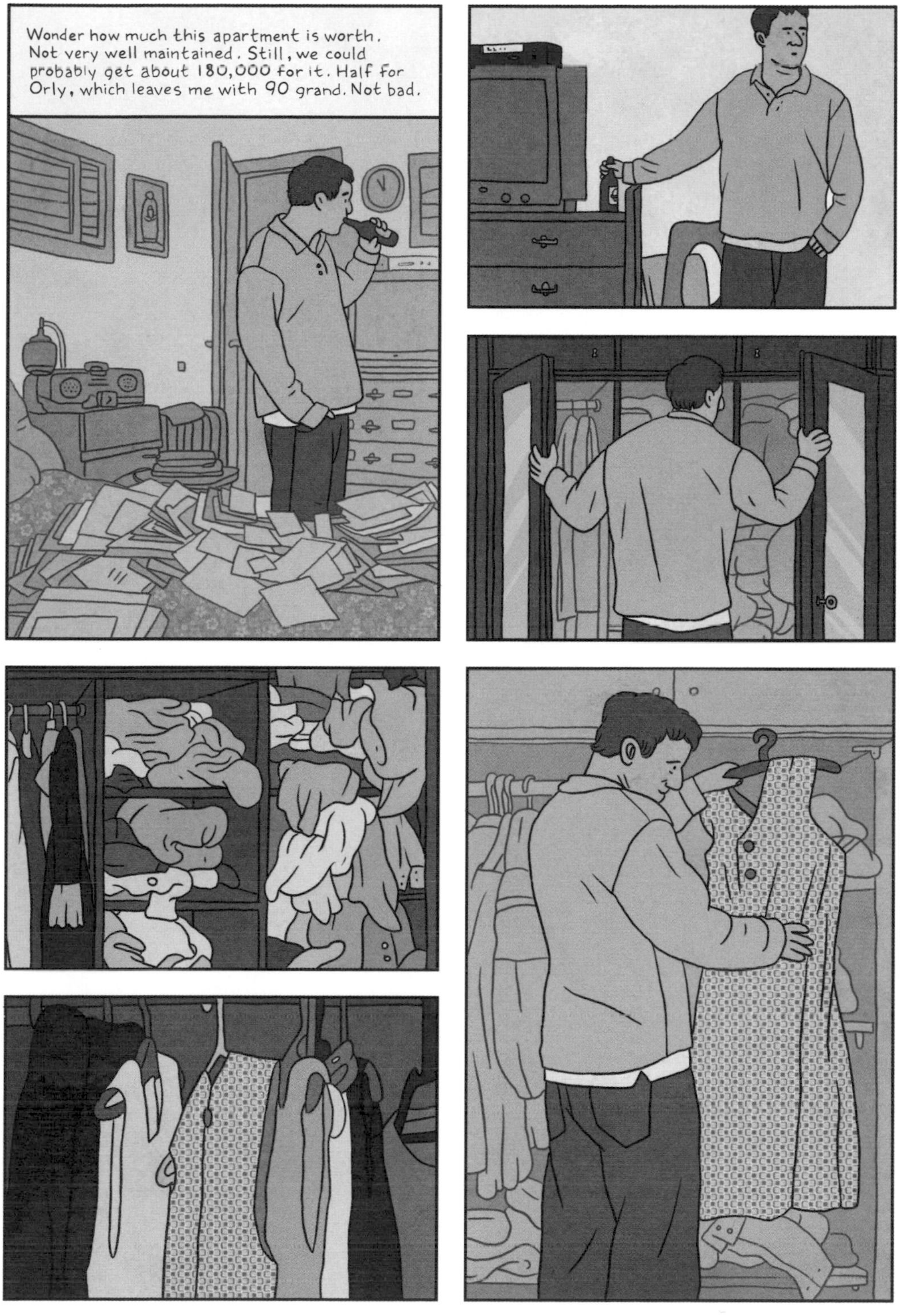
Wonder how much this apartment is worth. Not very well maintained. Still, we could probably get about 180,000 for it. Half for Orly, which leaves me with 90 grand. Not bad.

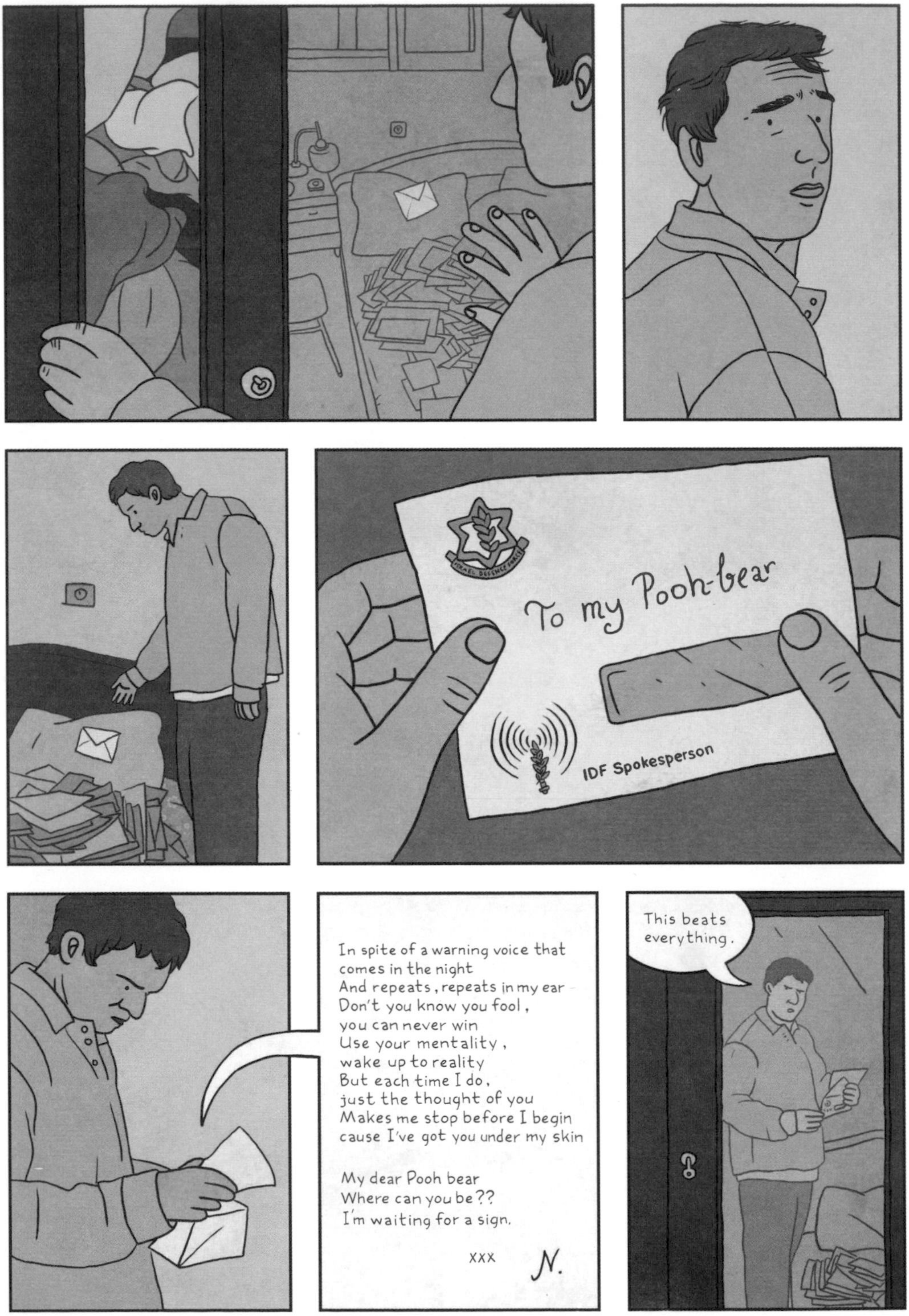
ISRAEL DEFENCE FORCES
To my Pooh-bear
IDF Spokesperson
In spite of a warning voice that comes in the night
And repeats, repeats in my ear
Don't you know you fool, you can never win
Use your mentality, wake up to reality
But each time I do, just the thought of you
Makes me stop before I begin
cause I've got you under my skin
My dear Pooh bear
Where can you be??
I'm waiting for a sign.
xxx N.
This beats everything.

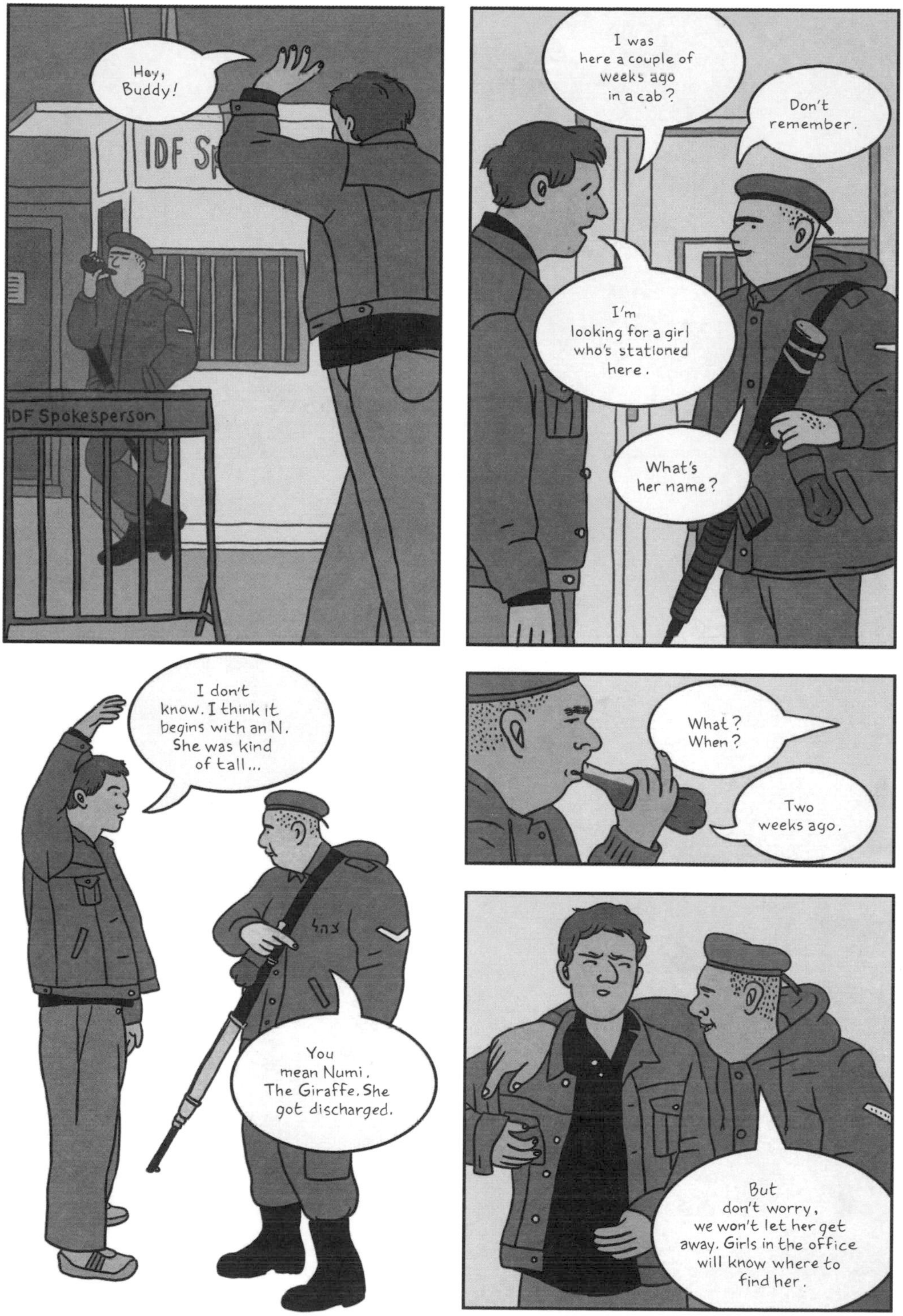
Hey, Buddy!
IDF Sp
IDF Spokesperson
I was here a couple of weeks ago in a cab?
Don't remember.
I'm looking for a girl who's stationed here.
What's her name?
I don't know. I think it begins with an N. She was kind of tall...
You mean Numi. The Giraffe. She got discharged.
What? When?
Two weeks ago.
But don't worry, we won't let her get away. Girls in the office will know where to find her.

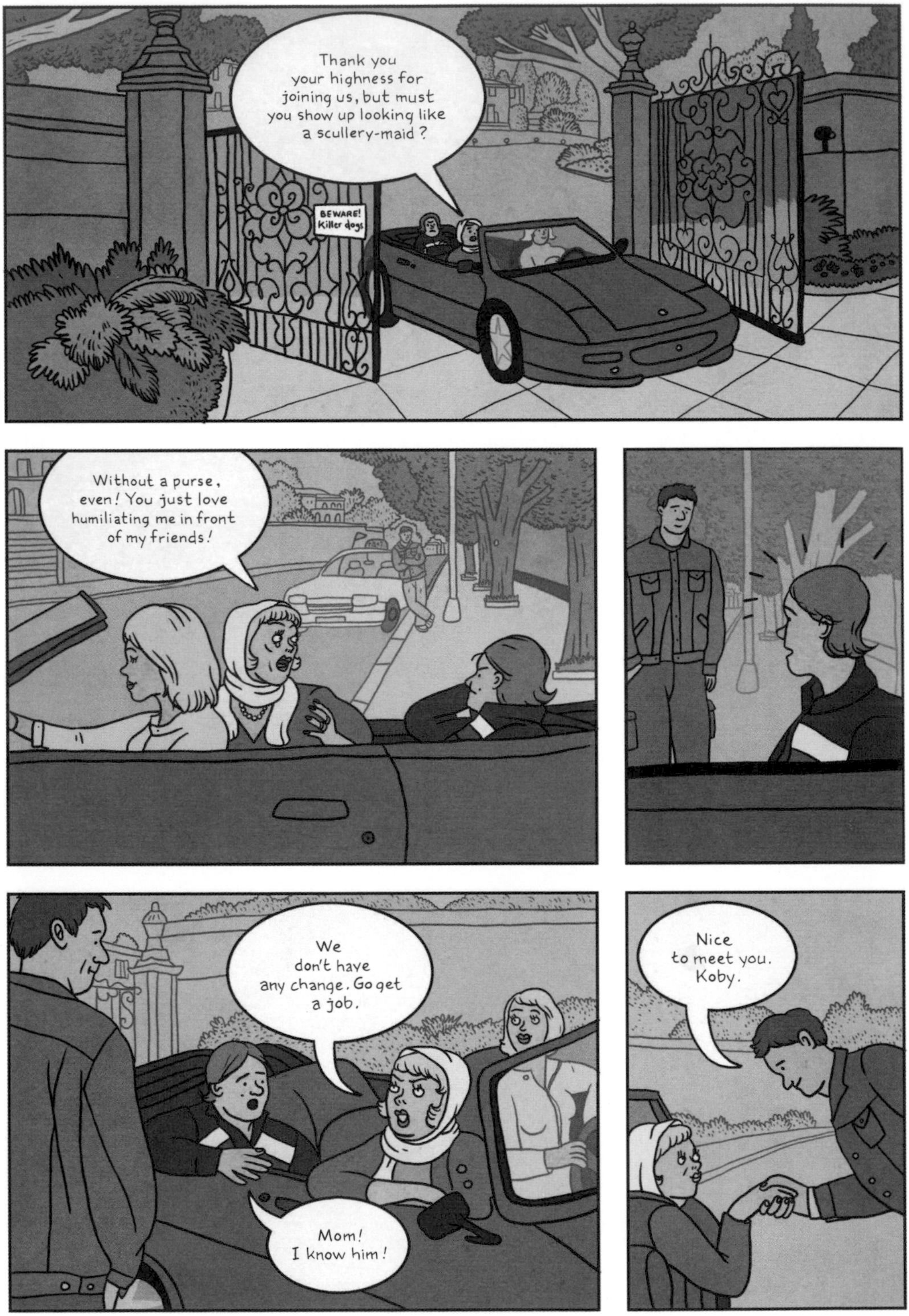
Thank you your highness for joining us, but must you show up looking like a scullery-maid?
BEWARE! Killer dogs
Without a purse, even! You just love humiliating me in front of my friends!
We don't have any change. Go get a job.
Mom! I know him!
Nice to meet you. Koby.

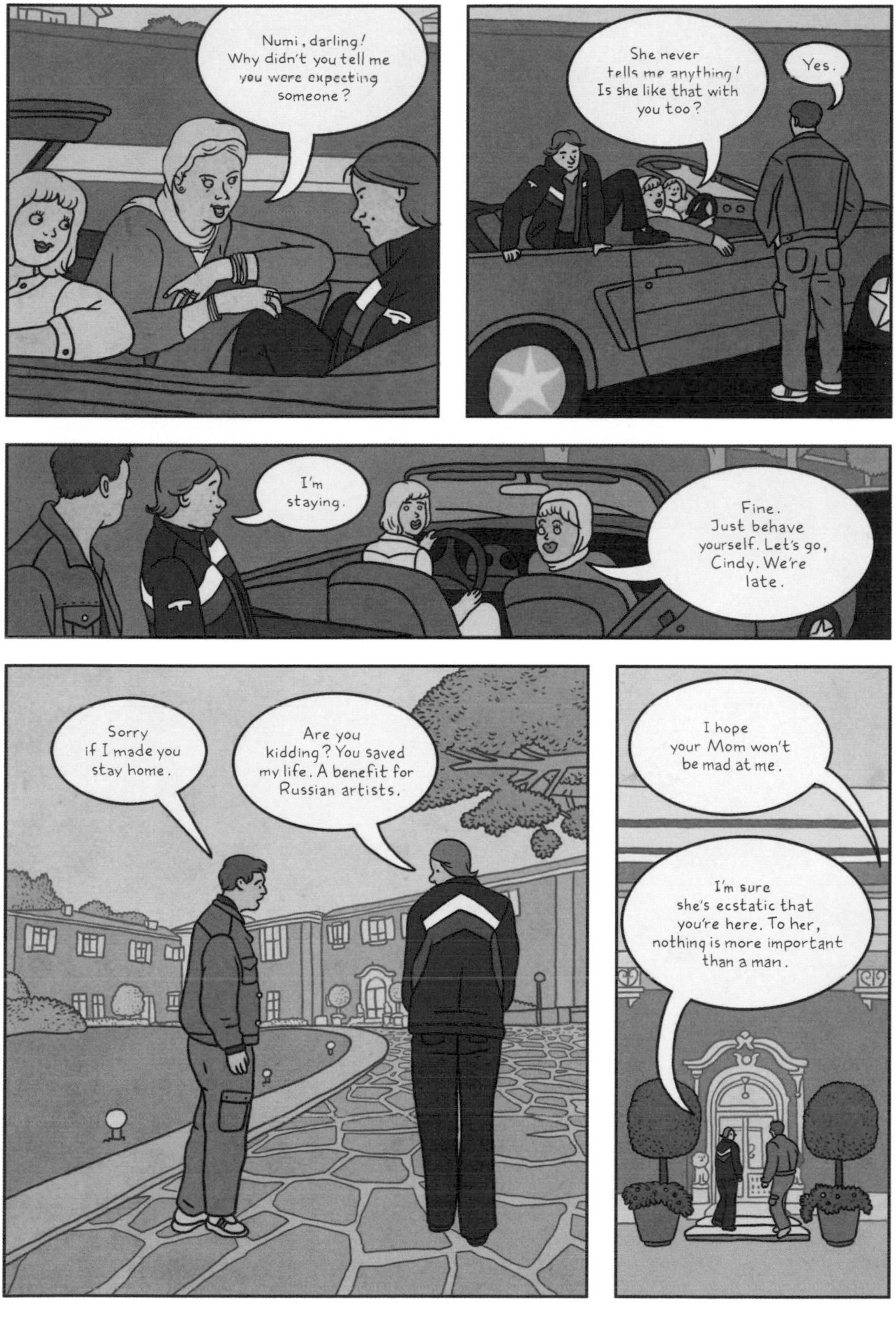
Numi, darling! Why didn't you tell me you were expecting someone?
She never tells me anything! Is she like that with you too?
Yes.
I'm staying.
Fine. Just behave yourself. Let's go, Cindy. We're late.
Sorry if I made you stay home.
Are you kidding? You saved my life. A benefit for Russian artists.
I hope your Mom won't be mad at me.
I'm sure she's ecstatic that you're here. To her, nothing is more important than a man.

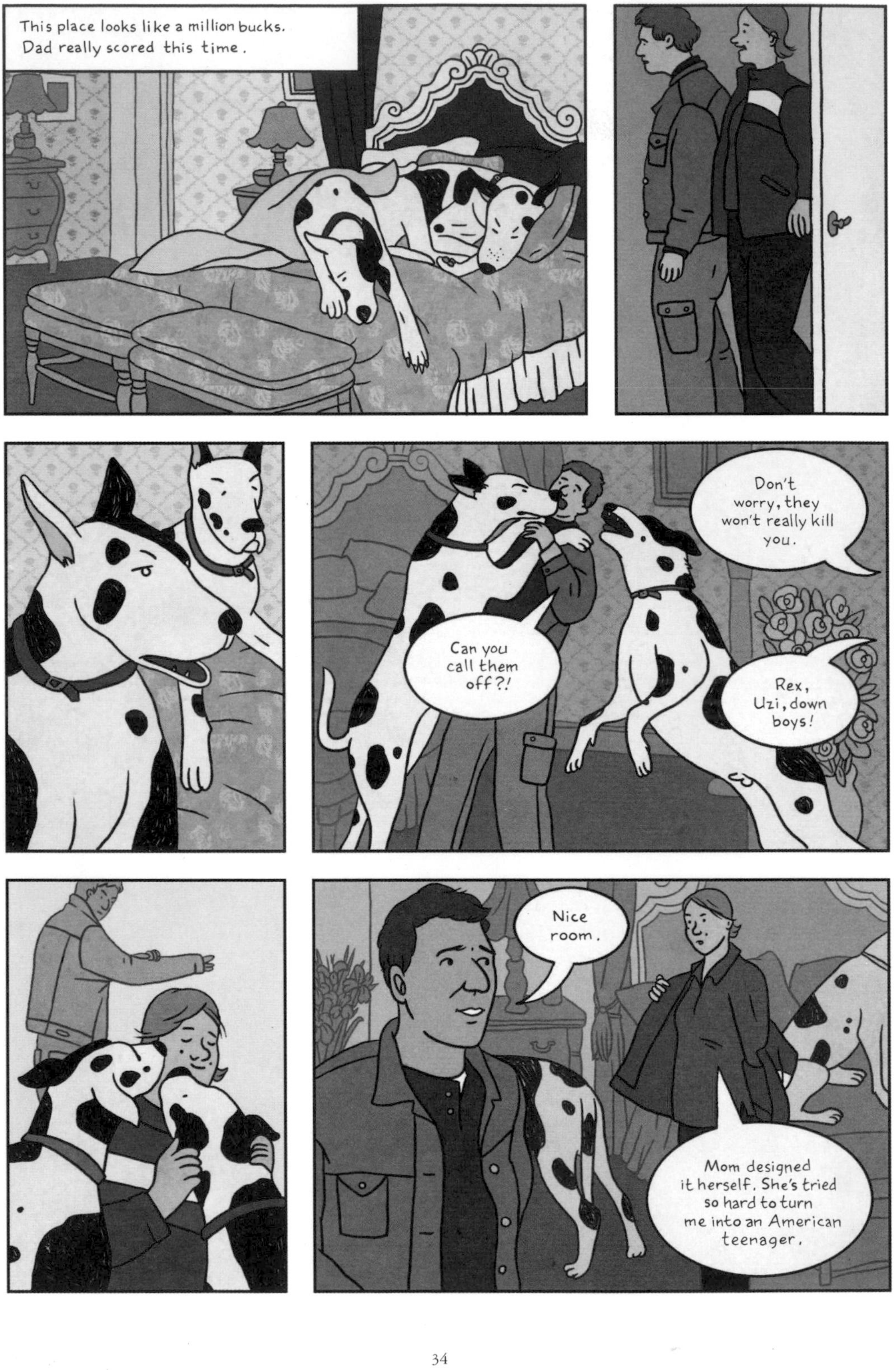
This place looks like a million bucks.
Dad really scored this time.
Don't worry, they won't really kill you.
Can you call them off?!
Rex, Uzi, down boys!
Nice room.
Mom designed it herself. She's tried so hard to turn me into an American teenager.

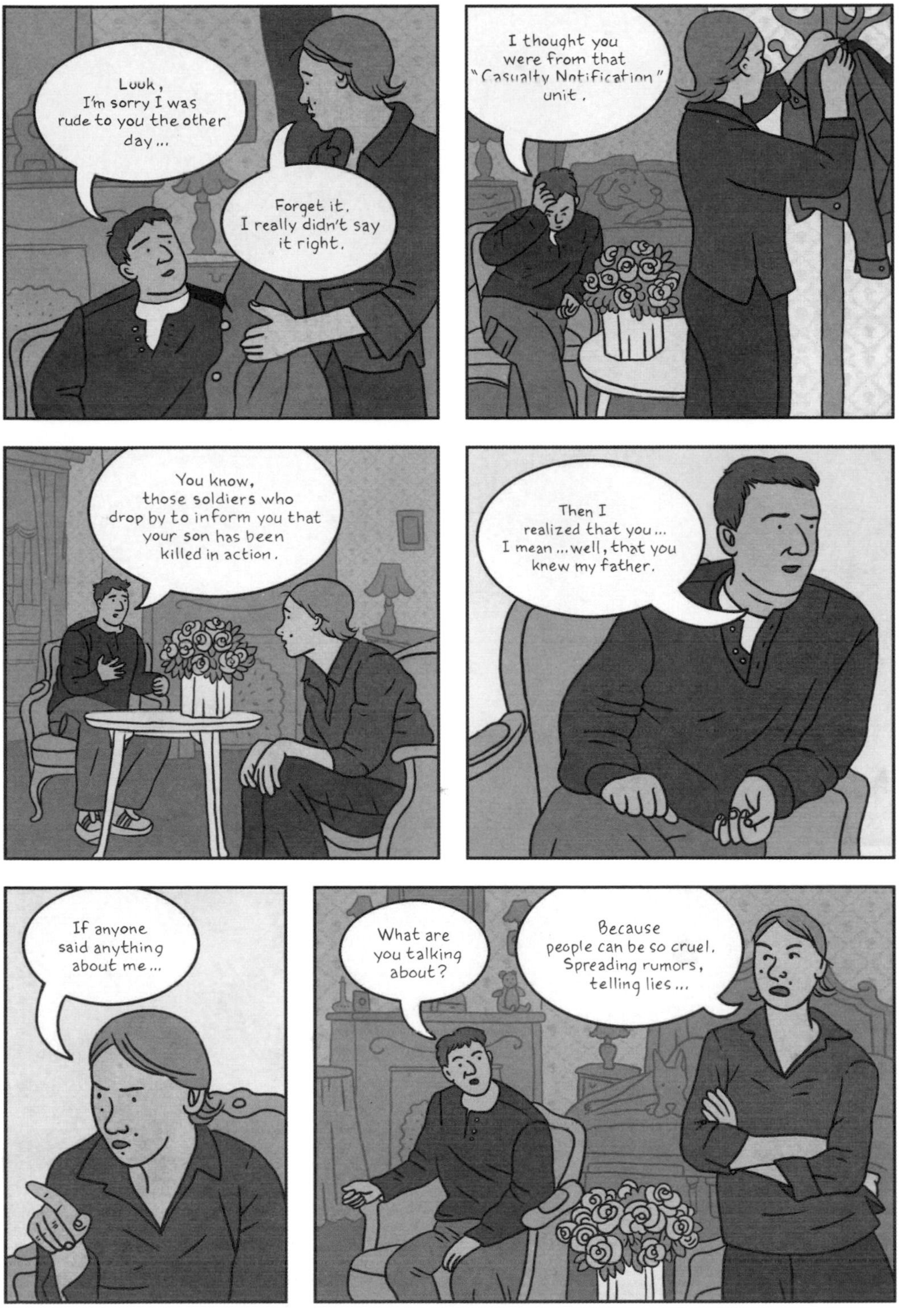
Look, I'm sorry I was rude to you the other day...
Forget it. I really didn't say it right.
I thought you were from that "Casualty Notification" unit.
You know, those soldiers who drop by to inform you that your son has been killed in action.
Then I realized that you... I mean... well, that you knew my father.
If anyone said anything about me...
What are you talking about?
Because people can be so cruel. Spreading rumors, telling lies...

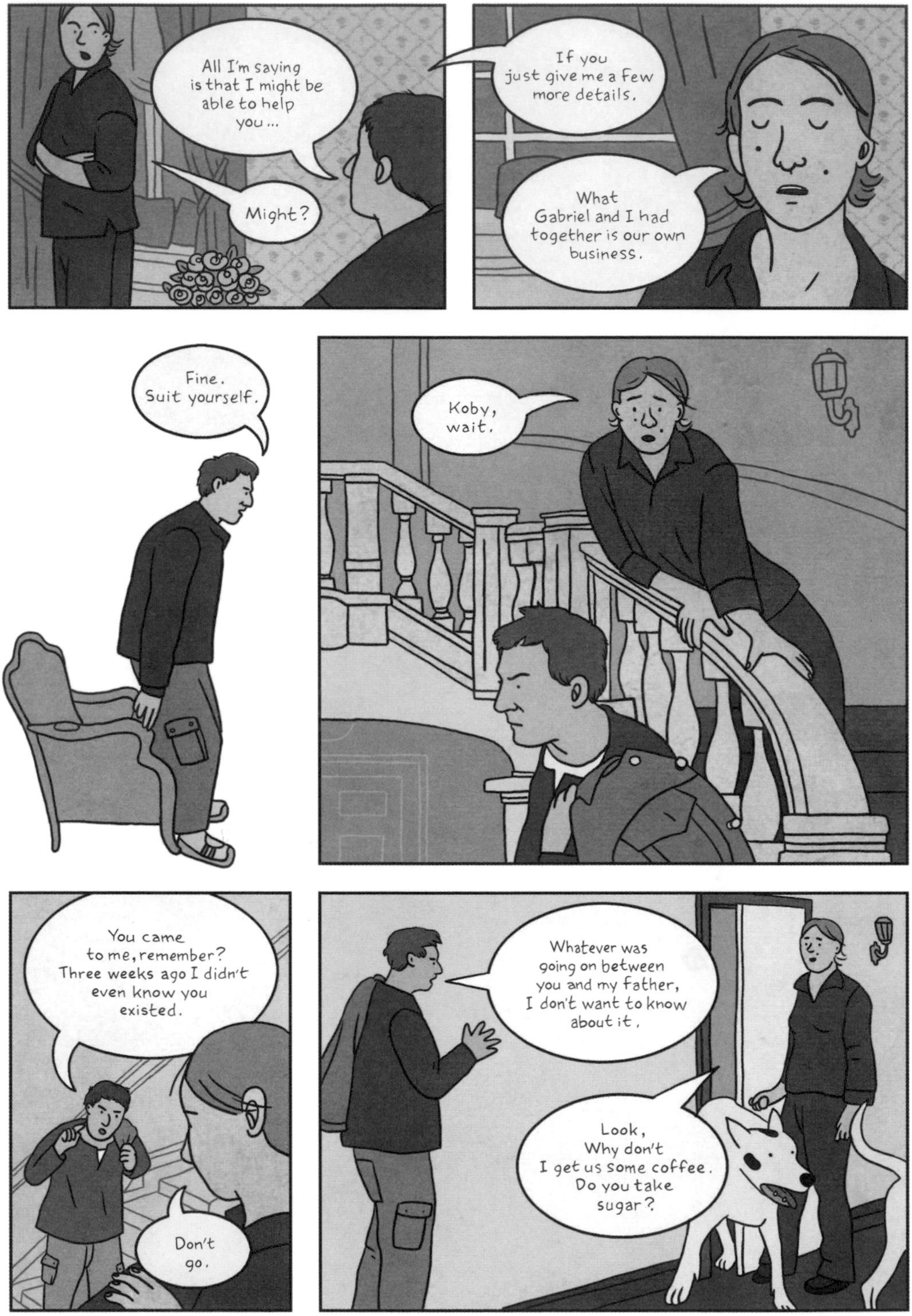
All I'm saying is that I might be able to help you...
Might?
If you just give me a few more details.
What Gabriel and I had together is our own business.
Fine. Suit yourself.
Koby, wait.
You came to me, remember? Three weeks ago I didn't even know you existed.
Don't go.
Whatever was going on between you and my father, I don't want to know about it.
Look, Why don't I get us some coffee. Do you take sugar?

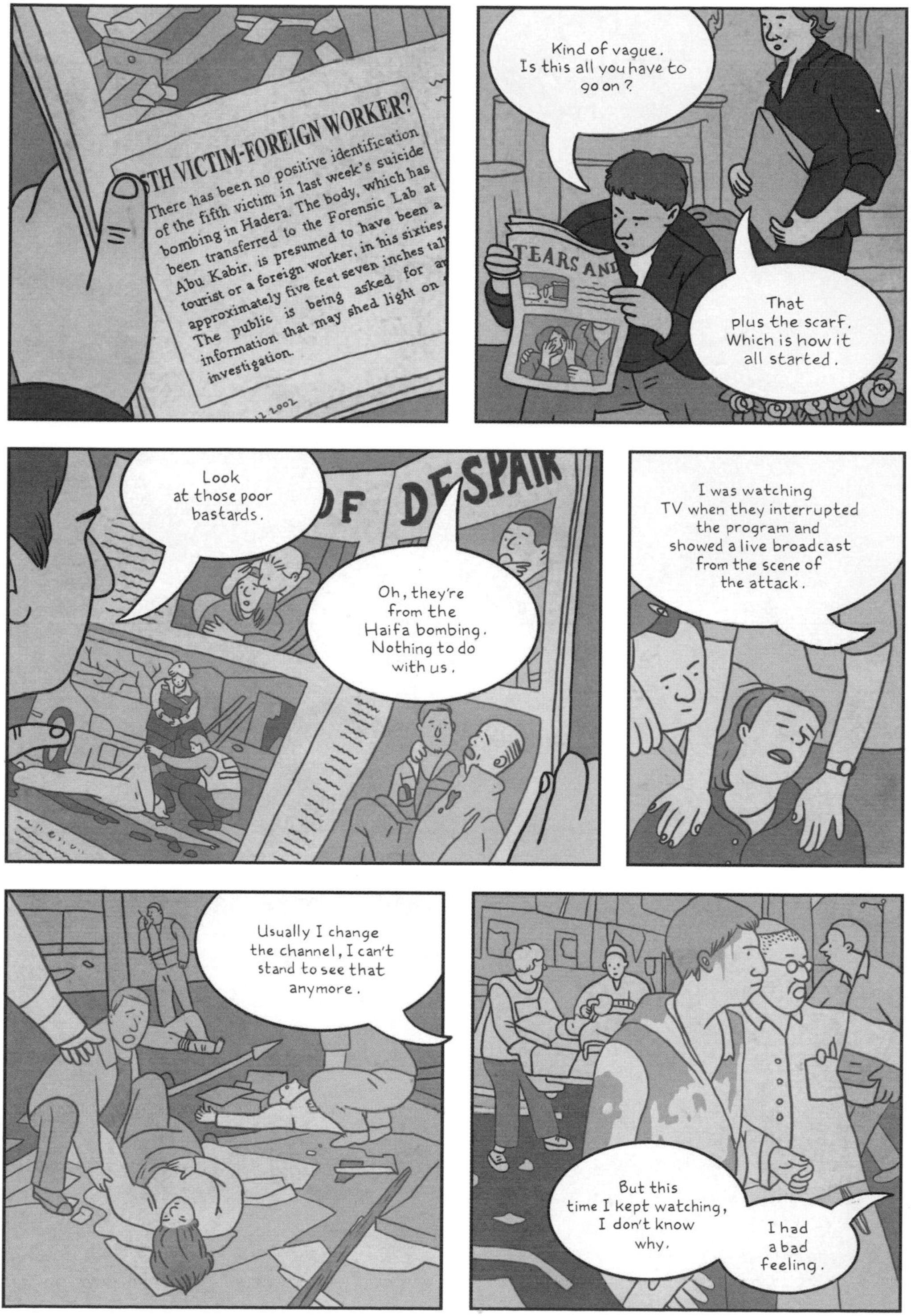
5TH VICTIM-FOREIGN WORKER?
There has been no positive identification of the fifth victim in last week's suicide bombing in Hadera. The body, which has been transferred to the Forensic Lab at Abu Kabir, is presumed to have been a tourist or a foreign worker, in his sixties, approximately five feet seven inches tal
The public is being asked for a
information that may shed light on
investigation.
TEARS AN
Kind of vague. Is this all you have to go on?
That plus the scarf. Which is how it all started.
OF DESPAIR
Look at those poor bastards.
Oh, they're from the Haifa bombing. Nothing to do with us.
I was watching TV when they interrupted the program and showed a live broadcast from the scene of the attack.
Usually I change the channel, I can't stand to see that anymore.
But this time I kept watching, I don't know why.
I had a bad feeling.

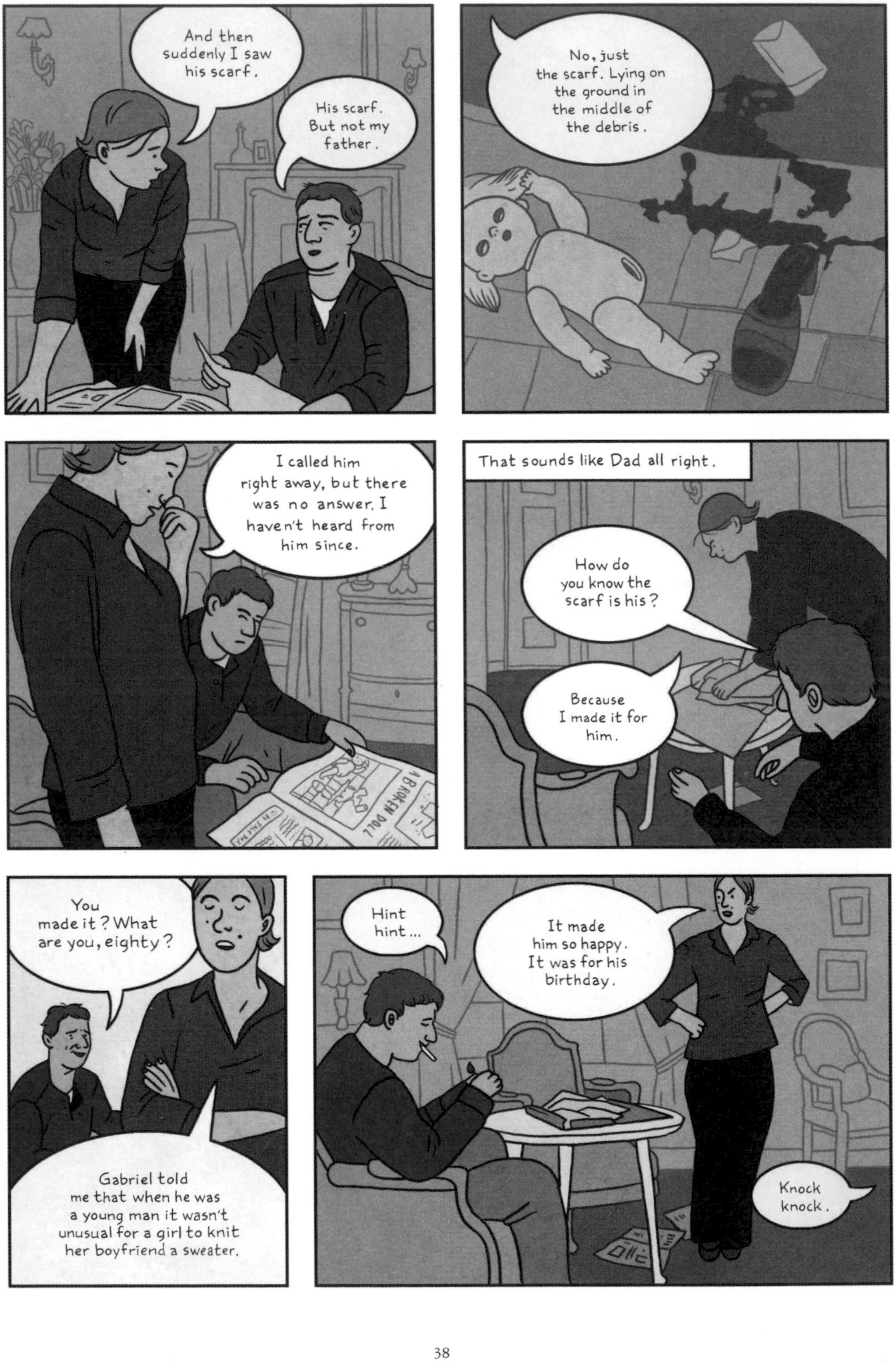
And then suddenly I saw his scarf.
His scarf. But not my father.
No, just the scarf. Lying on the ground in the middle of the debris.
I called him right away, but there was no answer. I haven't heard from him since.
A BROKEN DOLL
That sounds like Dad all right.
How do you know the scarf is his?
Because I made it for him.
You made it? What are you, eighty?
Gabriel told me that when he was a young man it wasn't unusual for a girl to knit her boyfriend a sweater.
Hint hint...
It made him so happy. It was for his birthday.
Knock knock.

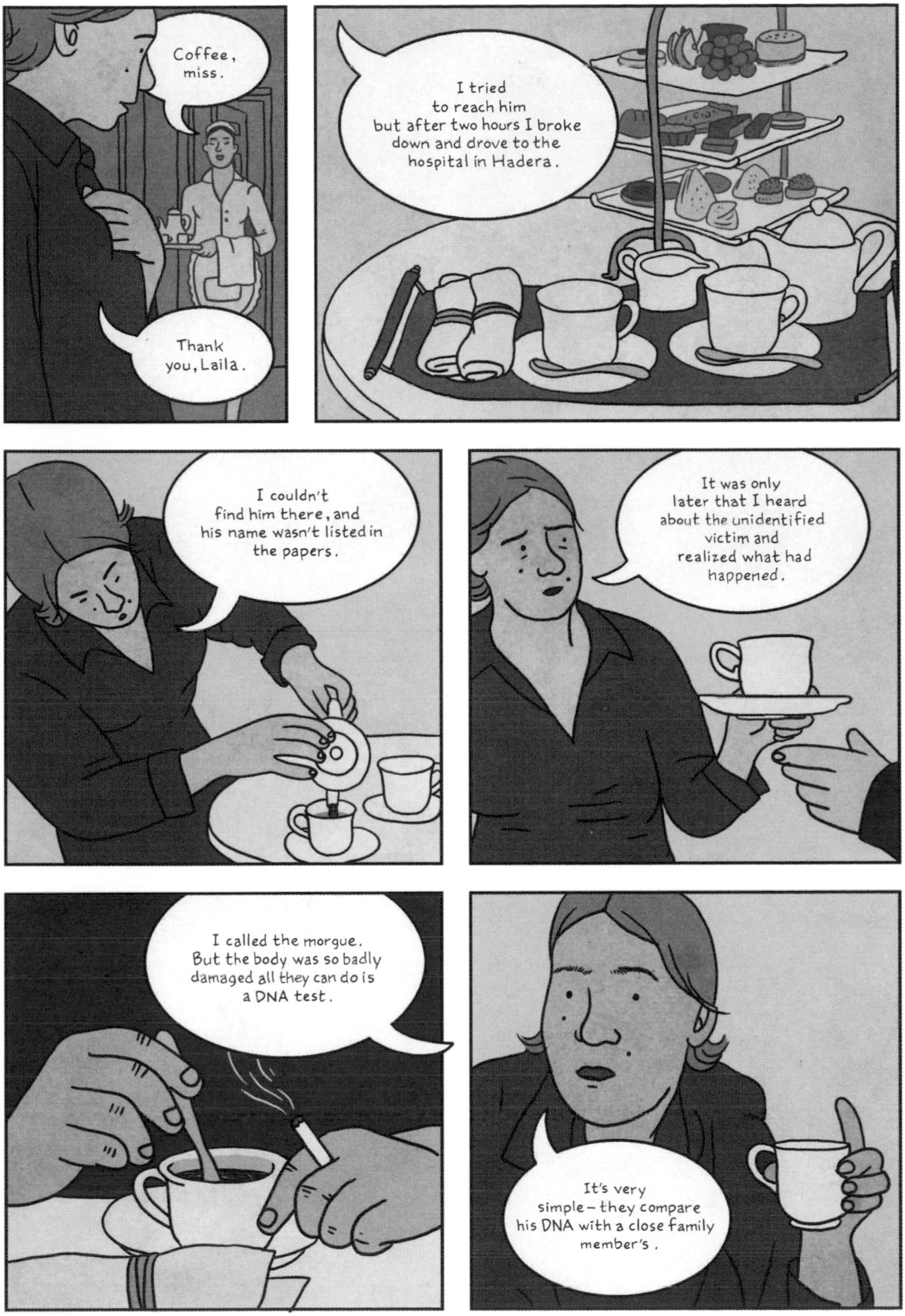
Coffee, miss.
Thank you, Laila.
I tried to reach him but after two hours I broke down and drove to the hospital in Hadera.
I couldn't find him there, and his name wasn't listed in the papers.
It was only later that I heard about the unidentified victim and realized what had happened.
I called the morgue. But the body was so badly damaged all they can do is a DNA test.
It's very simple – they compare his DNA with a close family member's.

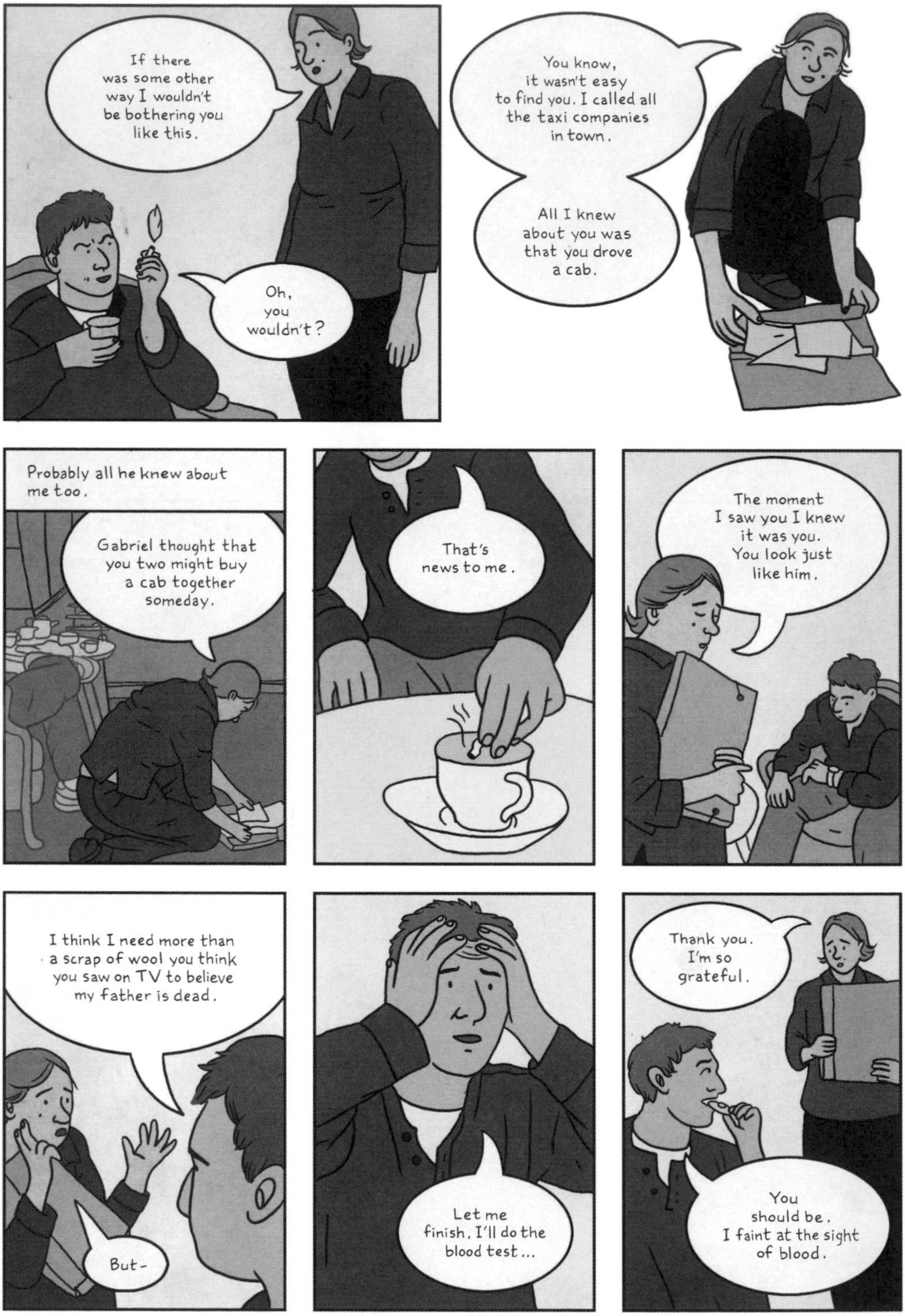
If there was some other way I wouldn't be bothering you like this.
Oh, you wouldn't?
You know, it wasn't easy to find you. I called all the taxi companies in town.
All I knew about you was that you drove a cab.
Probably all he knew about me too.
Gabriel thought that you two might buy a cab together someday.
That's news to me.
The moment I saw you I knew it was you. You look just like him.
I think I need more than a scrap of wool you think you saw on TV to believe my father is dead.
But-
Let me finish. I'll do the blood test...
Thank you. I'm so grateful.
You should be. I faint at the sight of blood.

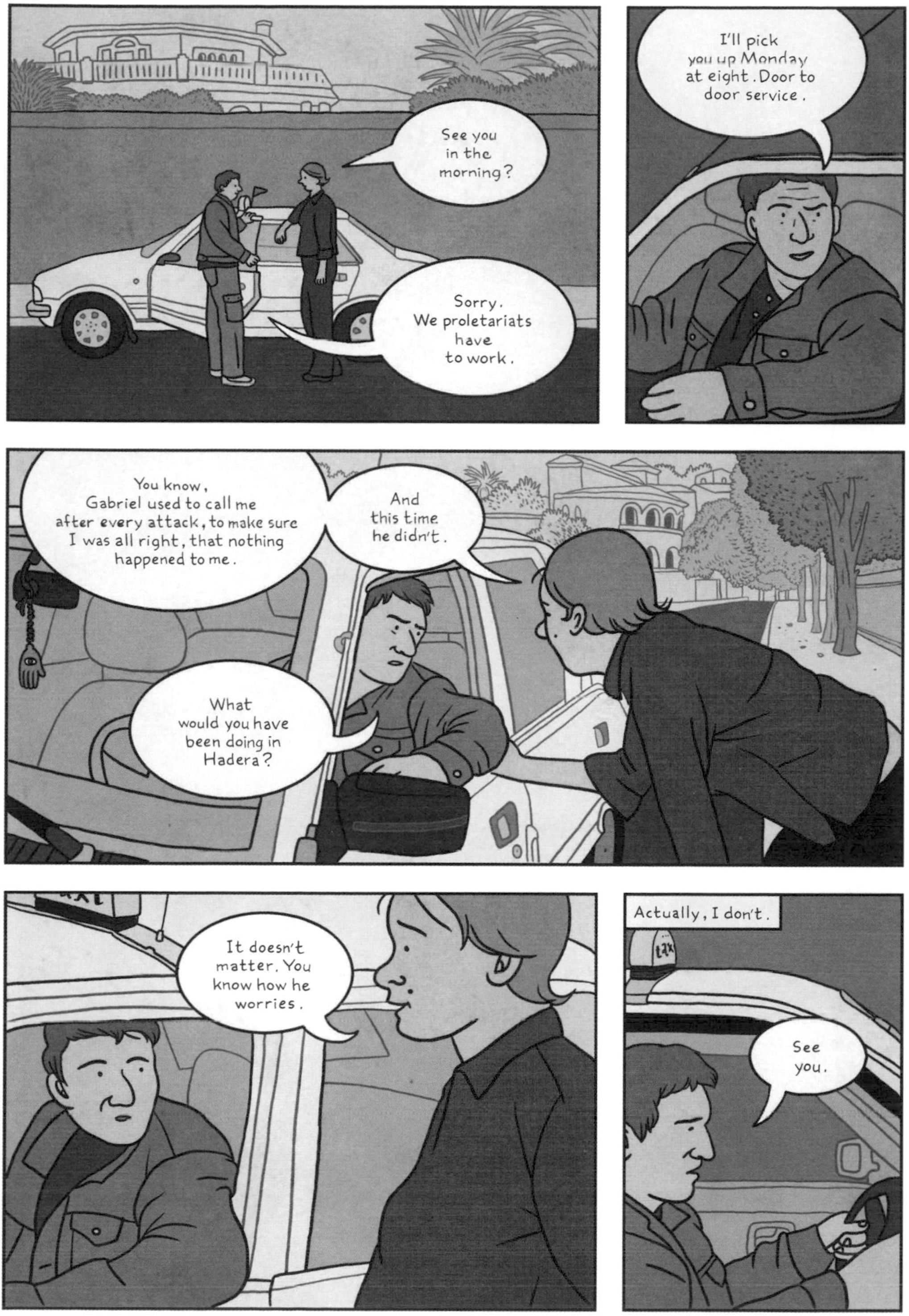
See you in the morning?
Sorry. We proletariats have to work.
I'll pick you up Monday at eight. Door to door service.
You know, Gabriel used to call me after every attack, to make sure I was all right, that nothing happened to me.
And this time he didn't.
What would you have been doing in Hadera?
It doesn't matter. You know how he worries.
Actually, I don't.
See you.

chapter two
my travels with the giraffe

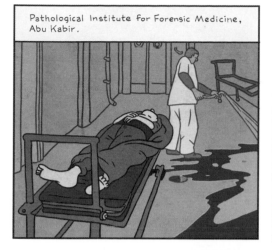

Pathological Institute for Forensic Medicine, Abu Kabir.

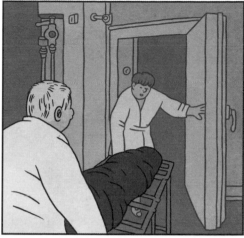

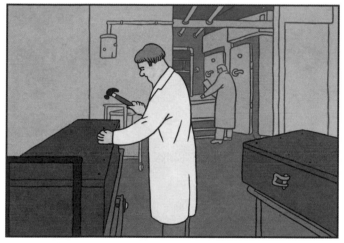

Any thoughts on lunch?

How about Chinese?

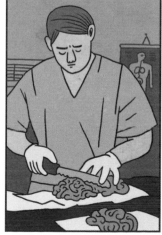

45

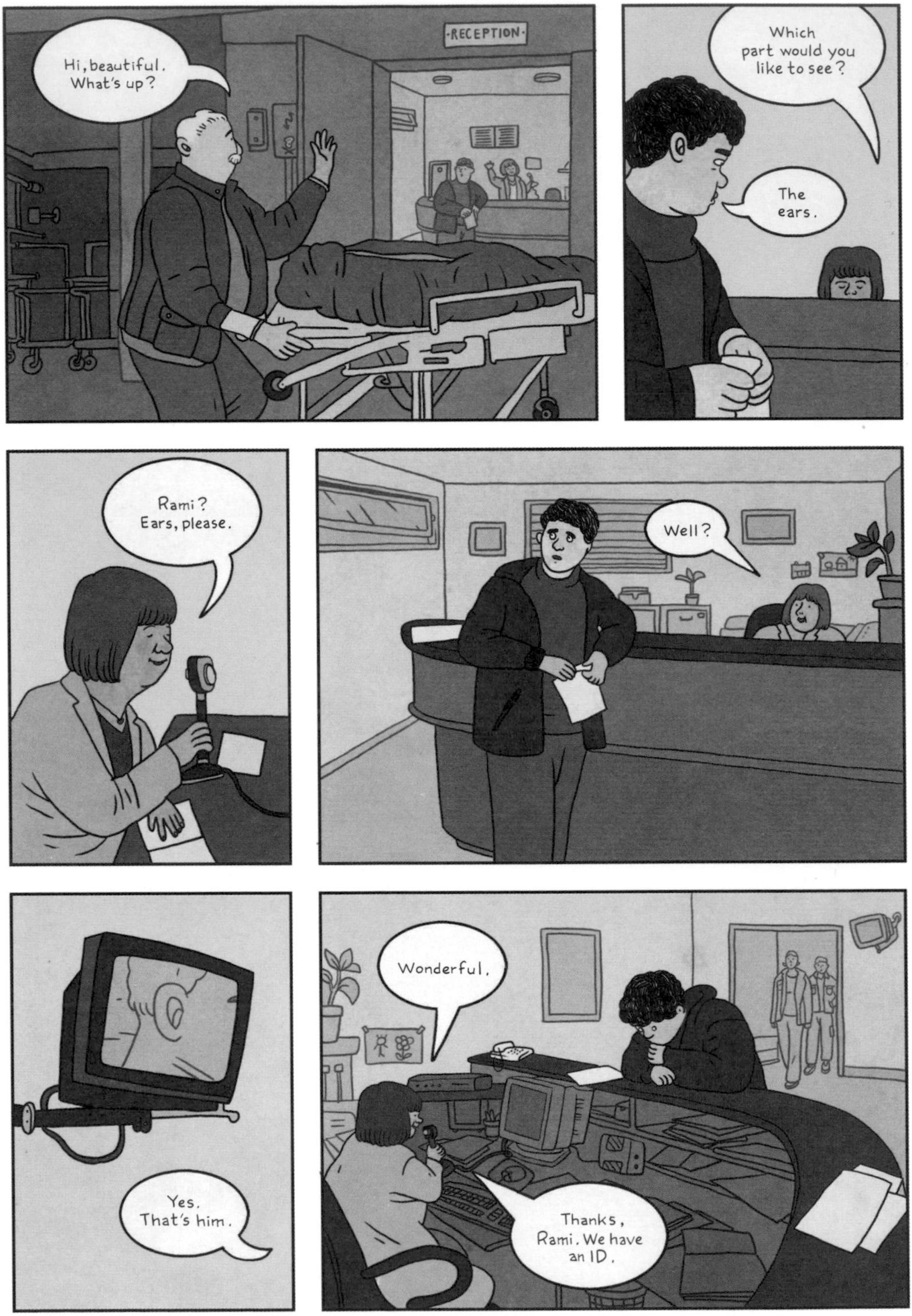
·RECEPTION·
Hi, beautiful. What's up?
Which part would you like to see?
The ears.
Rami? Ears, please.
Well?
Yes. That's him.
Wonderful.
Thanks, Rami. We have an ID.

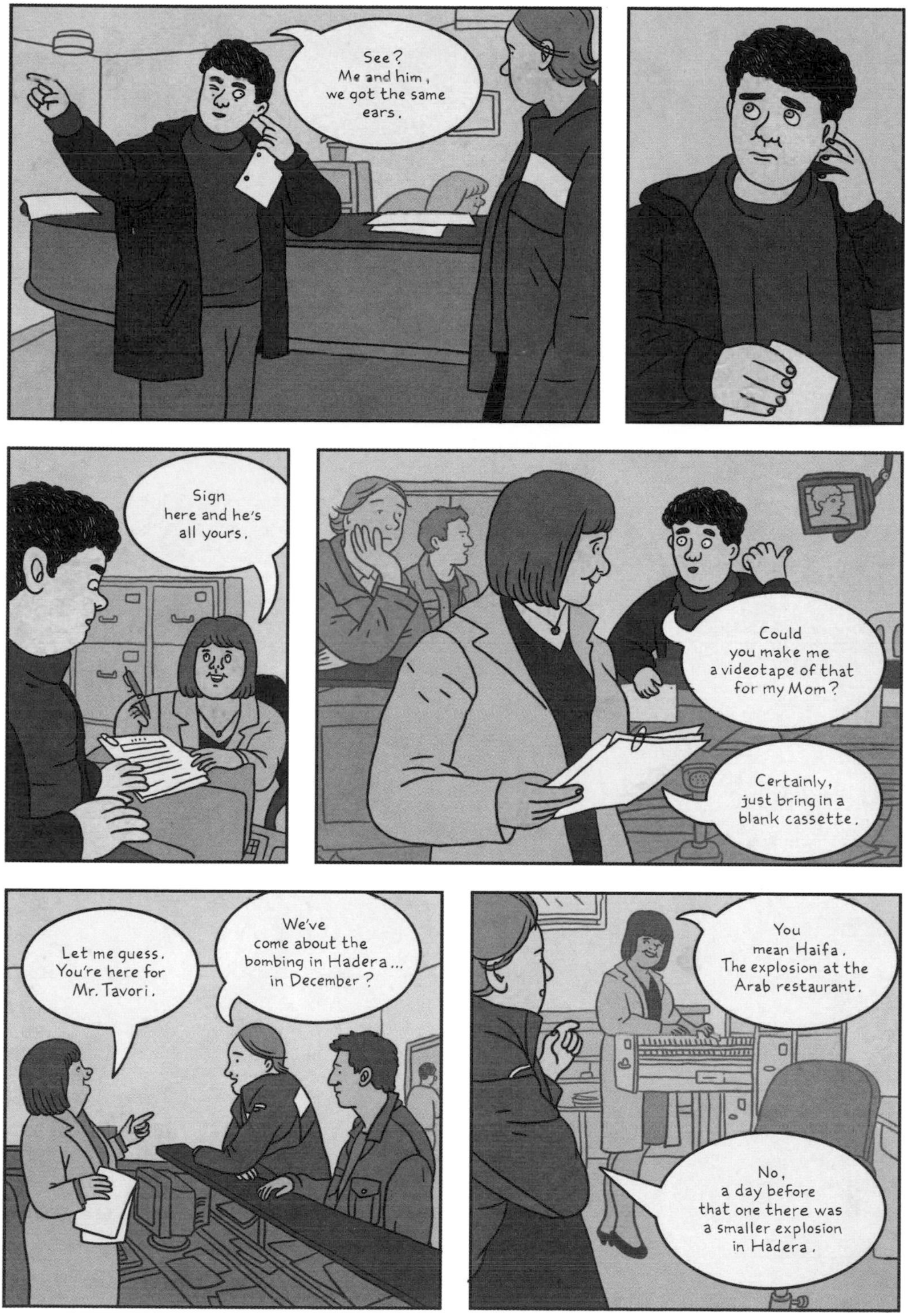
See? Me and him, we got the same ears.
Sign here and he's all yours.
Could you make me a videotape of that for my Mom?
Certainly, just bring in a blank cassette.
Let me guess. You're here for Mr. Tavori.
We've come about the bombing in Hadera... in December?
You mean Haifa. The explosion at the Arab restaurant.
No, a day before that one there was a smaller explosion in Hadera.

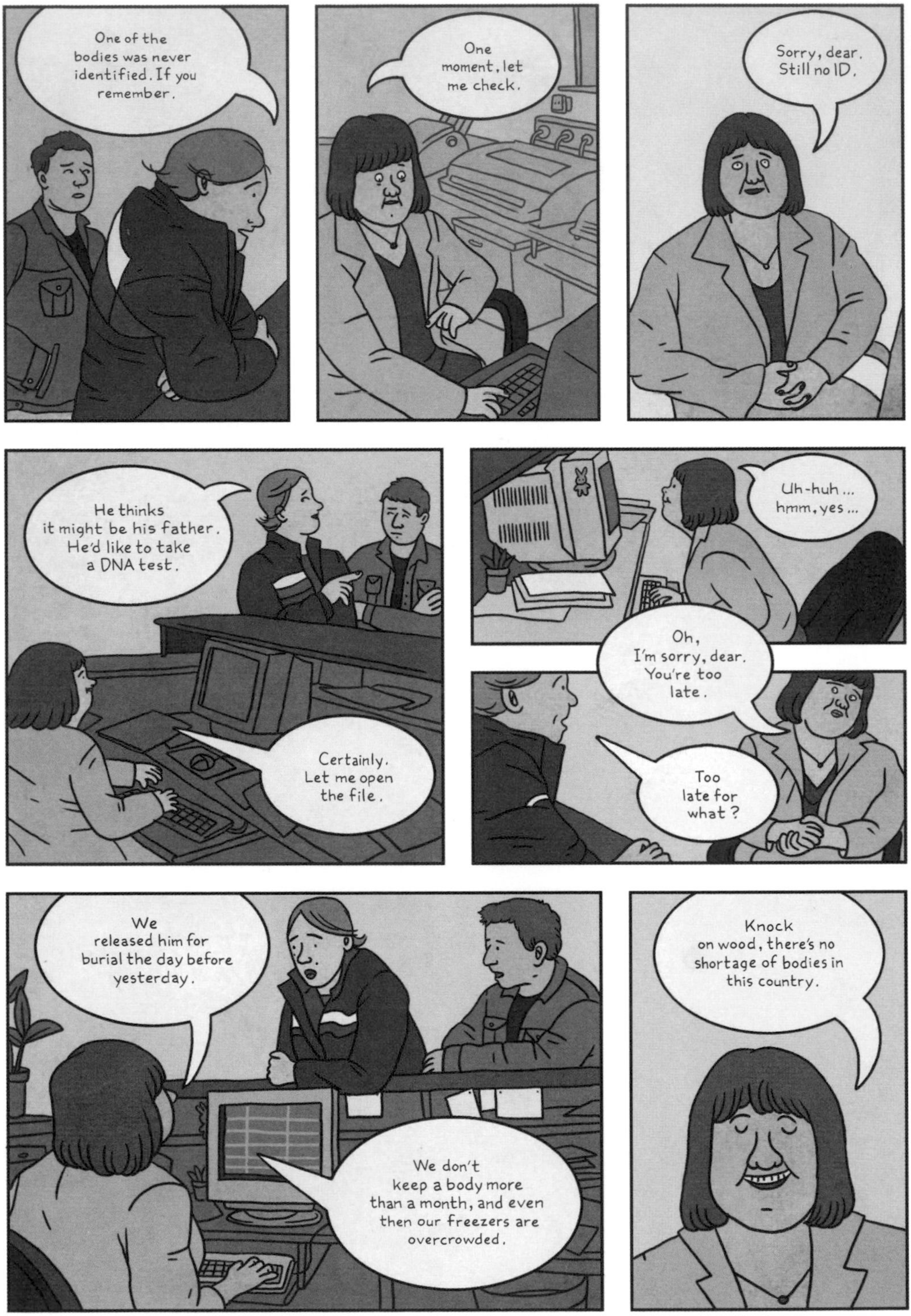
One of the bodies was never identified. If you remember.
One moment, let me check.
Sorry, dear. Still no ID.
He thinks it might be his father. He'd like to take a DNA test.
Certainly. Let me open the file.
Uh-huh ... hmm, yes ...
Oh, I'm sorry, dear. You're too late.
Too late for what?
We released him for burial the day before yesterday.
We don't keep a body more than a month, and even then our freezers are overcrowded.
Knock on wood, there's no shortage of bodies in this country.

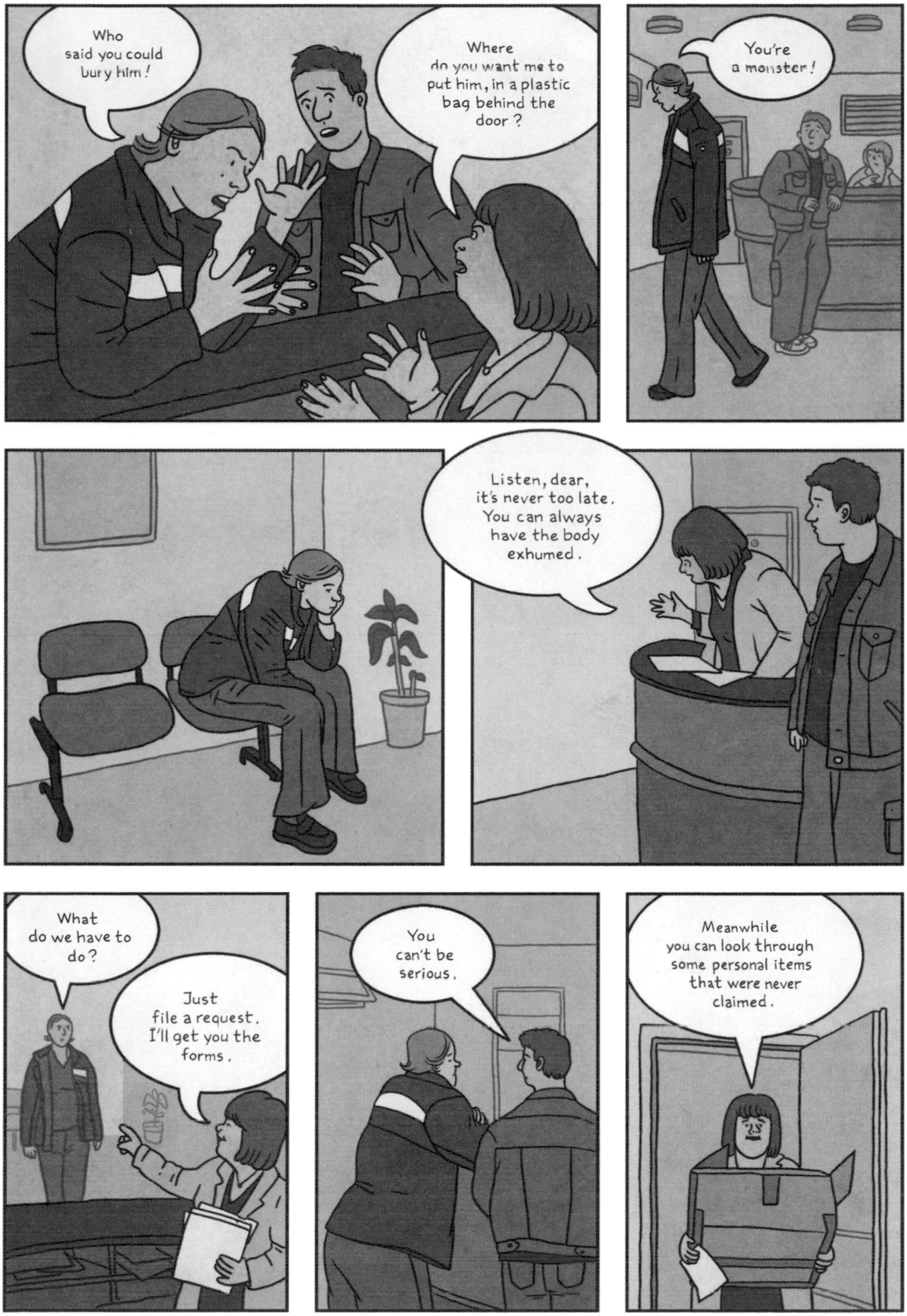

Who said you could bury him!
Where do you want me to put him, in a plastic bag behind the door?
You're a monster!
Listen, dear, it's never too late. You can always have the body exhumed.
What do we have to do?
Just file a request. I'll get you the forms.
You can't be serious.
Meanwhile you can look through some personal items that were never claimed.

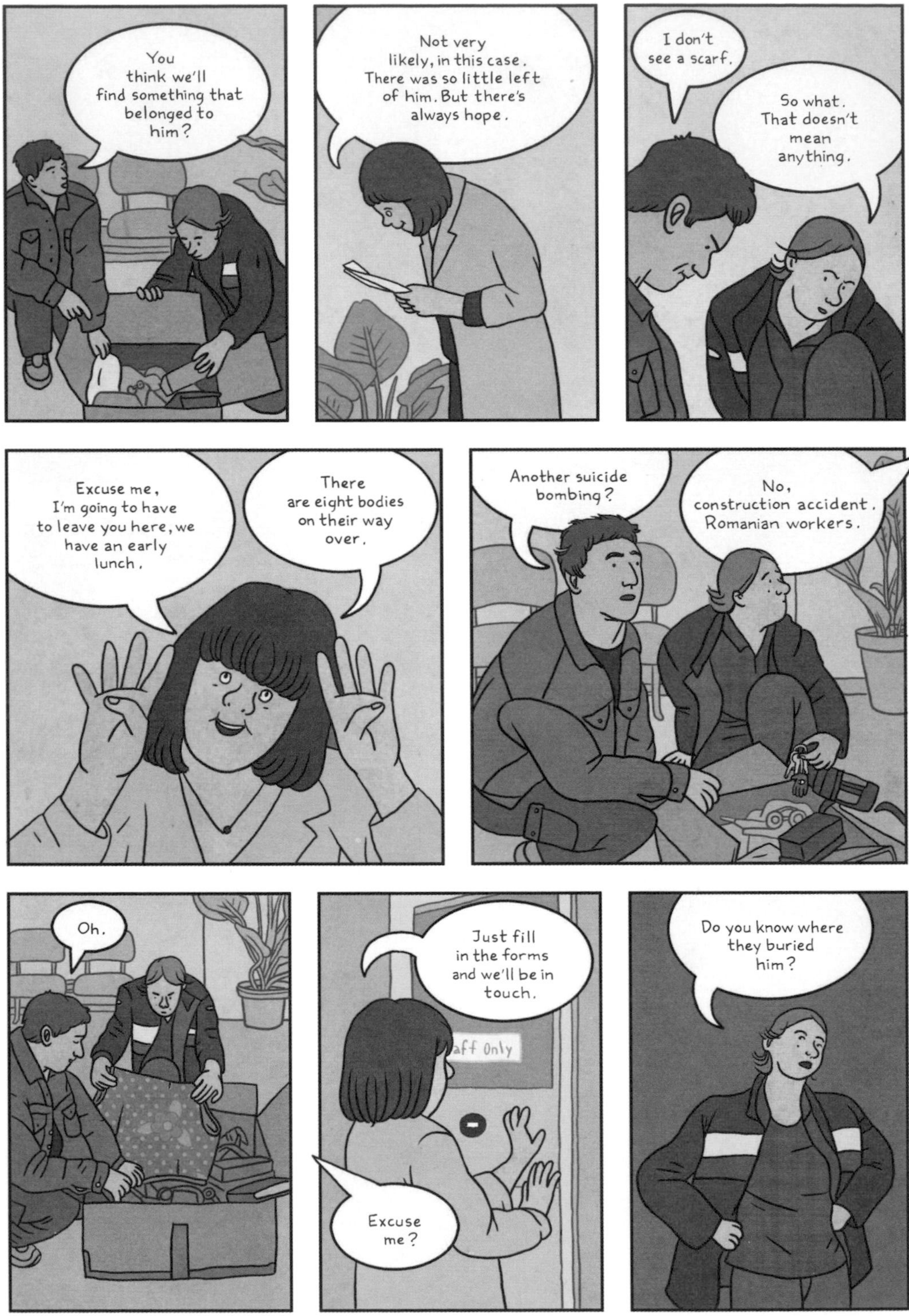
You think we'll find something that belonged to him?
Not very likely, in this case. There was so little left of him. But there's always hope.
I don't see a scarf.
So what. That doesn't mean anything.
Excuse me, I'm going to have to leave you here, we have an early lunch.
There are eight bodies on their way over.
Another suicide bombing?
No, construction accident. Romanian workers.
Oh.
Just fill in the forms and we'll be in touch.
aff Only
Excuse me?
Do you know where they buried him?

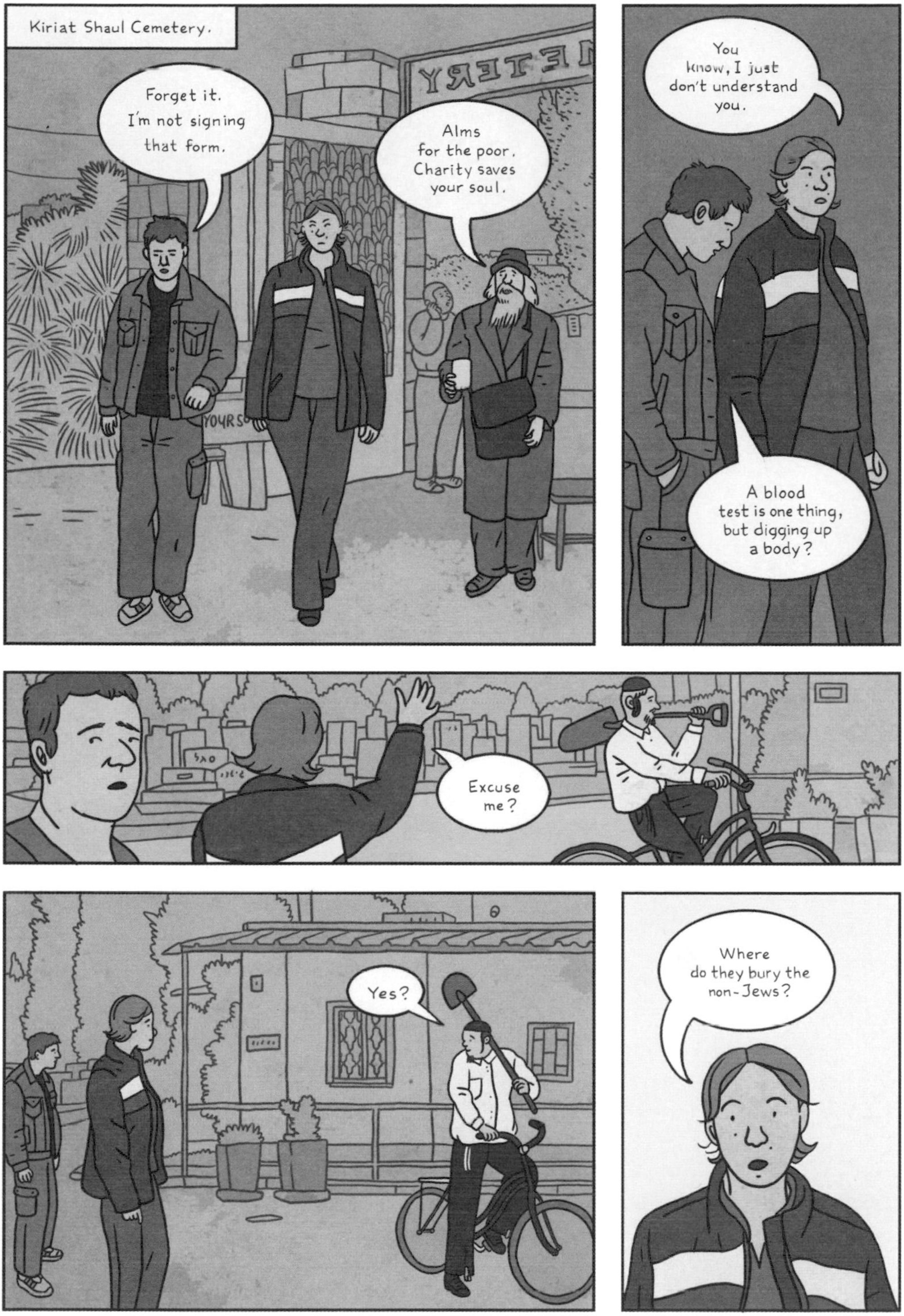
Kiriat Shaul Cemetery.
Forget it. I'm not signing that form.
Alms for the poor. Charity saves your soul.
You know, I just don't understand you.
A blood test is one thing, but digging up a body?
Excuse me?
Yes?
Where do they bury the non-Jews?

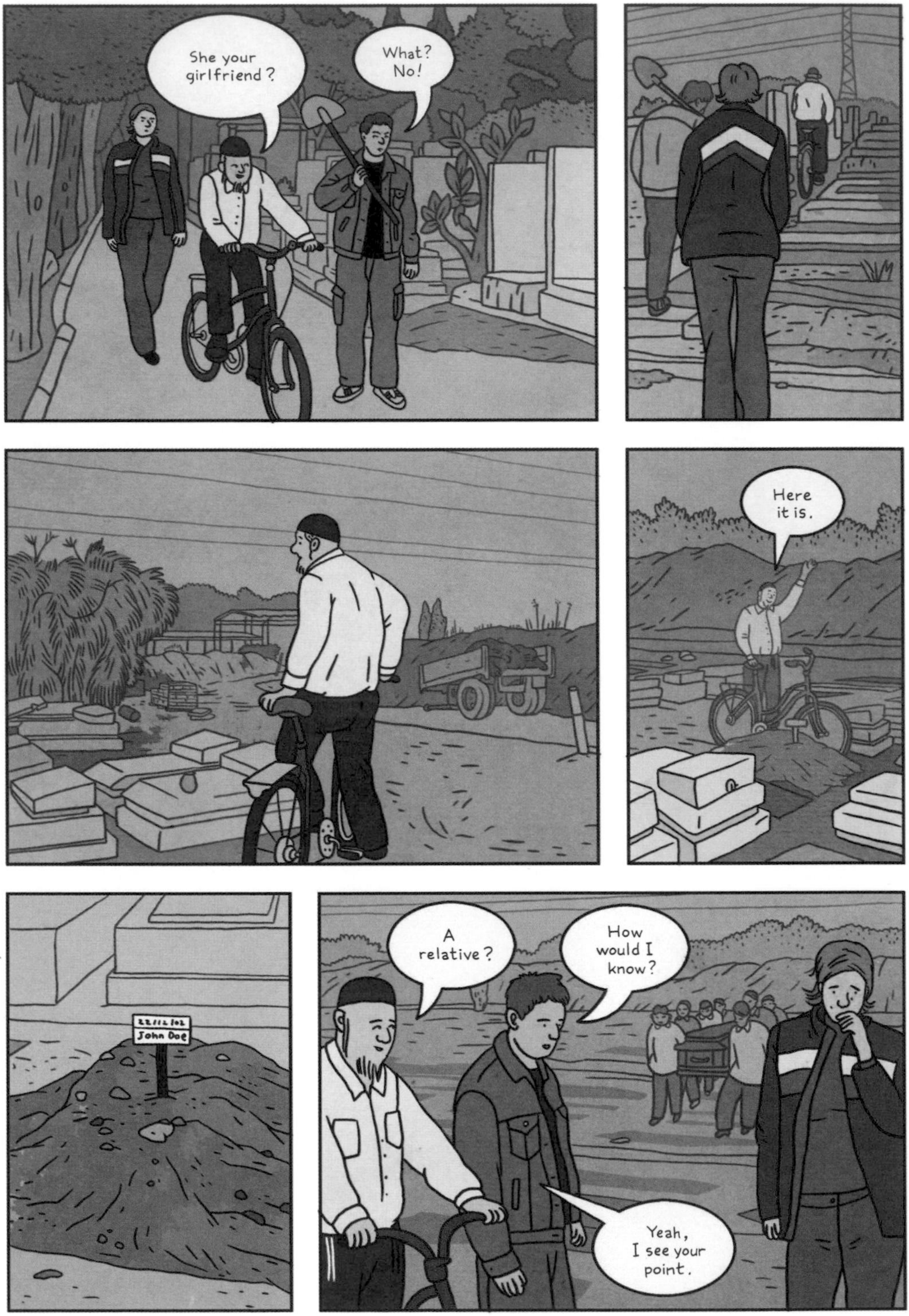
She your girlfriend?
What? No!
Here it is.
22/12/02
John Doe
A relative?
How would I know?
Yeah, I see your point.

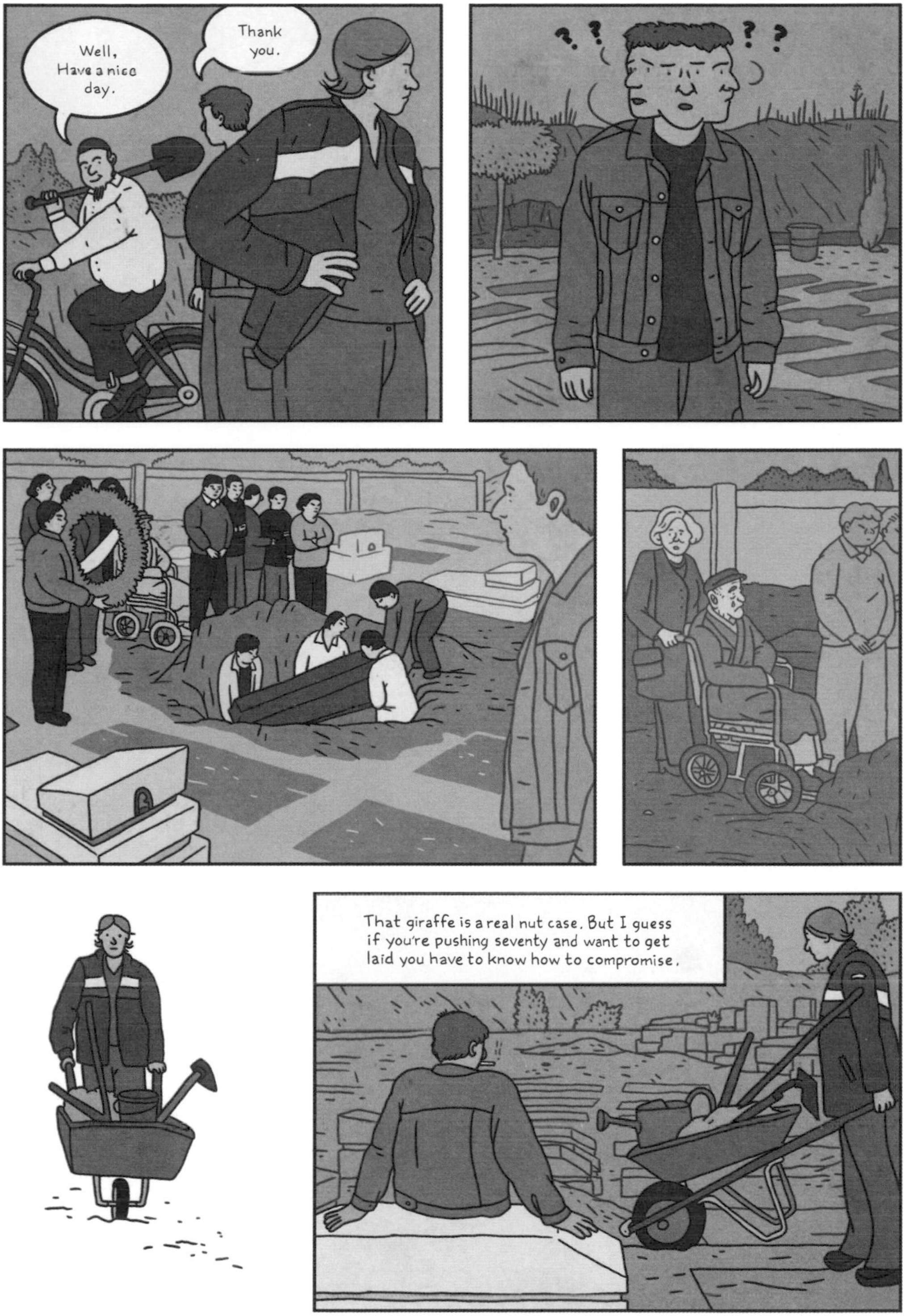
Well, Have a nice day.
Thank you.
That giraffe is a real nut case. But I guess if you're pushing seventy and want to get laid you have to know how to compromise.

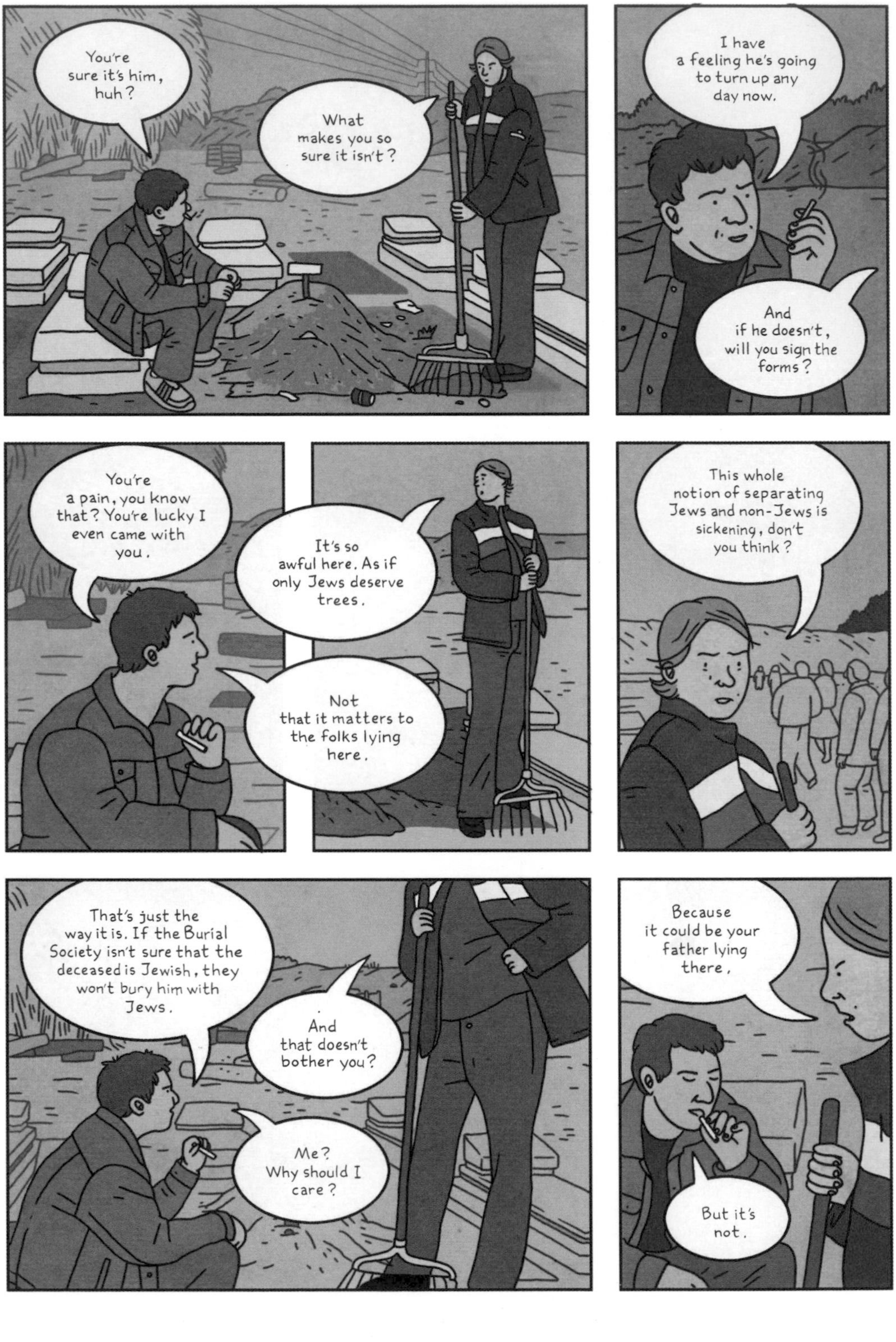
You're sure it's him, huh?
What makes you so sure it isn't?
I have a feeling he's going to turn up any day now.
And if he doesn't, will you sign the forms?
You're a pain, you know that? You're lucky I even came with you.
It's so awful here. As if only Jews deserve trees.
Not that it matters to the folks lying here.
This whole notion of separating Jews and non-Jews is sickening, don't you think?
That's just the way it is. If the Burial Society isn't sure that the deceased is Jewish, they won't bury him with Jews.
And that doesn't bother you?
Me? Why should I care?
Because it could be your father lying there,
But it's not.

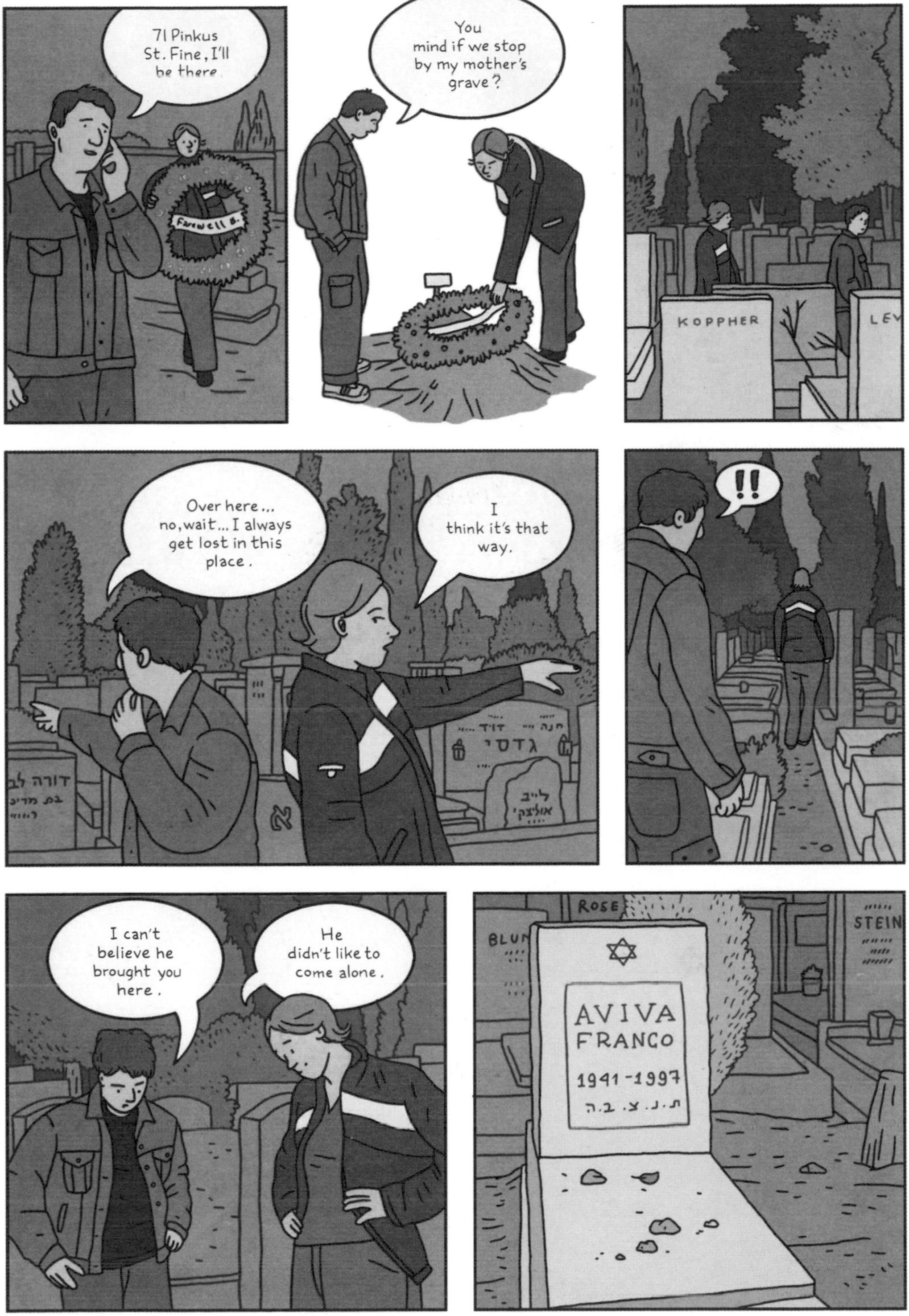

71 Pinkus St. Fine, I'll be there.
Farewell B.
You mind if we stop by my mother's grave?
KOPPHER
LEV
Over here... no, wait... I always get lost in this place.
I think it's that way.
דורה לב
גדסי
!!
I can't believe he brought you here.
He didn't like to come alone.
ROSE
BLUN
STEIN
AVIVA FRANCO
1941-1997
ת.נ.צ.ב.ה

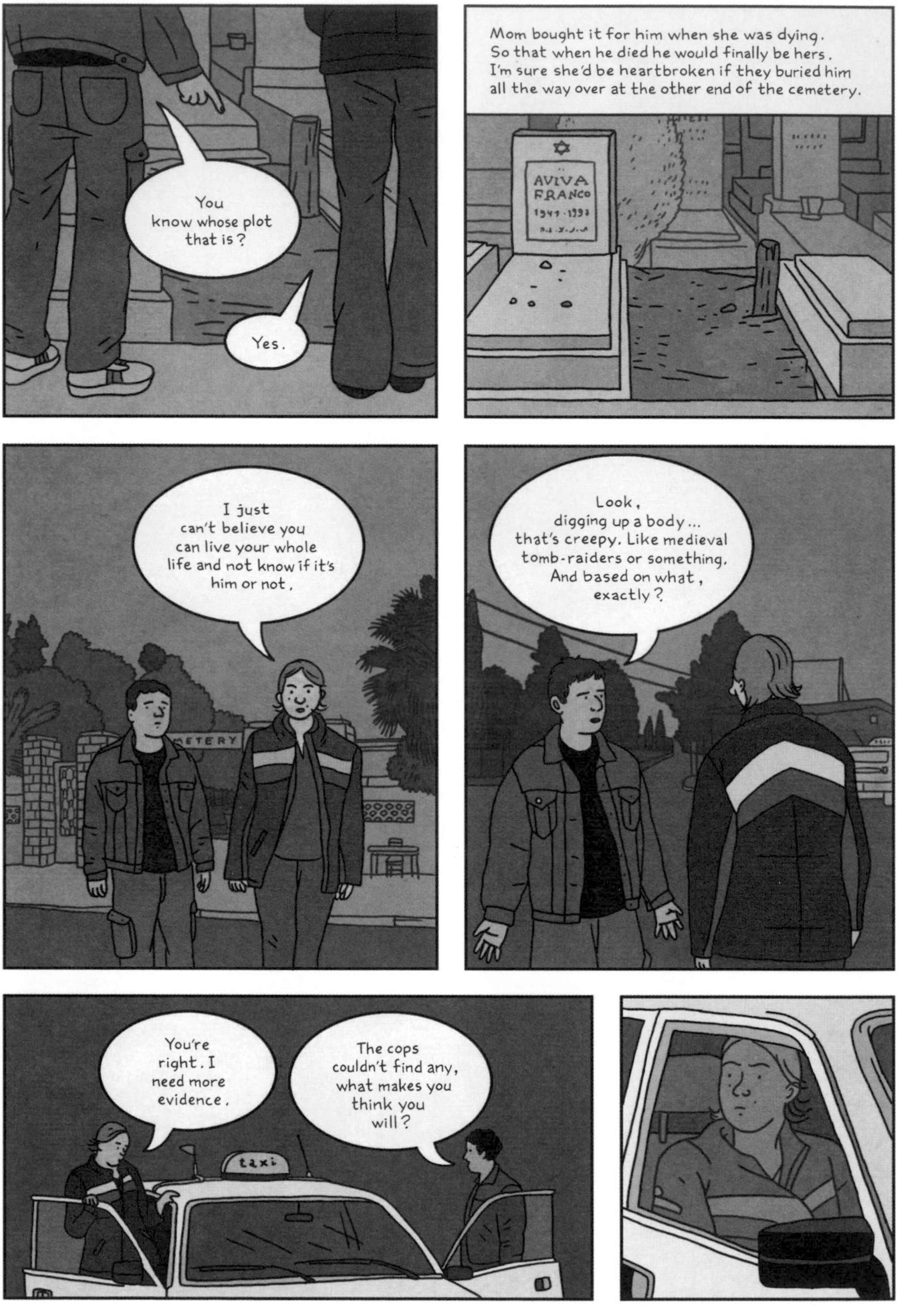
You know whose plot that is?
Yes.
Mom bought it for him when she was dying. So that when he died he would finally be hers. I'm sure she'd be heartbroken if they buried him all the way over at the other end of the cemetery.
AVIVA FRANCO
I just can't believe you can live your whole life and not know if it's him or not.
Look, digging up a body... that's creepy. Like medieval tomb-raiders or something. And based on what, exactly?
You're right. I need more evidence.
The cops couldn't find any, what makes you think you will?
taxi

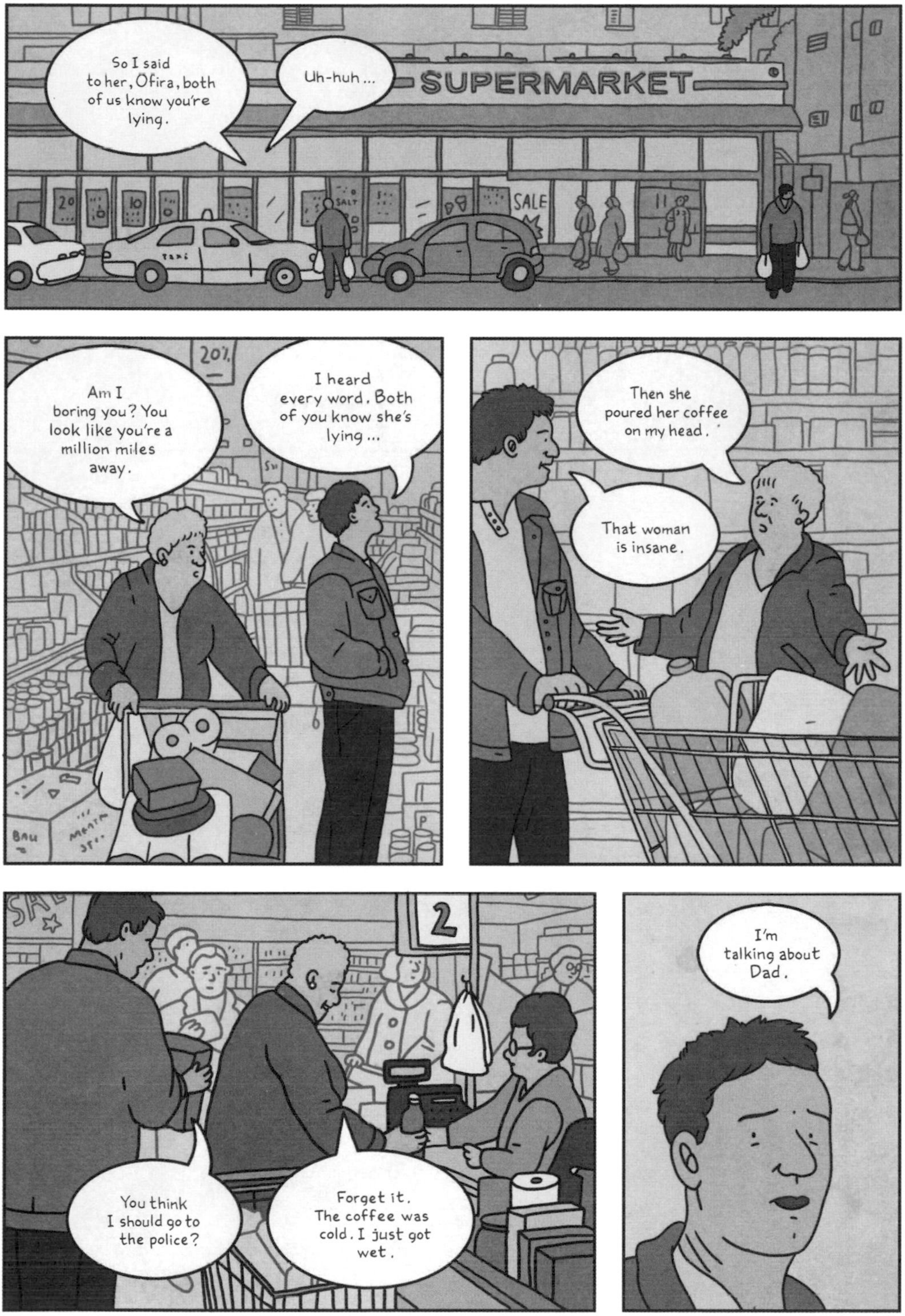
So I said to her, Ofira, both of us know you're lying.
Uh-huh ...
SUPERMARKET
SALE
Am I boring you? You look like you're a million miles away.
I heard every word. Both of us know she's lying ...
Then she poured her coffee on my head.
That woman is insane.
You think I should go to the police?
Forget it. The coffee was cold. I just got wet.
I'm talking about Dad.

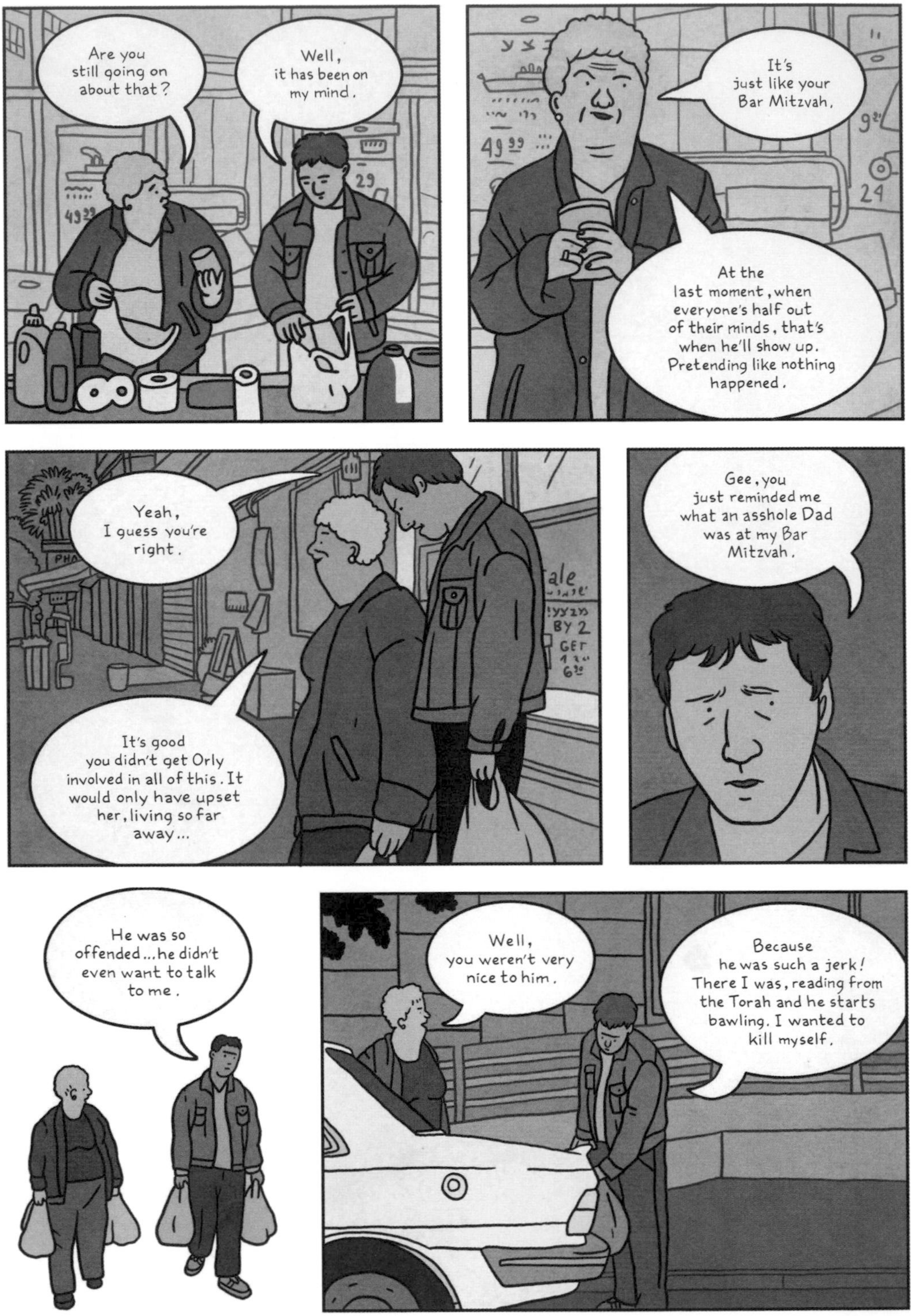
Are you still going on about that?
Well, it has been on my mind.
It's just like your Bar Mitzvah.
At the last moment, when everyone's half out of their minds, that's when he'll show up. Pretending like nothing happened.
Yeah, I guess you're right.
It's good you didn't get Orly involved in all of this. It would only have upset her, living so far away...
Gee, you just reminded me what an asshole Dad was at my Bar Mitzvah.
He was so offended...he didn't even want to talk to me.
Well, you weren't very nice to him.
Because he was such a jerk! There I was, reading from the Torah and he starts bawling. I wanted to kill myself.

It's a very emotional moment for a father.
Yeah, sure.
You should know that your parents cashed in a savings account so you could have a decent Bar Mitzvah.
Like I asked for it.
Kids never appreciate what their parents do for them.
So now you're on his side?
I'm just saying that you were no angel either.
I was thirteen years old!
BANG
תי את מקדשי בתוכם לעולם
Come on, Aunt Ruthie.

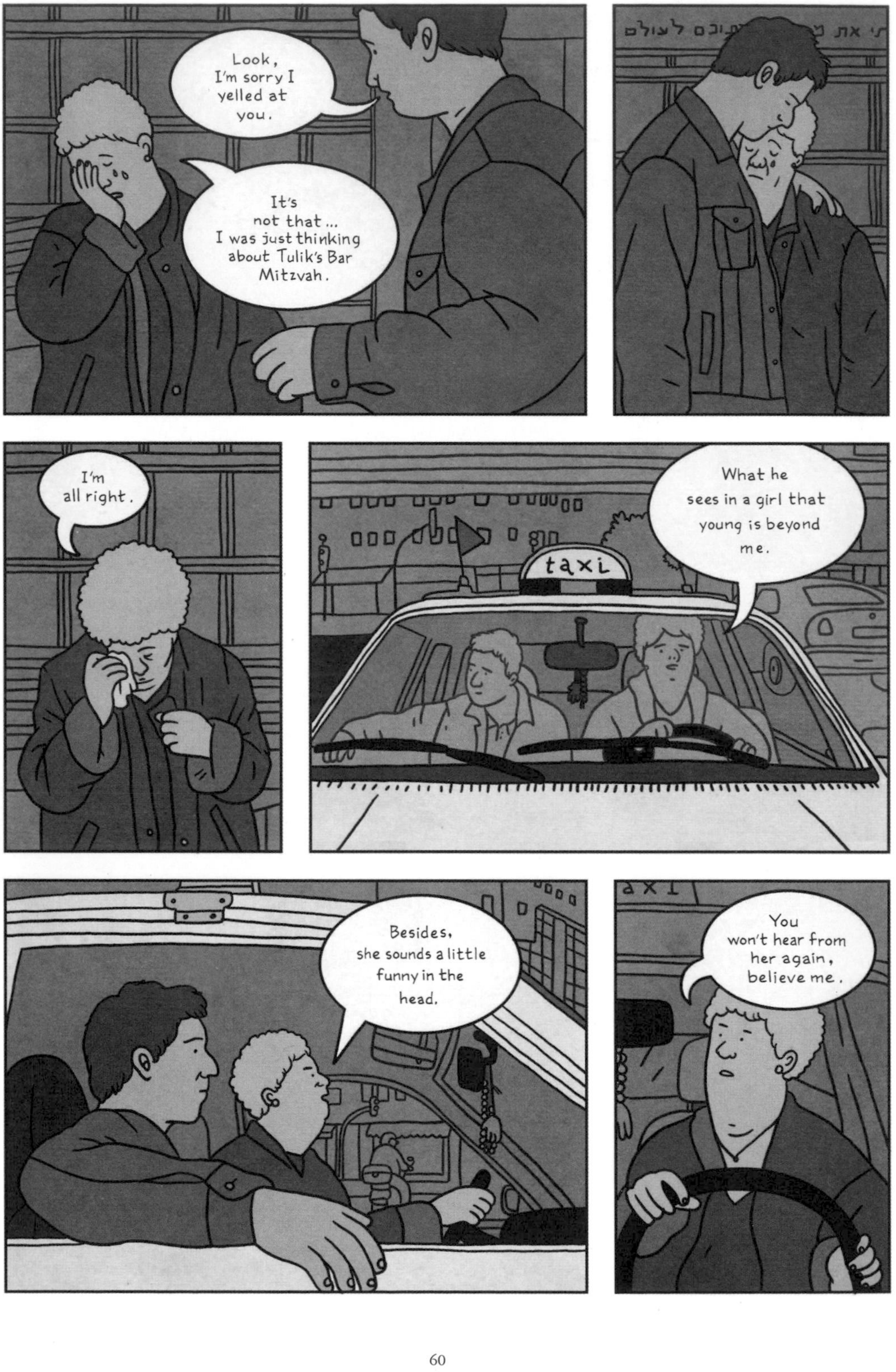
Look, I'm sorry I yelled at you.
It's not that... I was just thinking about Tulik's Bar Mitzvah.
I'm all right.
taxi
What he sees in a girl that young is beyond me.
Besides, she sounds a little funny in the head.
You won't hear from her again, believe me.

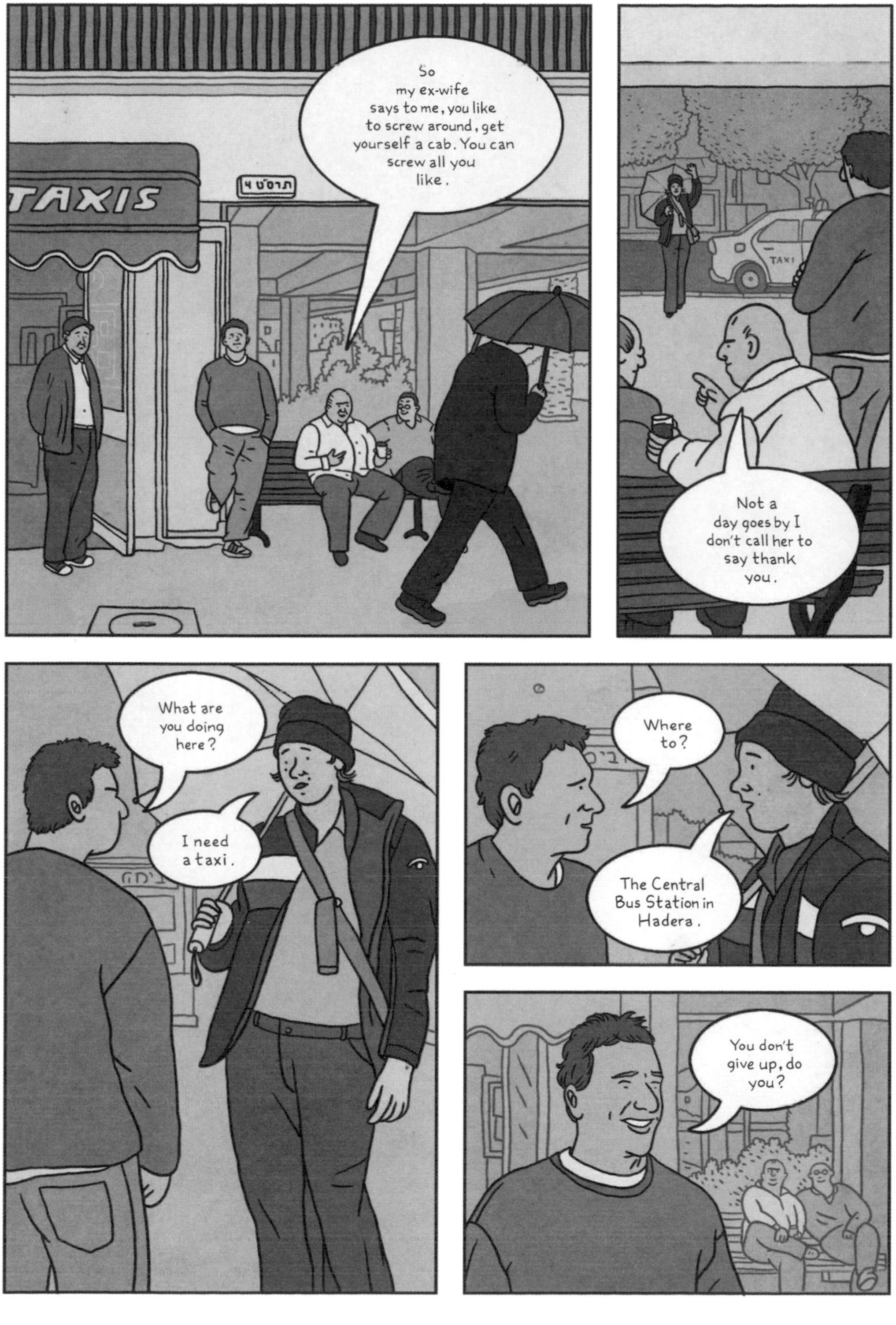
So my ex-wife says to me, you like to screw around, get yourself a cab. You can screw all you like.
TAXIS
Not a day goes by I don't call her to say thank you.
What are you doing here?
I need a taxi.
Where to?
The Central Bus Station in Hadera.
You don't give up, do you?

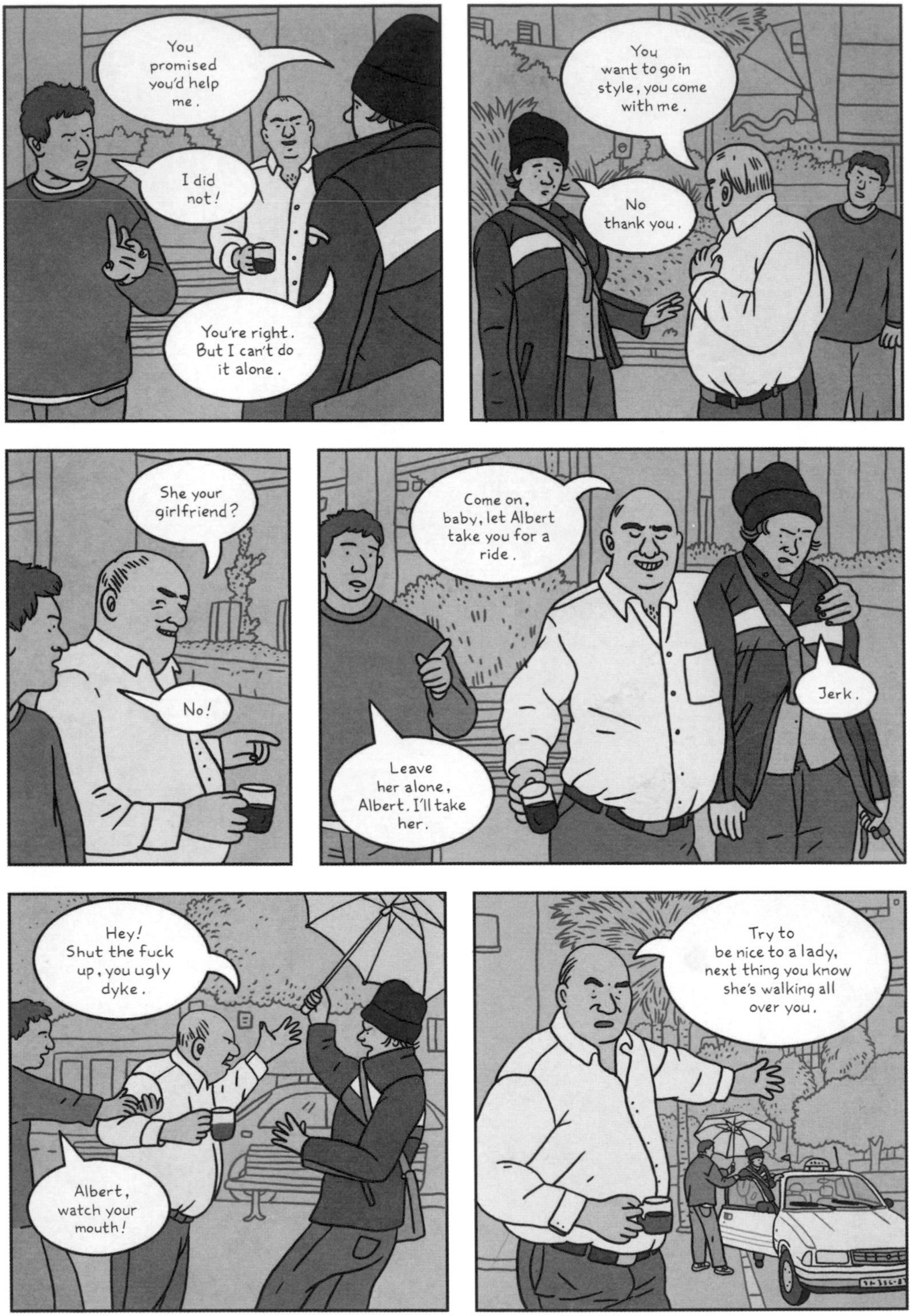
You promised you'd help me.
I did not!
You're right. But I can't do it alone.
You want to go in style, you come with me.
No thank you.
She your girlfriend?
No!
Come on, baby, let Albert take you for a ride.
Jerk.
Leave her alone, Albert. I'll take her.
Hey! Shut the fuck up, you ugly dyke.
Albert, watch your mouth!
Try to be nice to a lady, next thing you know she's walking all over you.

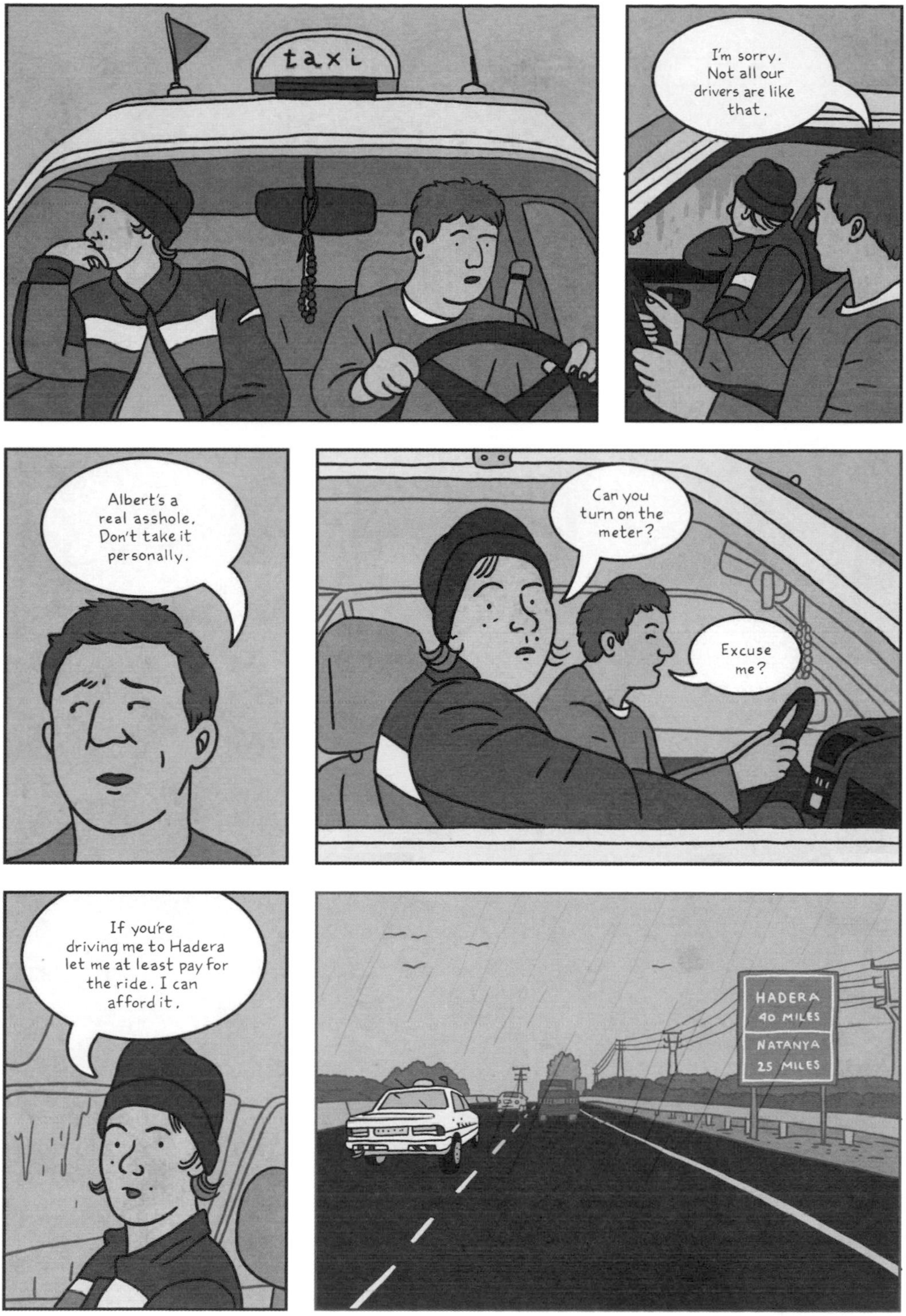
taxi
I'm sorry. Not all our drivers are like that.
Albert's a real asshole. Don't take it personally.
Can you turn on the meter?
Excuse me?
If you're driving me to Hadera let me at least pay for the ride. I can afford it.
HADERA 40 MILES
NATANYA 25 MILES

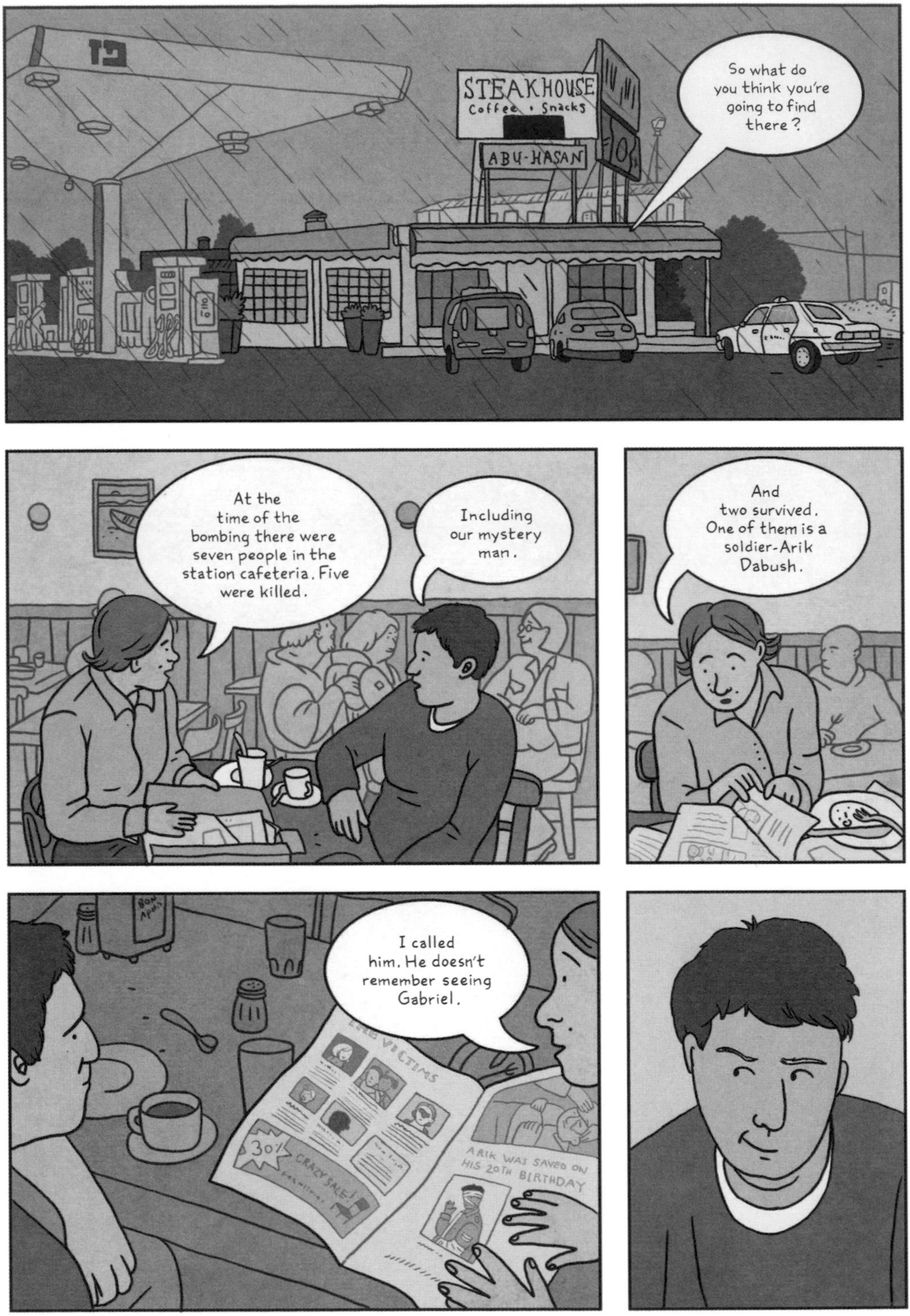
STEAKHOUSE
Coffee • Snacks
ABU-HASAN
So what do you think you're going to find there?
At the time of the bombing there were seven people in the station cafeteria. Five were killed.
Including our mystery man.
And two survived. One of them is a soldier-Arik Dabush.
I called him. He doesn't remember seeing Gabriel.
VICTIMS
30%
CRAZY SALE!
ARIK WAS SAVED ON HIS 20TH BIRTHDAY

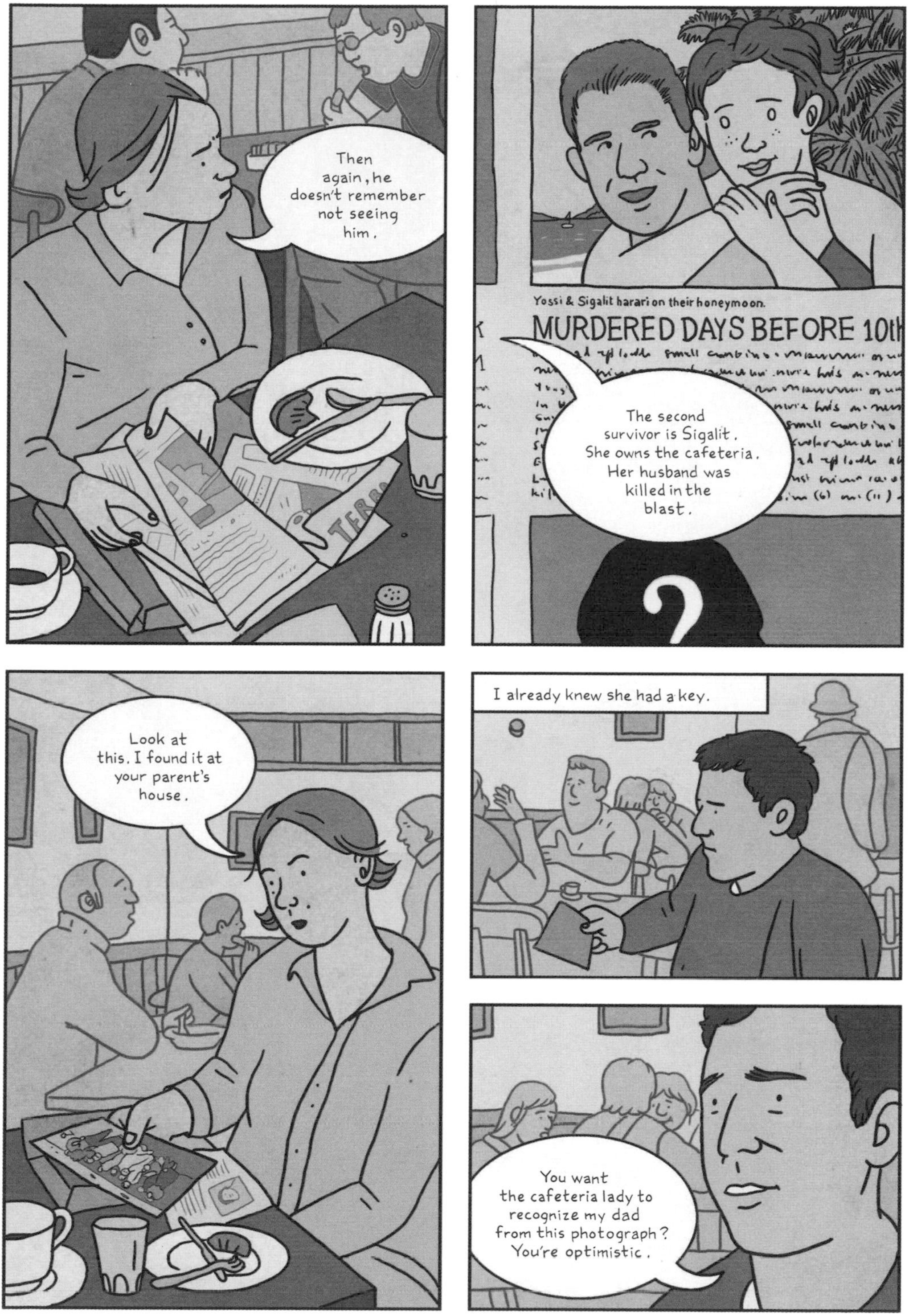
Then again, he doesn't remember not seeing him.
Yossi & Sigalit harari on their honeymoon.
MURDERED DAYS BEFORE 10th
The second survivor is Sigalit. She owns the cafeteria. Her husband was killed in the blast.
Look at this. I found it at your parent's house.
I already knew she had a key.
You want the cafeteria lady to recognize my dad from this photograph? You're optimistic.

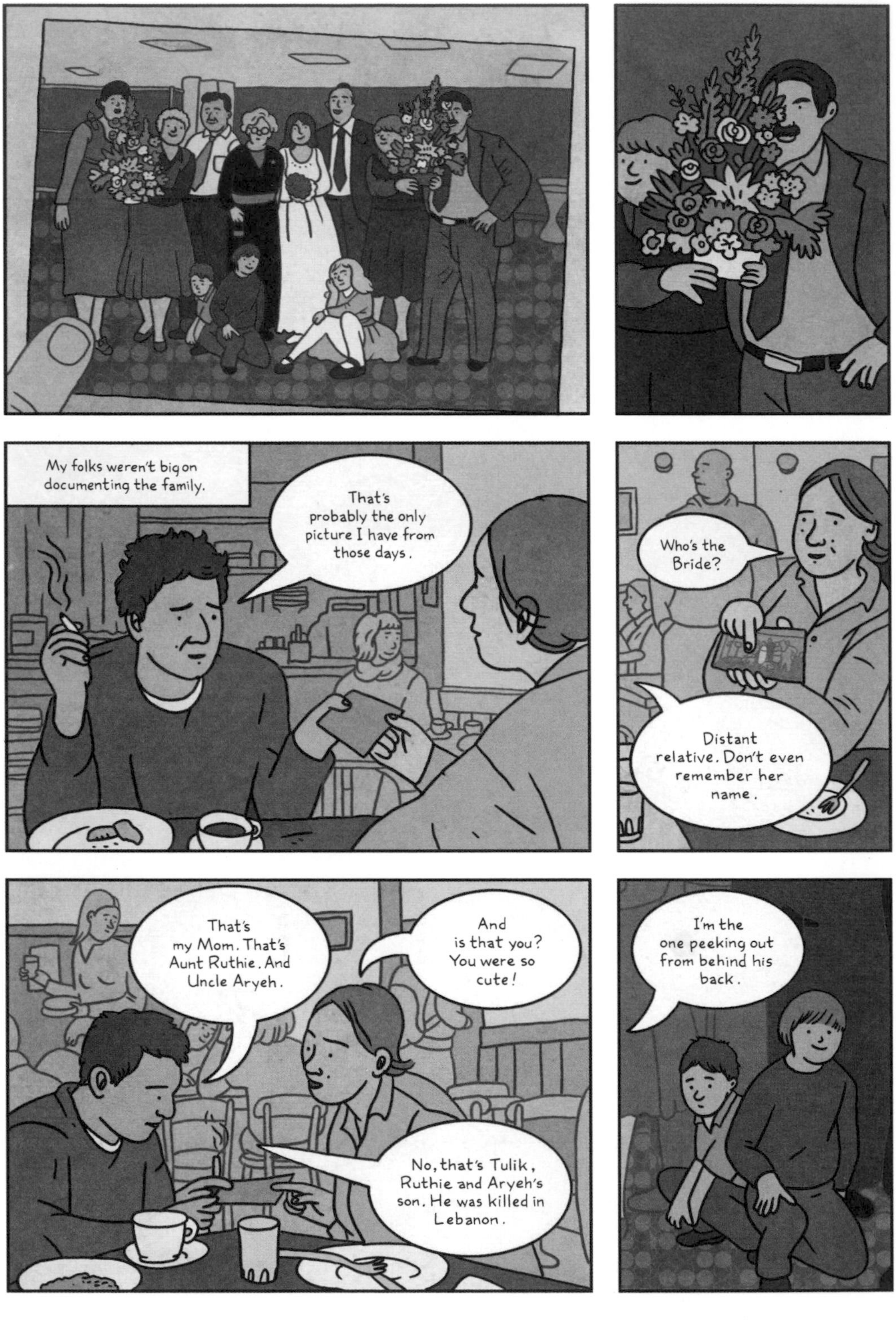
My folks weren't big on documenting the family.
That's probably the only picture I have from those days.
Who's the Bride?
Distant relative. Don't even remember her name.
That's my Mom. That's Aunt Ruthie. And Uncle Aryeh.
And is that you? You were so cute!
No, that's Tulik, Ruthie and Aryeh's son. He was killed in Lebanon.
I'm the one peeking out from behind his back.

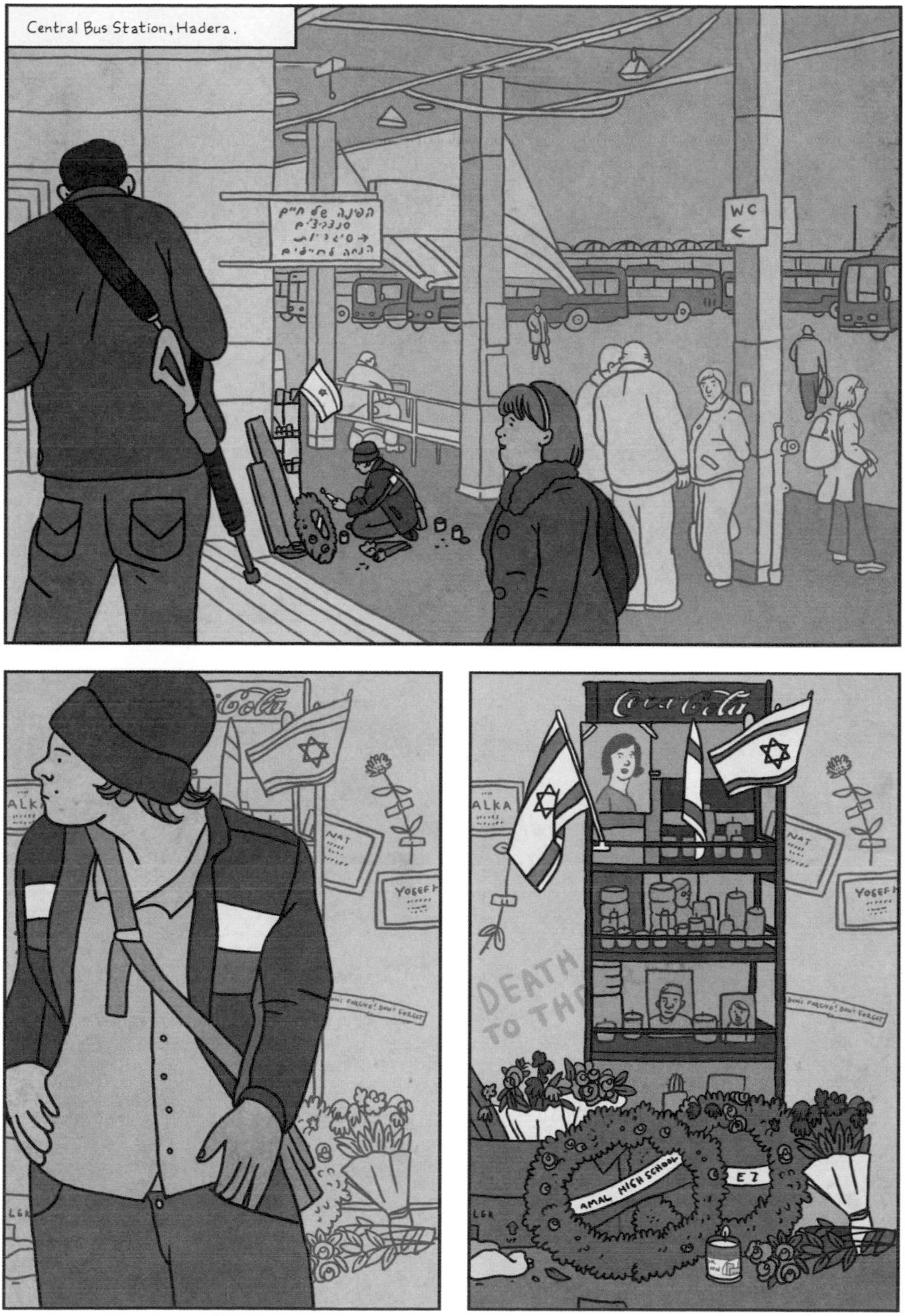
Central Bus Station, Hadera.
WC
DEATH
AMAL HIGH SCHOOL
EZ

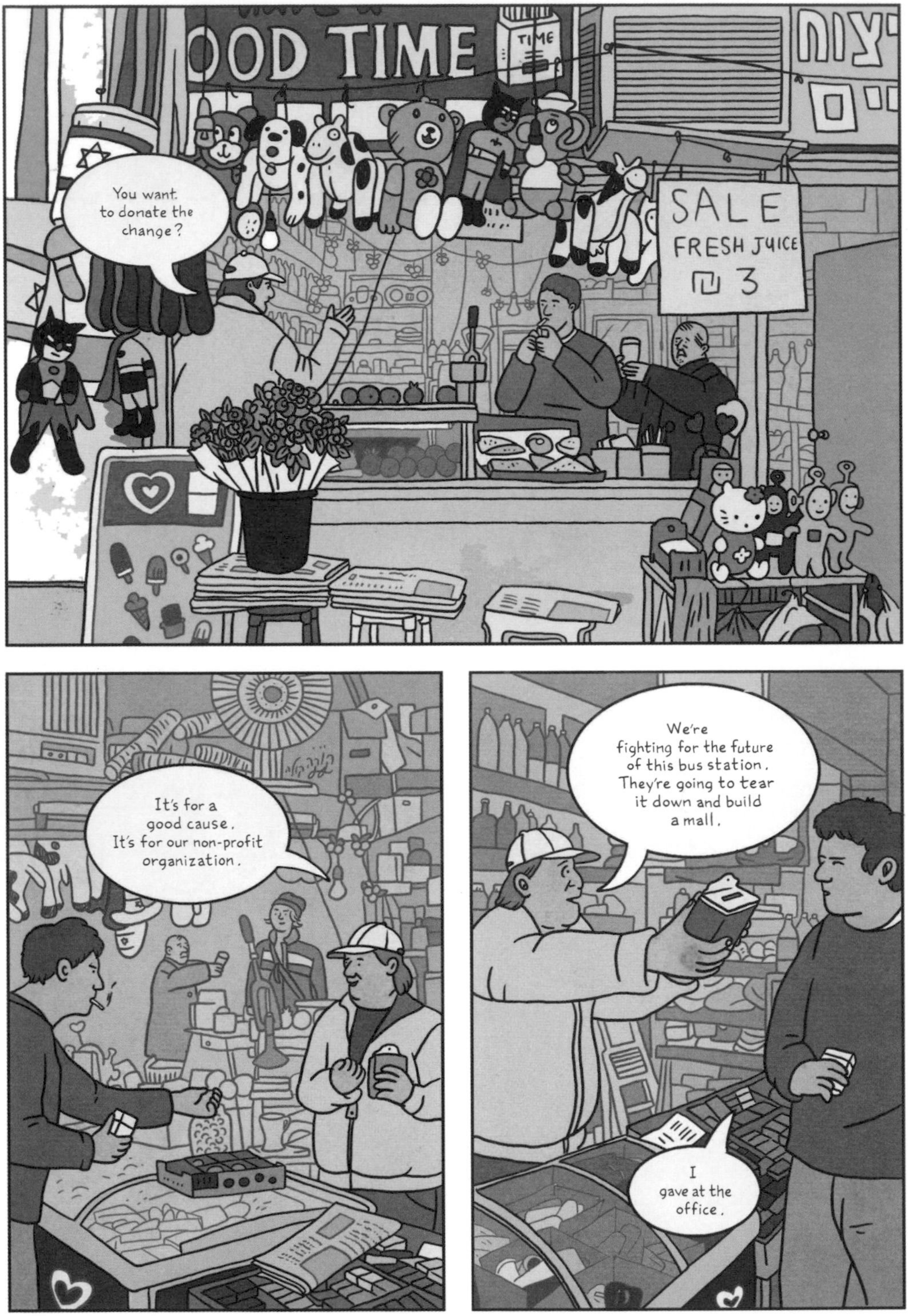

OOD TIME
TIME
SALE
FRESH JUICE
₪ 3
You want to donate the change?
It's for a good cause. It's for our non-profit organization.
We're fighting for the future of this bus station. They're going to tear it down and build a mall.
I gave at the office.

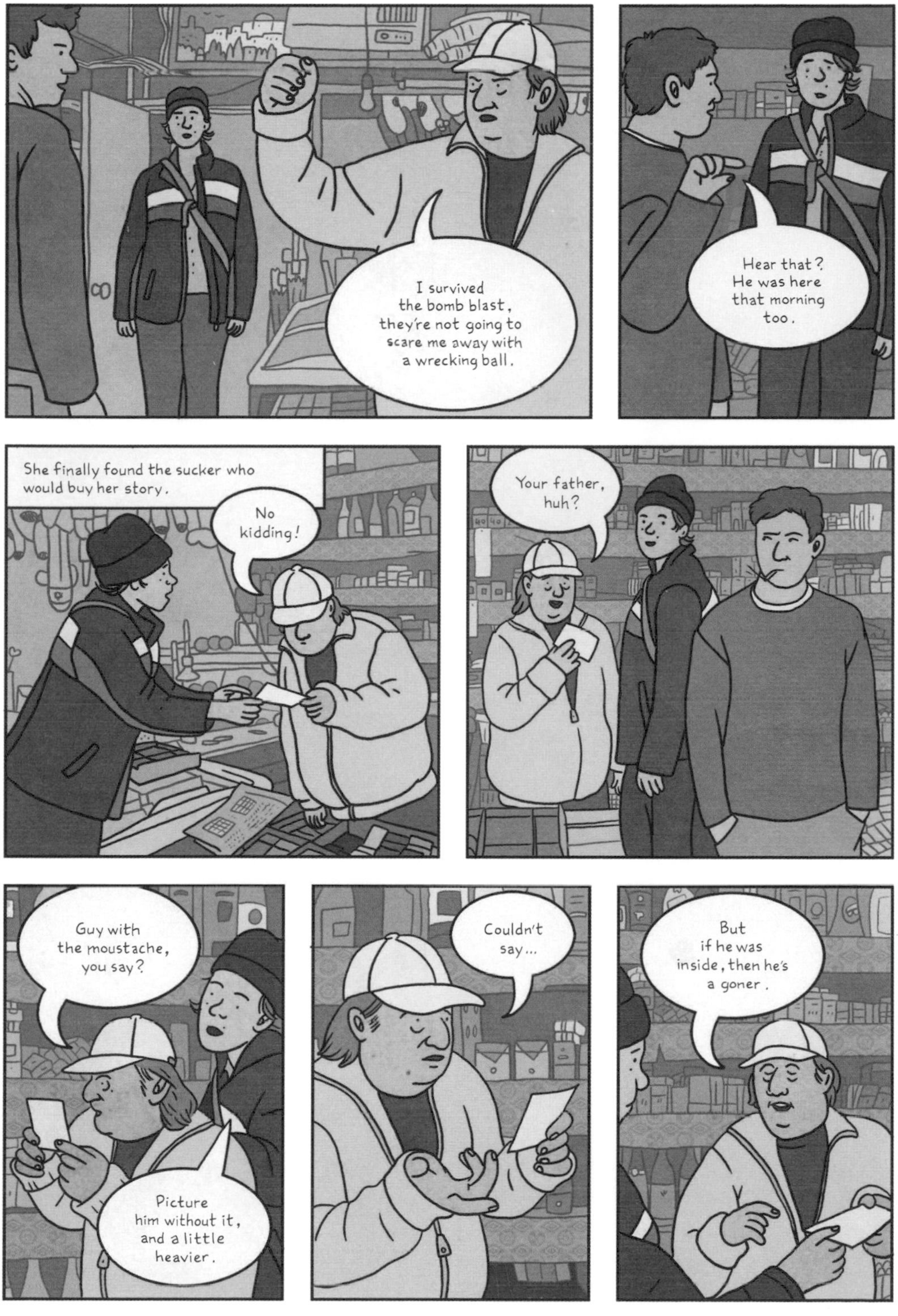
I survived the bomb blast, they're not going to scare me away with a wrecking ball.
Hear that? He was here that morning too.
She finally found the sucker who would buy her story.
No kidding!
Your father, huh?
Guy with the moustache, you say?
Picture him without it, and a little heavier.
Couldn't say...
But if he was inside, then he's a goner.

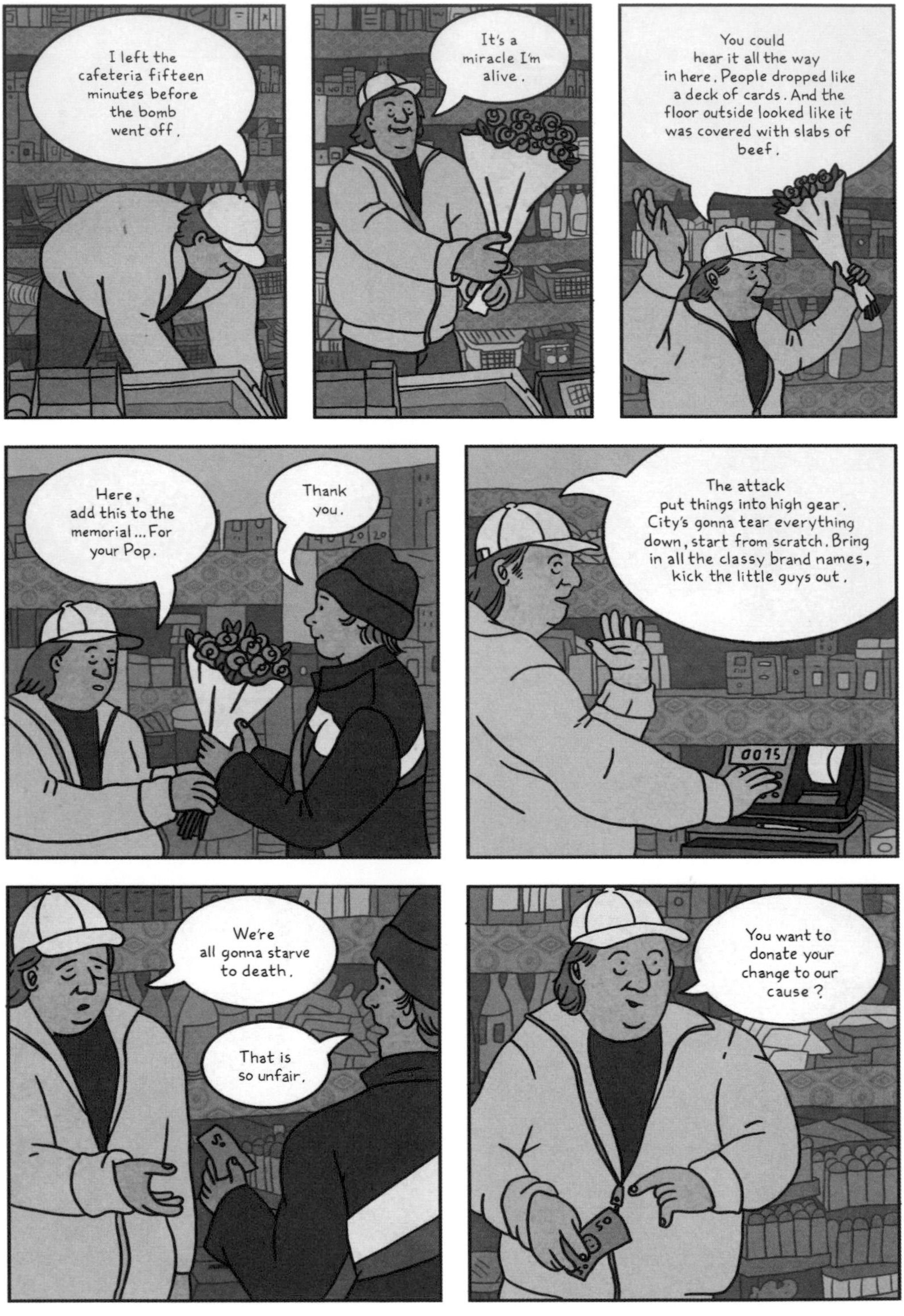

I left the cafeteria fifteen minutes before the bomb went off.
It's a miracle I'm alive.
You could hear it all the way in here. People dropped like a deck of cards. And the floor outside looked like it was covered with slabs of beef.
Here, add this to the memorial... For your Pop.
Thank you.
The attack put things into high gear. City's gonna tear everything down, start from scratch. Bring in all the classy brand names, kick the little guys out.
0015
We're all gonna starve to death.
That is so unfair.
You want to donate your change to our cause?

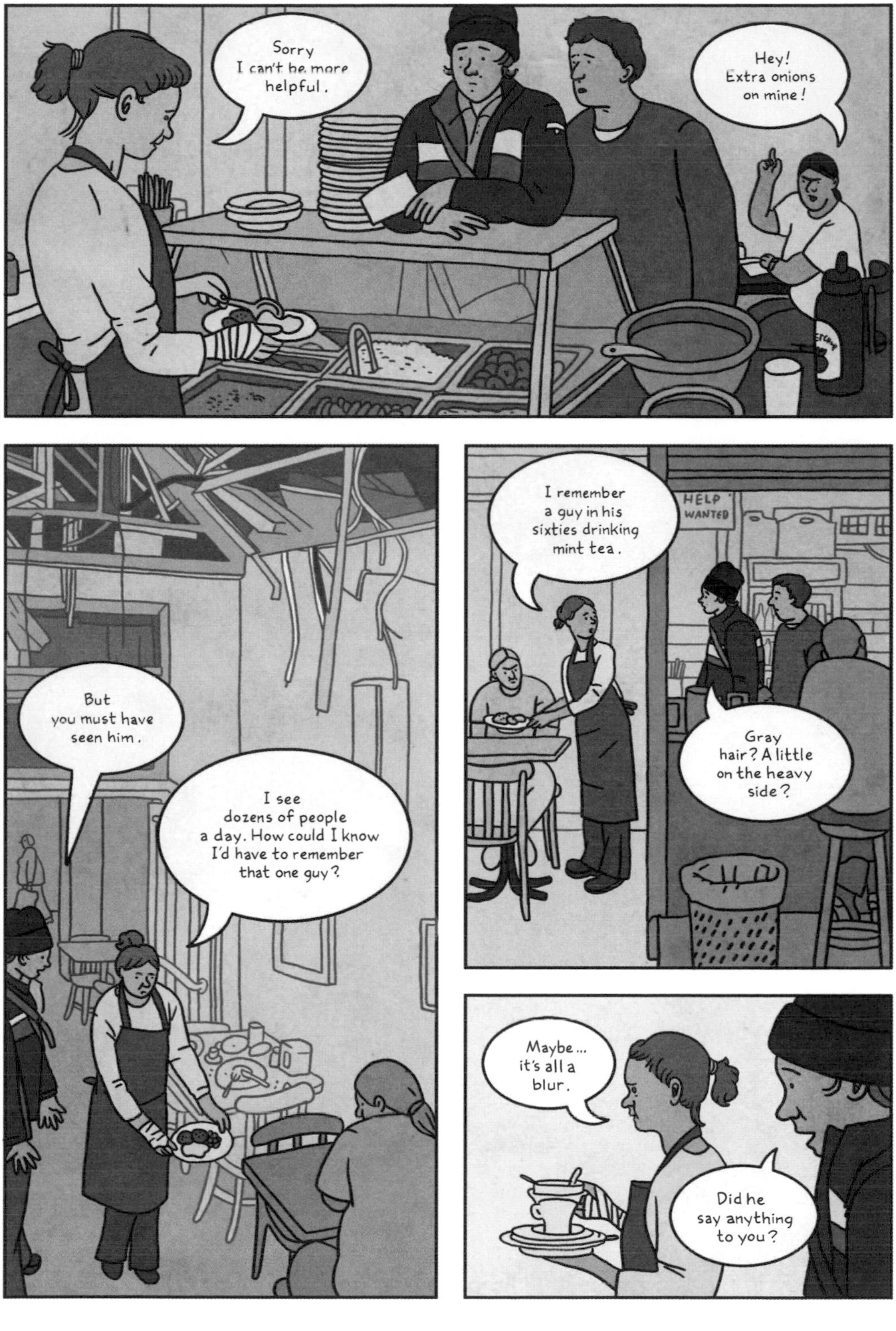

Sorry I can't be more helpful.
Hey! Extra onions on mine!
But you must have seen him.
I see dozens of people a day. How could I know I'd have to remember that one guy?
I remember a guy in his sixties drinking mint tea.
HELP WANTED
Gray hair? A little on the heavy side?
Maybe... it's all a blur.
Did he say anything to you?

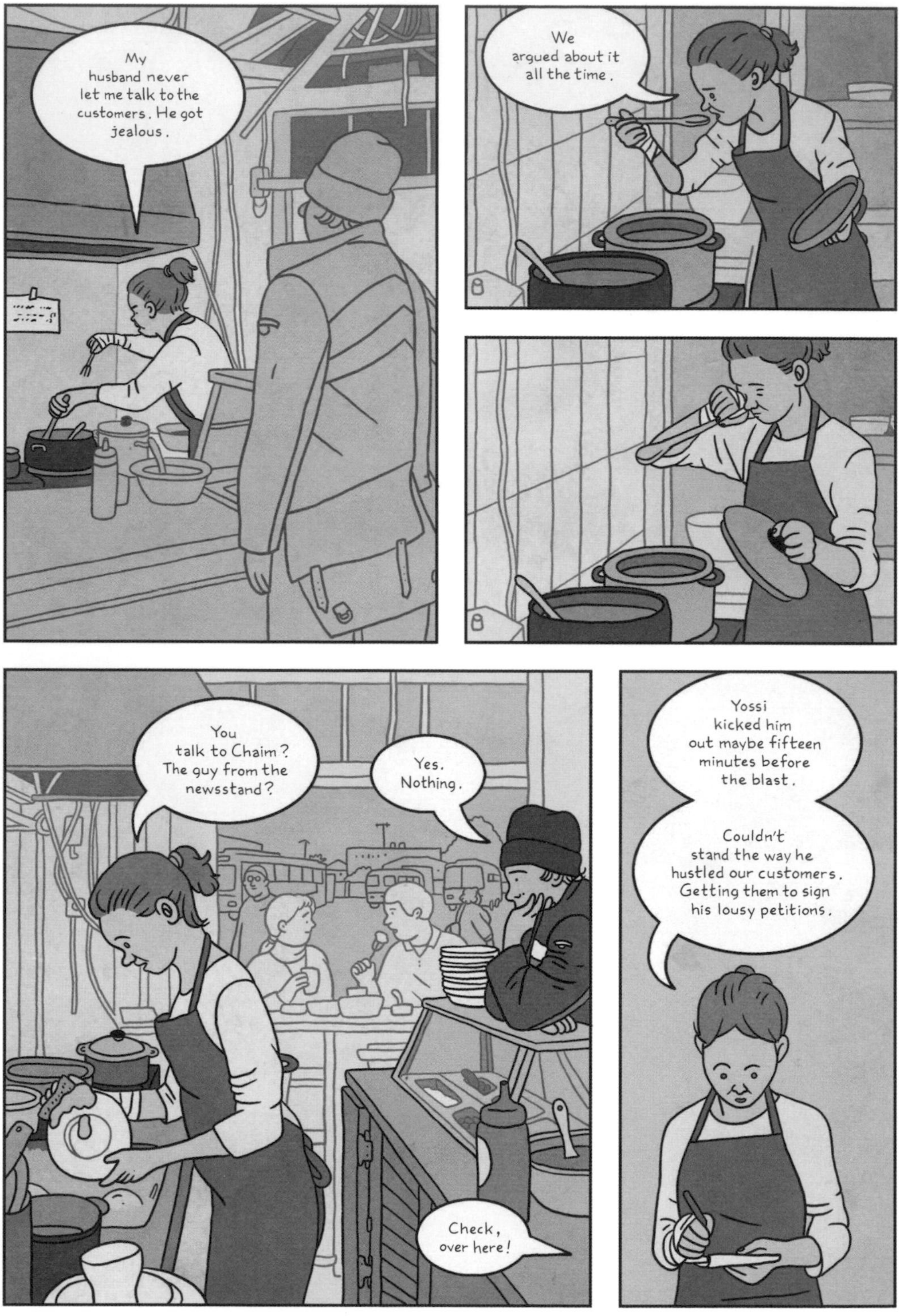
My husband never let me talk to the customers. He got jealous.
We argued about it all the time.
You talk to Chaim? The guy from the newsstand?
Yes. Nothing.
Check, over here!
Yossi kicked him out maybe fifteen minutes before the blast.
Couldn't stand the way he hustled our customers. Getting them to sign his lousy petitions.

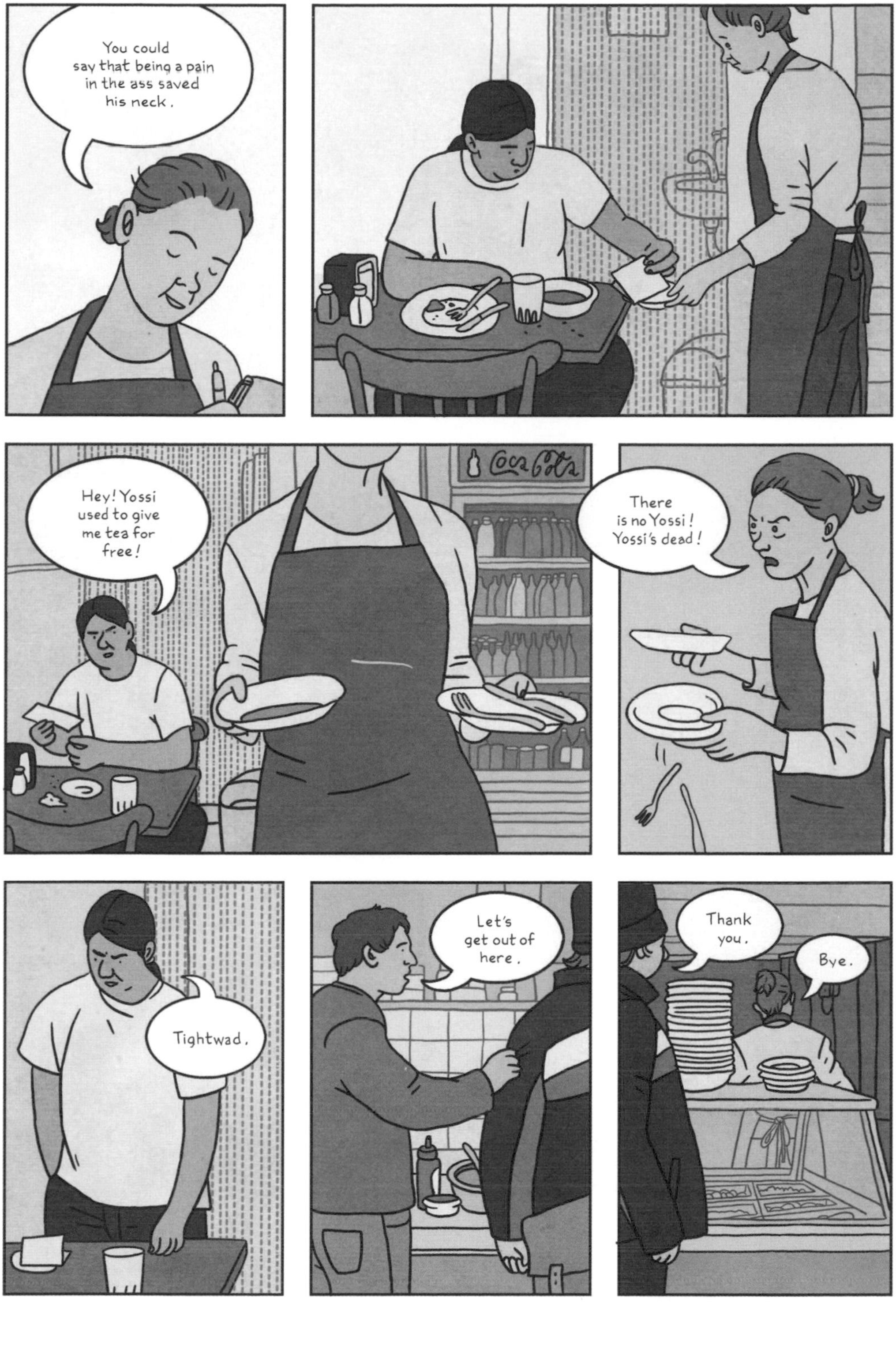
You could say that being a pain in the ass saved his neck.
Hey! Yossi used to give me tea for free!
There is no Yossi! Yossi's dead!
Tightwad.
Let's get out of here.
Thank you.
Bye.

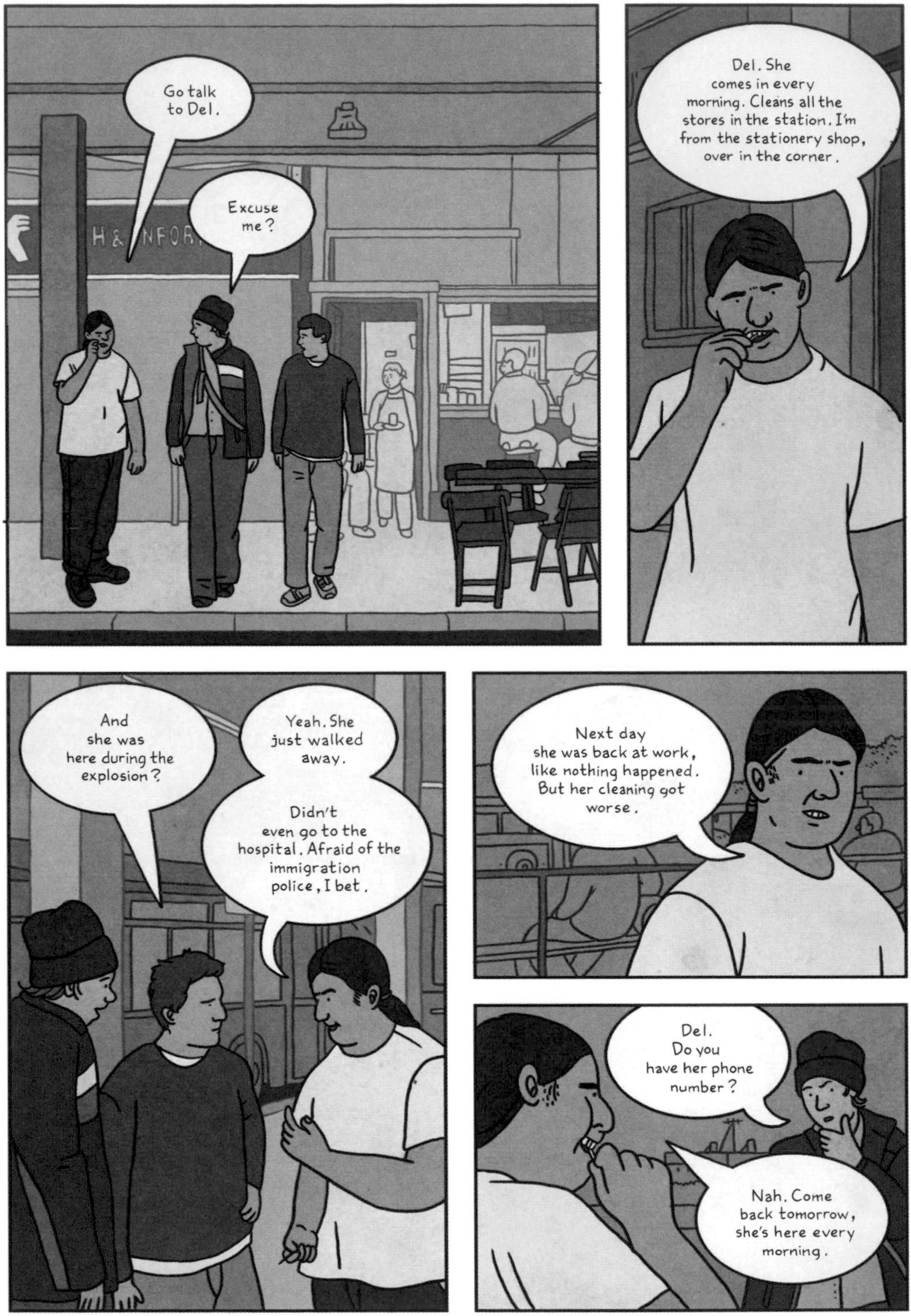
Go talk to Del.
Excuse me?
H & INFOR
Del. She comes in every morning. Cleans all the stores in the station. I'm from the stationery shop, over in the corner.
And she was here during the explosion?
Yeah. She just walked away.
Didn't even go to the hospital. Afraid of the immigration police, I bet.
Next day she was back at work, like nothing happened. But her cleaning got worse.
Del. Do you have her phone number?
Nah. Come back tomorrow, she's here every morning.

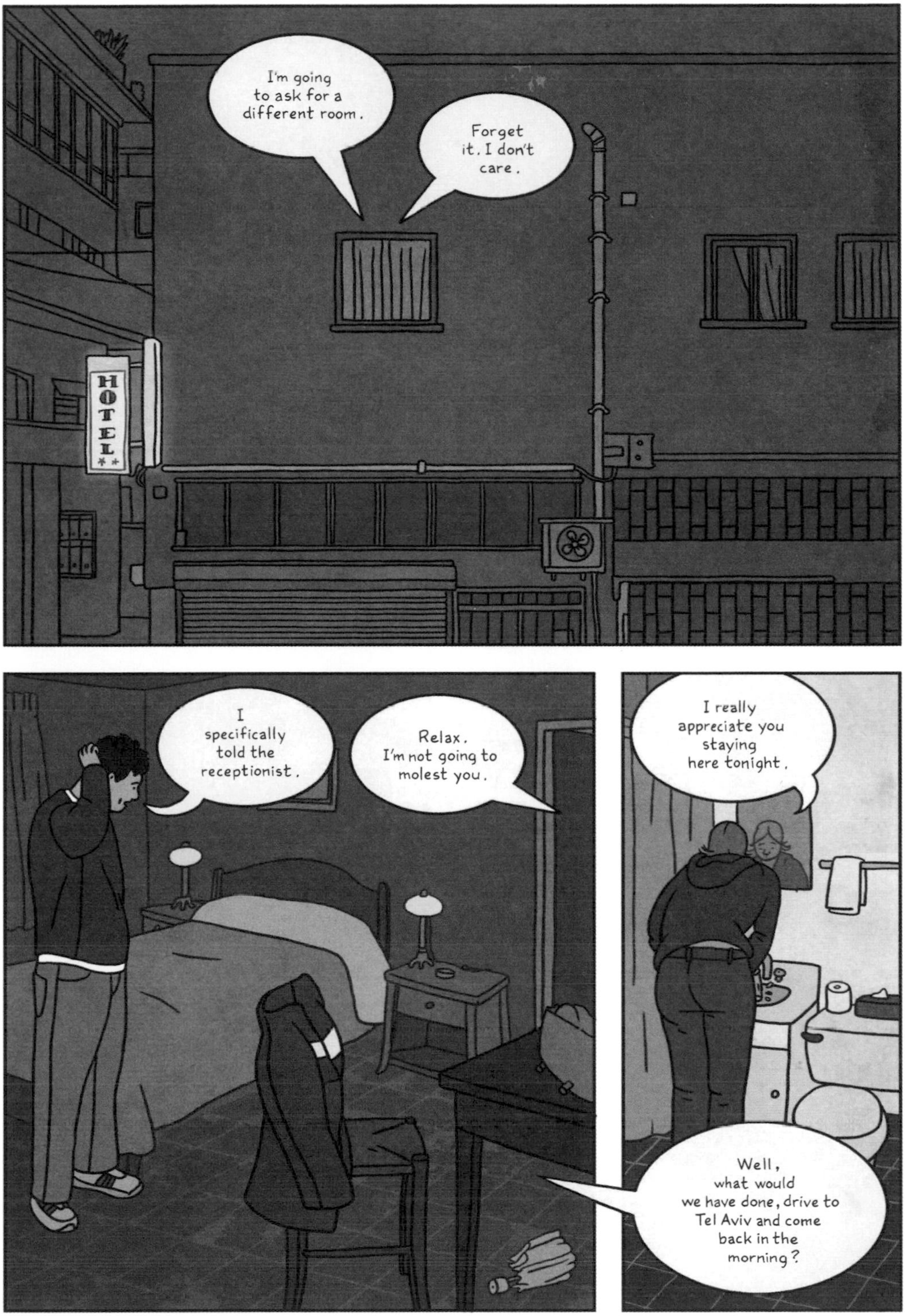
HOTEL
I'm going to ask for a different room.
Forget it. I don't care.
I specifically told the receptionist.
Relax. I'm not going to molest you.
I really appreciate you staying here tonight.
Well, what would we have done, drive to Tel Aviv and come back in the morning?

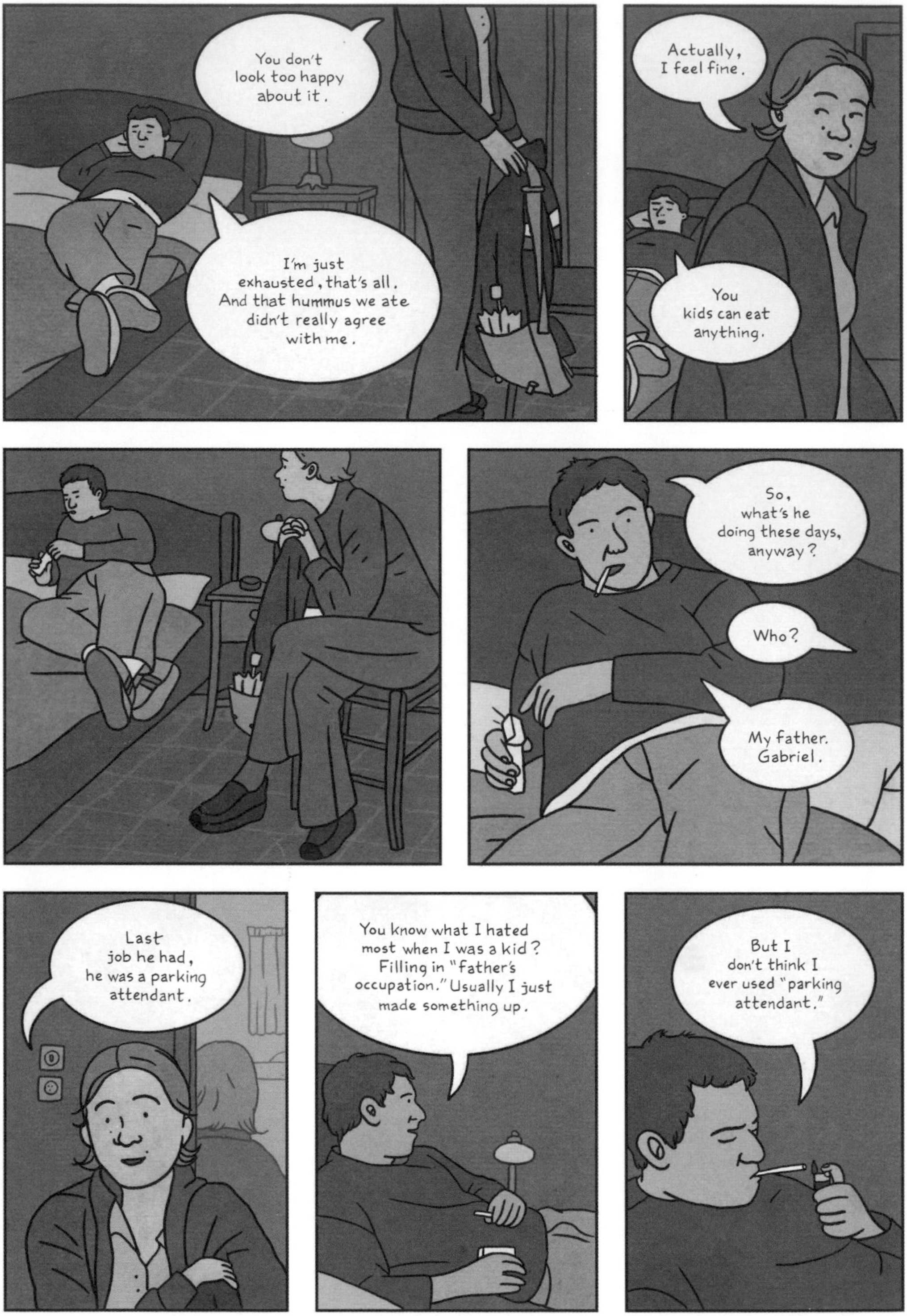
You don't look too happy about it.
I'm just exhausted, that's all. And that hummus we ate didn't really agree with me.
Actually, I feel fine.
You kids can eat anything.
So, what's he doing these days, anyway?
Who?
My father. Gabriel.
Last job he had, he was a parking attendant.
You know what I hated most when I was a kid? Filling in "father's occupation." Usually I just made something up.
But I don't think I ever used "parking attendant."

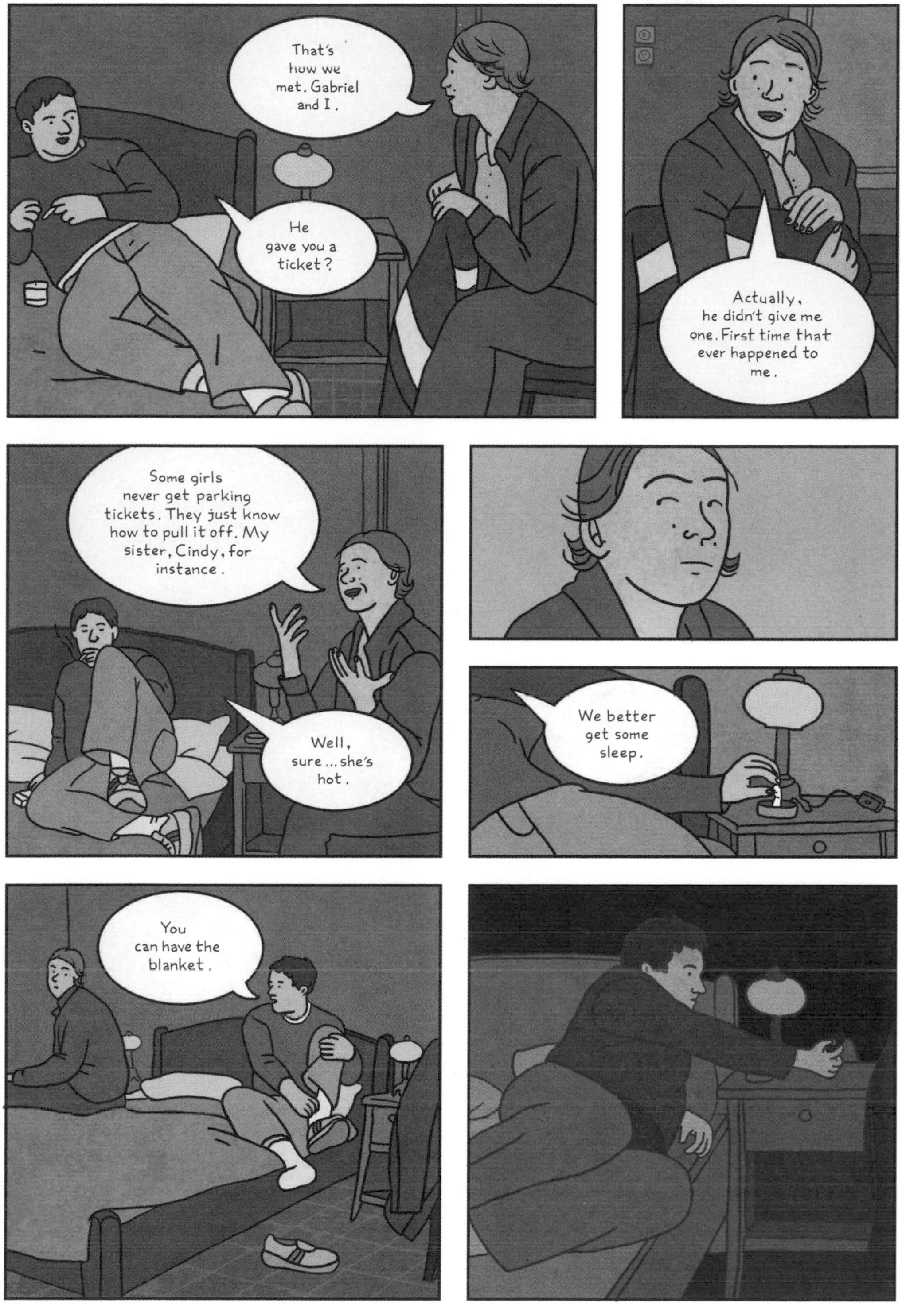
That's how we met. Gabriel and I.
He gave you a ticket?
Actually, he didn't give me one. First time that ever happened to me.
Some girls never get parking tickets. They just know how to pull it off. My sister, Cindy, for instance.
Well, sure ... she's hot.
We better get some sleep.
You can have the blanket.

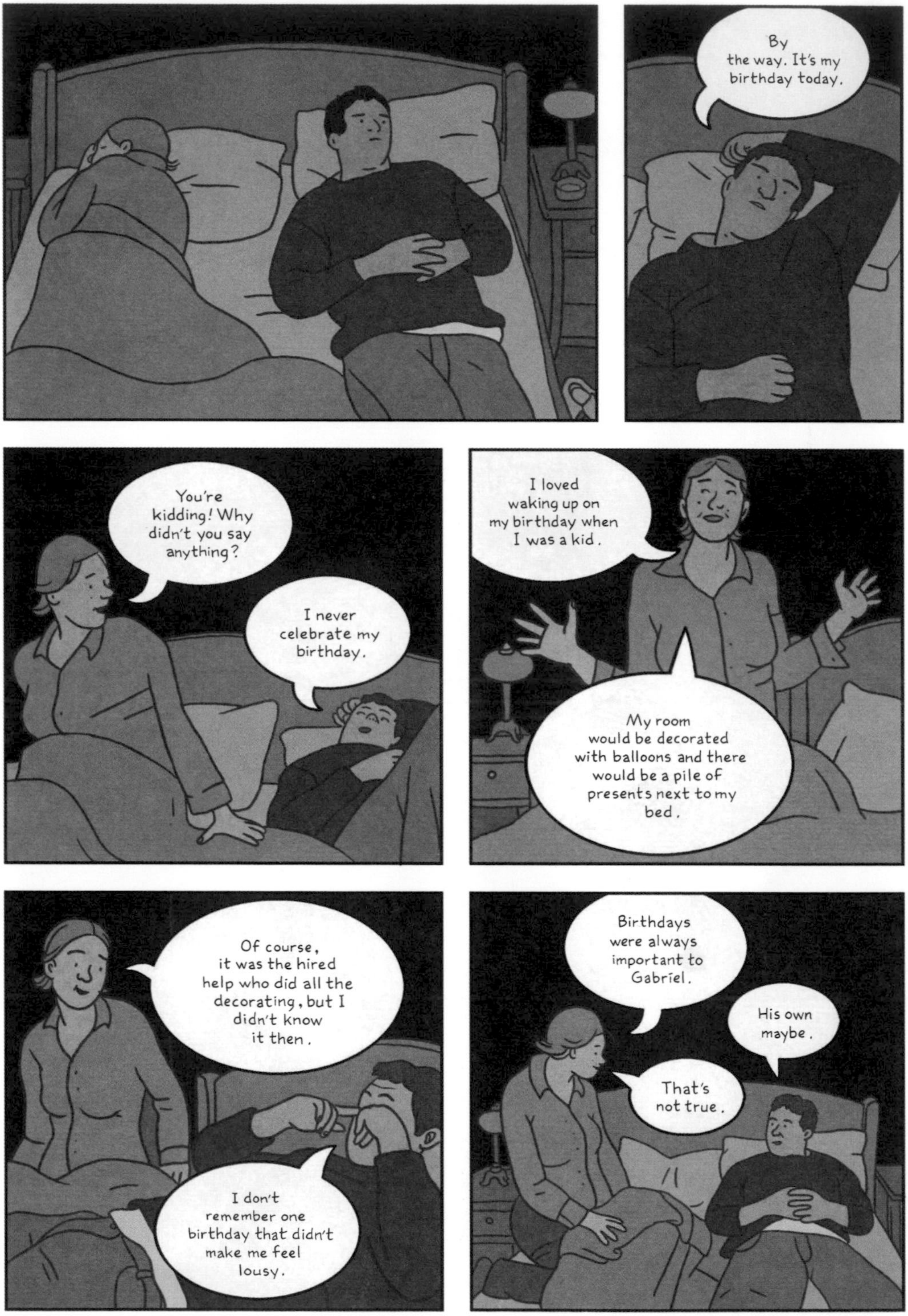
By the way. It's my birthday today.
You're kidding! Why didn't you say anything?
I never celebrate my birthday.
I loved waking up on my birthday when I was a kid.
My room would be decorated with balloons and there would be a pile of presents next to my bed.
Of course, it was the hired help who did all the decorating, but I didn't know it then.
I don't remember one birthday that didn't make me feel lousy.
Birthdays were always important to Gabriel.
His own maybe.
That's not true.

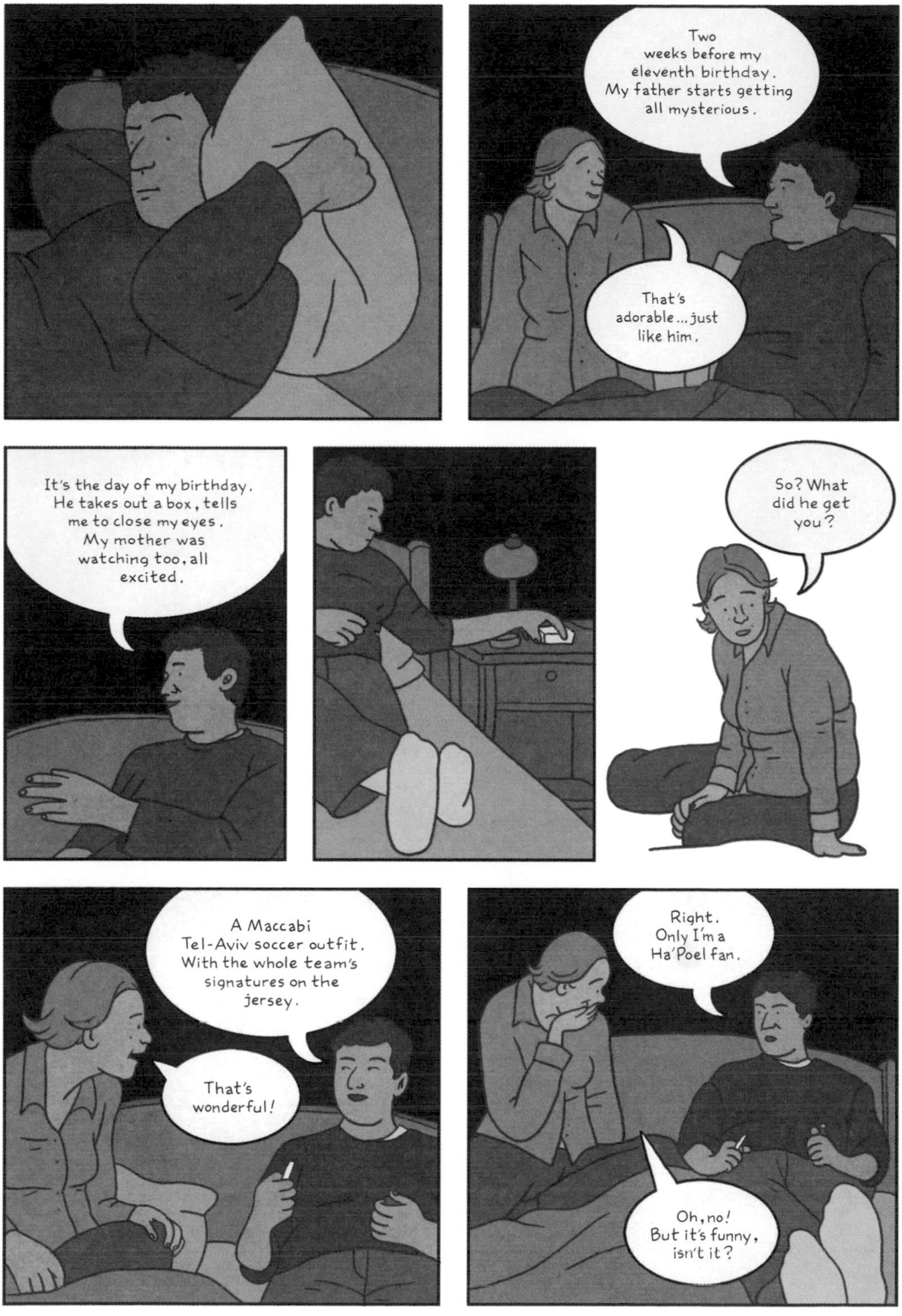
Two weeks before my eleventh birthday. My father starts getting all mysterious.
That's adorable... just like him.
It's the day of my birthday. He takes out a box, tells me to close my eyes. My mother was watching too, all excited.
So? What did he get you?
A Maccabi Tel-Aviv soccer outfit. With the whole team's signatures on the jersey.
That's wonderful!
Right. Only I'm a Ha'Poel fan.
Oh, no! But it's funny, isn't it?

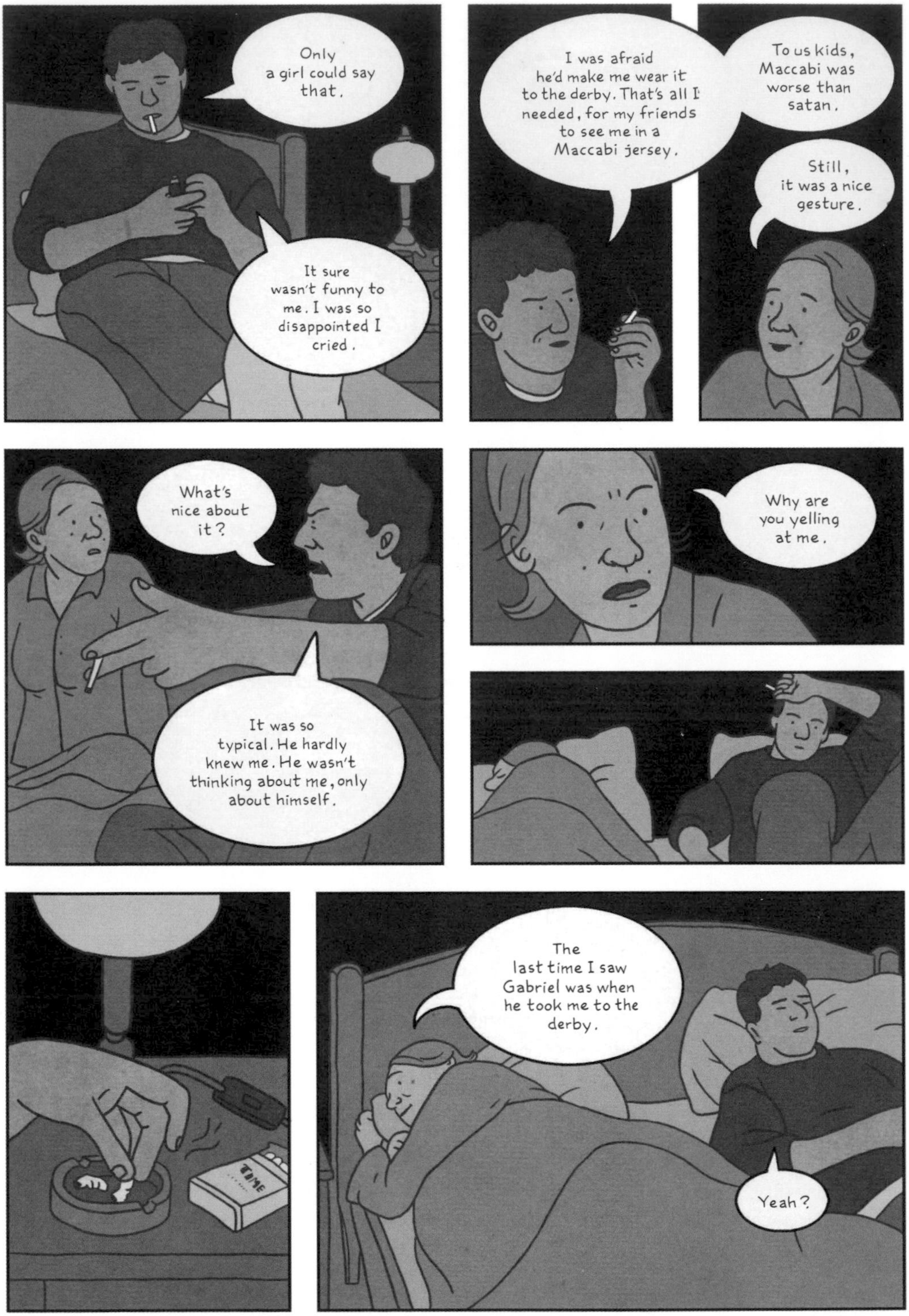
Only a girl could say that.
It sure wasn't funny to me. I was so disappointed I cried.
I was afraid he'd make me wear it to the derby. That's all I needed, for my friends to see me in a Maccabi jersey.
To us kids, Maccabi was worse than satan.
Still, it was a nice gesture.
What's nice about it?
It was so typical. He hardly knew me. He wasn't thinking about me, only about himself.
Why are you yelling at me.
The last time I saw Gabriel was when he took me to the derby.
Yeah?

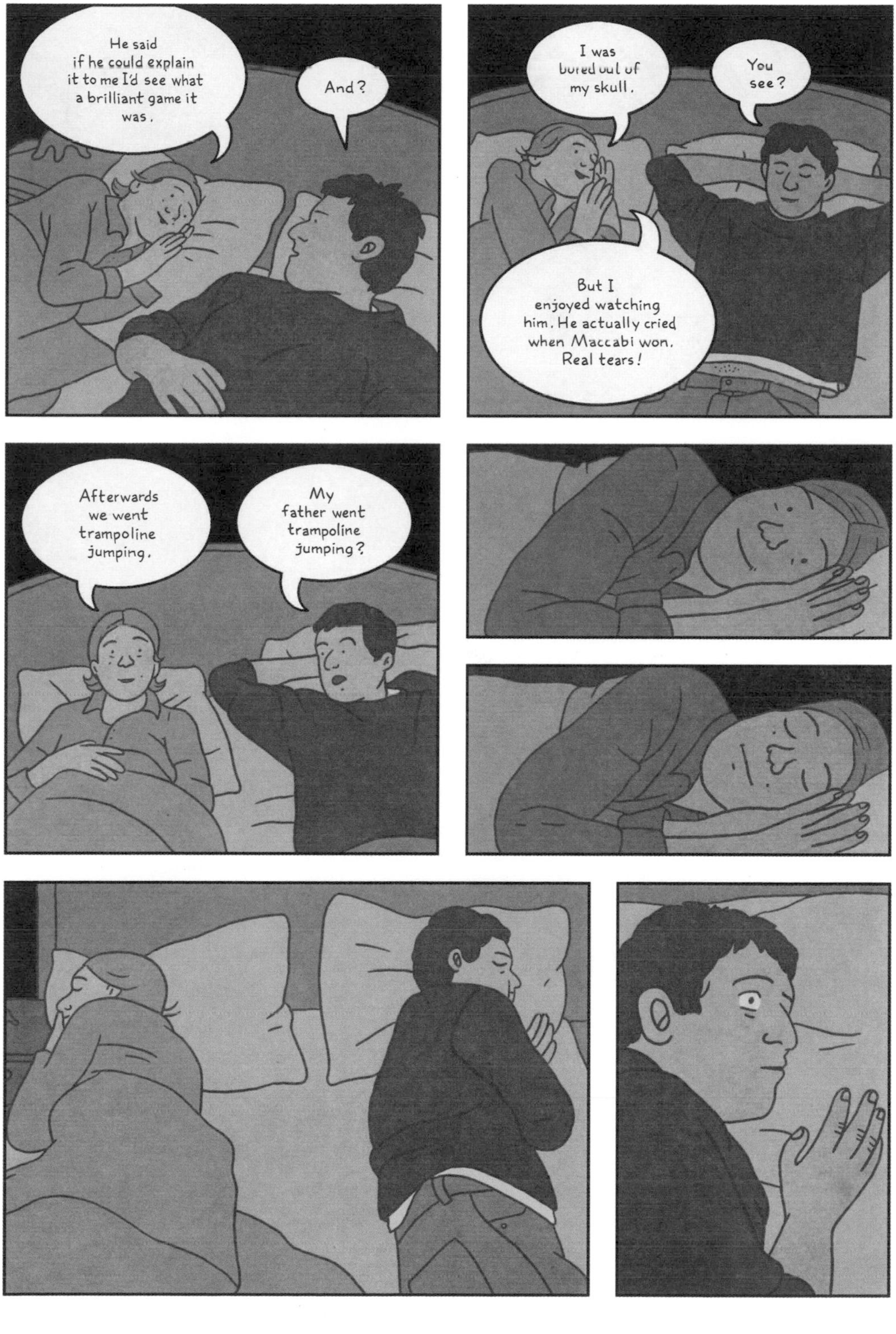
He said if he could explain it to me I'd see what a brilliant game it was.
And?
I was bored out of my skull.
You see?
But I enjoyed watching him. He actually cried when Maccabi won. Real tears!
Afterwards we went trampoline jumping.
My father went trampoline jumping?

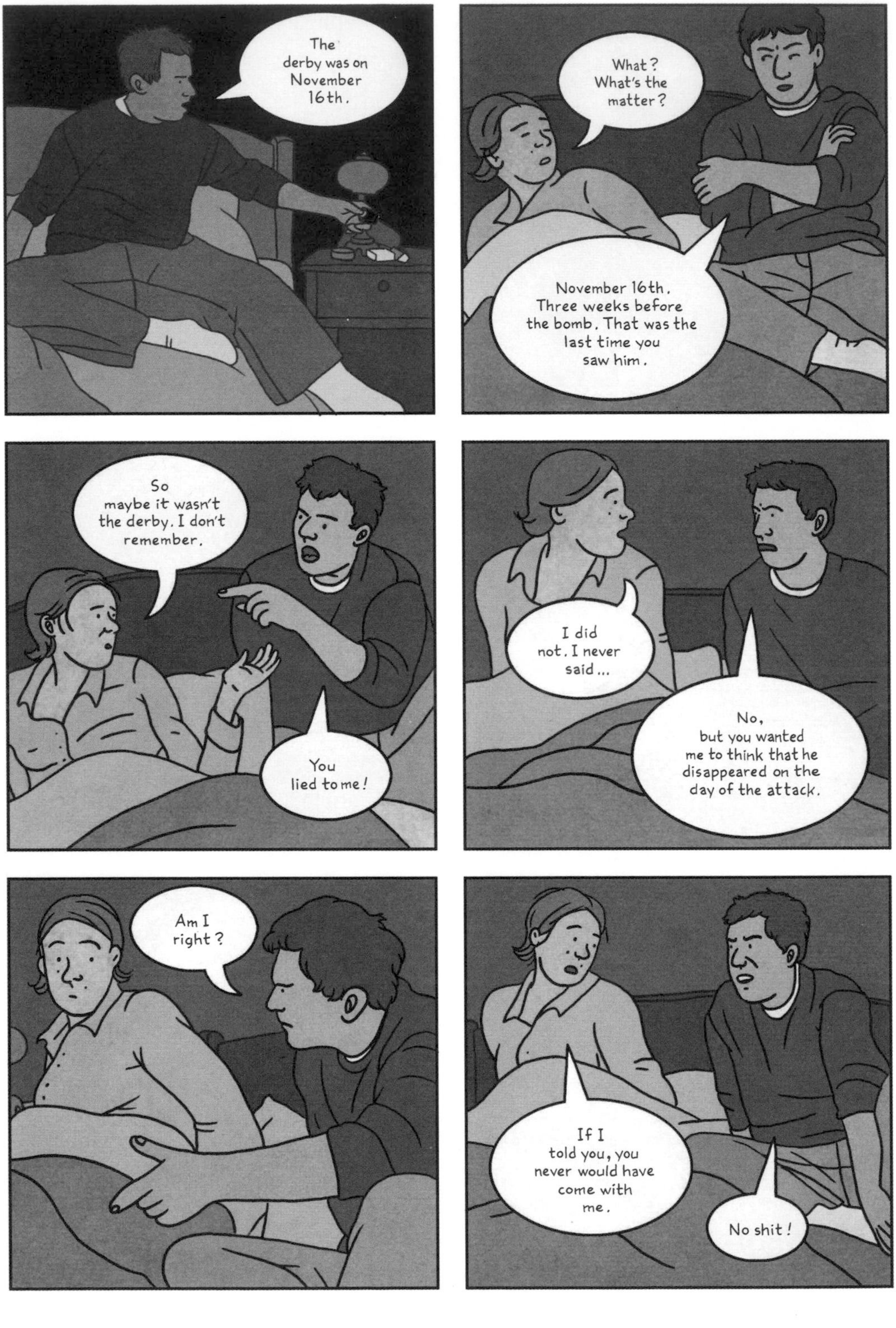
The derby was on November 16th.
What? What's the matter?
November 16th. Three weeks before the bomb. That was the last time you saw him.
So maybe it wasn't the derby. I don't remember.
You lied to me!
I did not. I never said...
No, but you wanted me to think that he disappeared on the day of the attack.
Am I right?
If I told you, you never would have come with me.
No shit!

And anyway what difference does it make? If he was alive he would have called me already.

What are you doing?

I'm going back to Tel-Aviv.

You can't leave me here.

So where is he, you tell me! Where is Gabriel?

The guy ditched you. Simple as that.

103

You're so sure! Why, because I'm not "hot"?

What are you talking about?

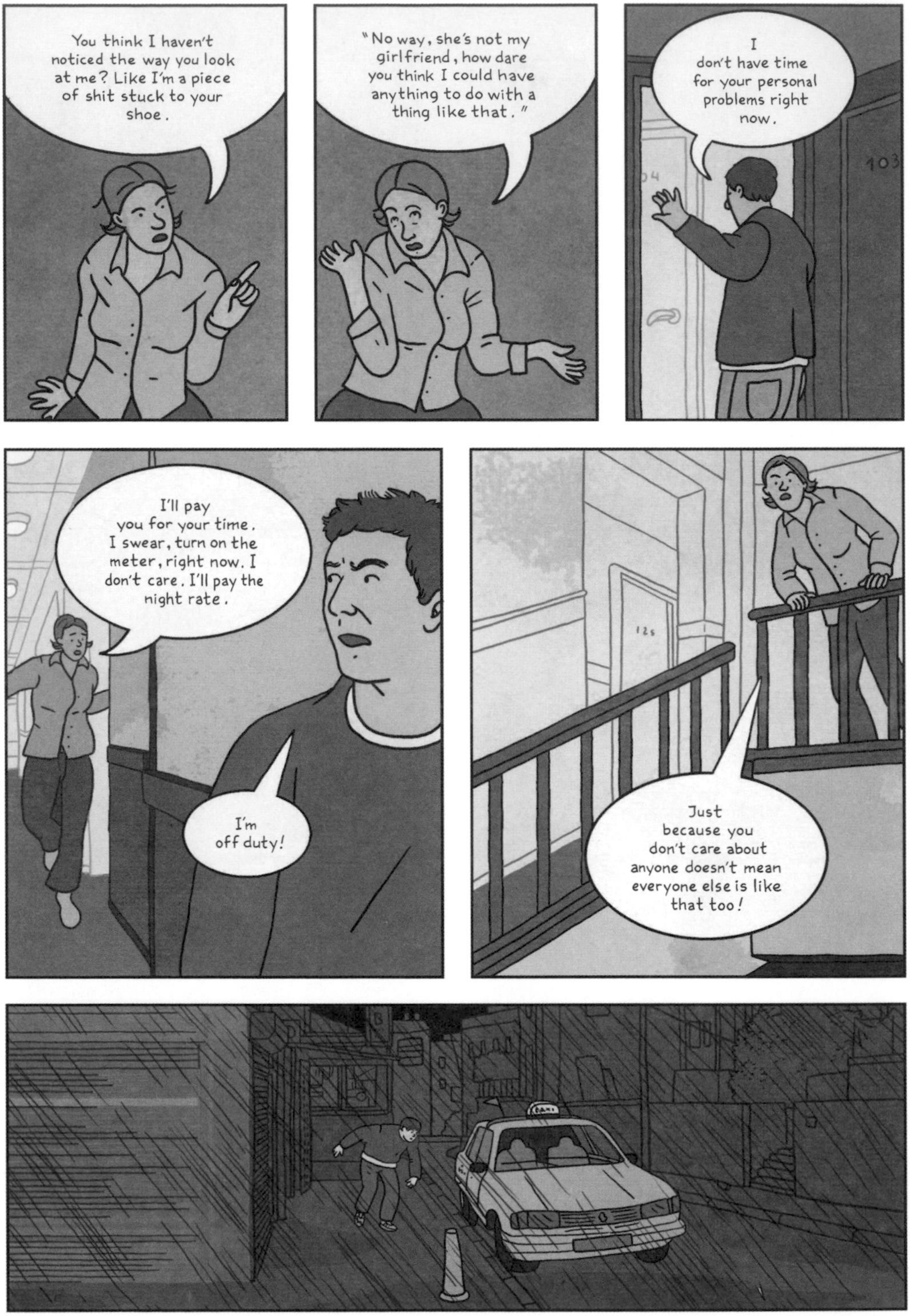
You think I haven't noticed the way you look at me? Like I'm a piece of shit stuck to your shoe.
"No way, she's not my girlfriend, how dare you think I could have anything to do with a thing like that."
I don't have time for your personal problems right now.
I'll pay you for your time. I swear, turn on the meter, right now. I don't care. I'll pay the night rate.
I'm off duty!
Just because you don't care about anyone doesn't mean everyone else is like that too!

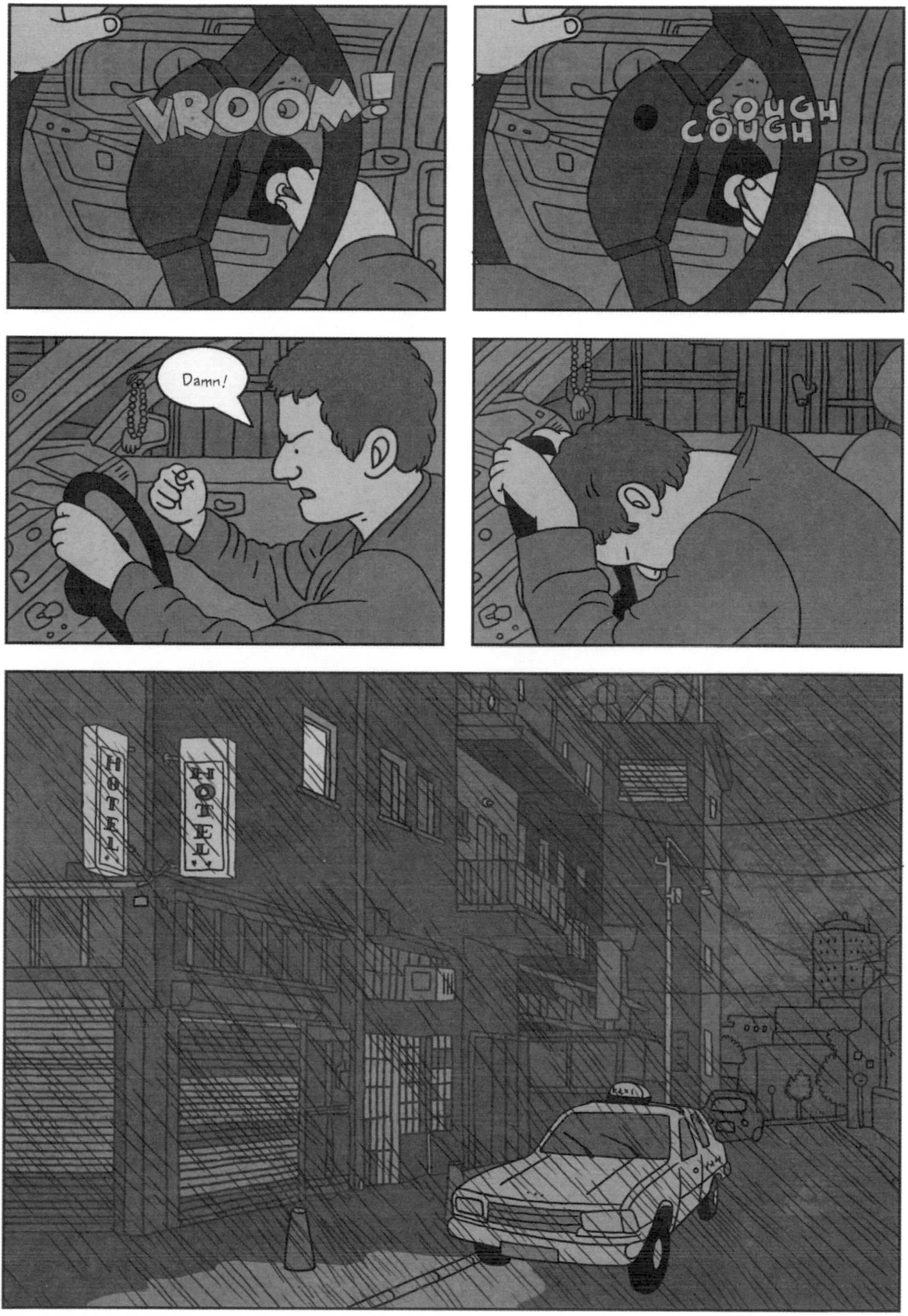
VROOM!
COUGH COUGH
Damn!
HOTEL
HOTEL

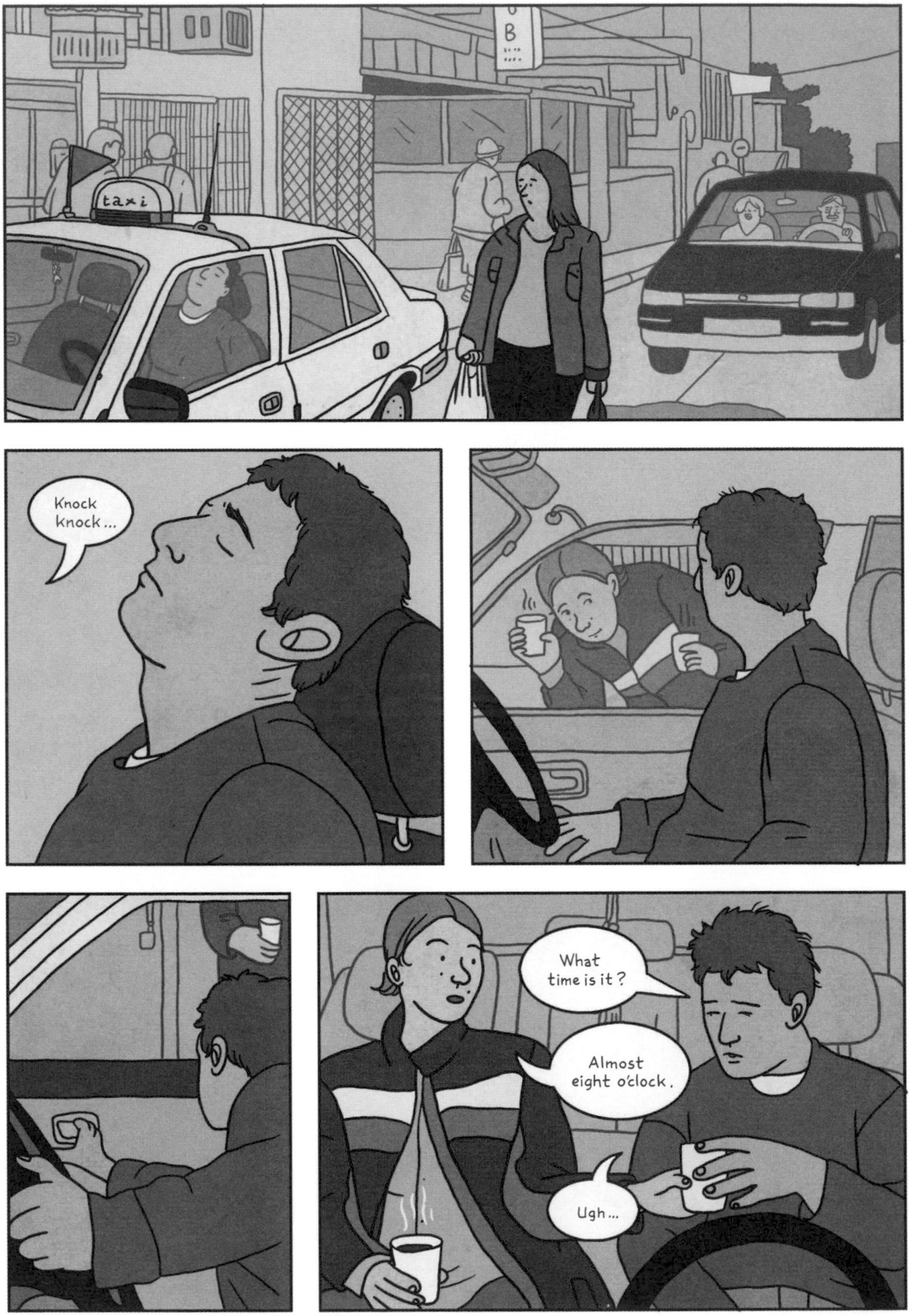
taxi
Knock knock...
What time is it?
Almost eight o'clock.
Ugh...

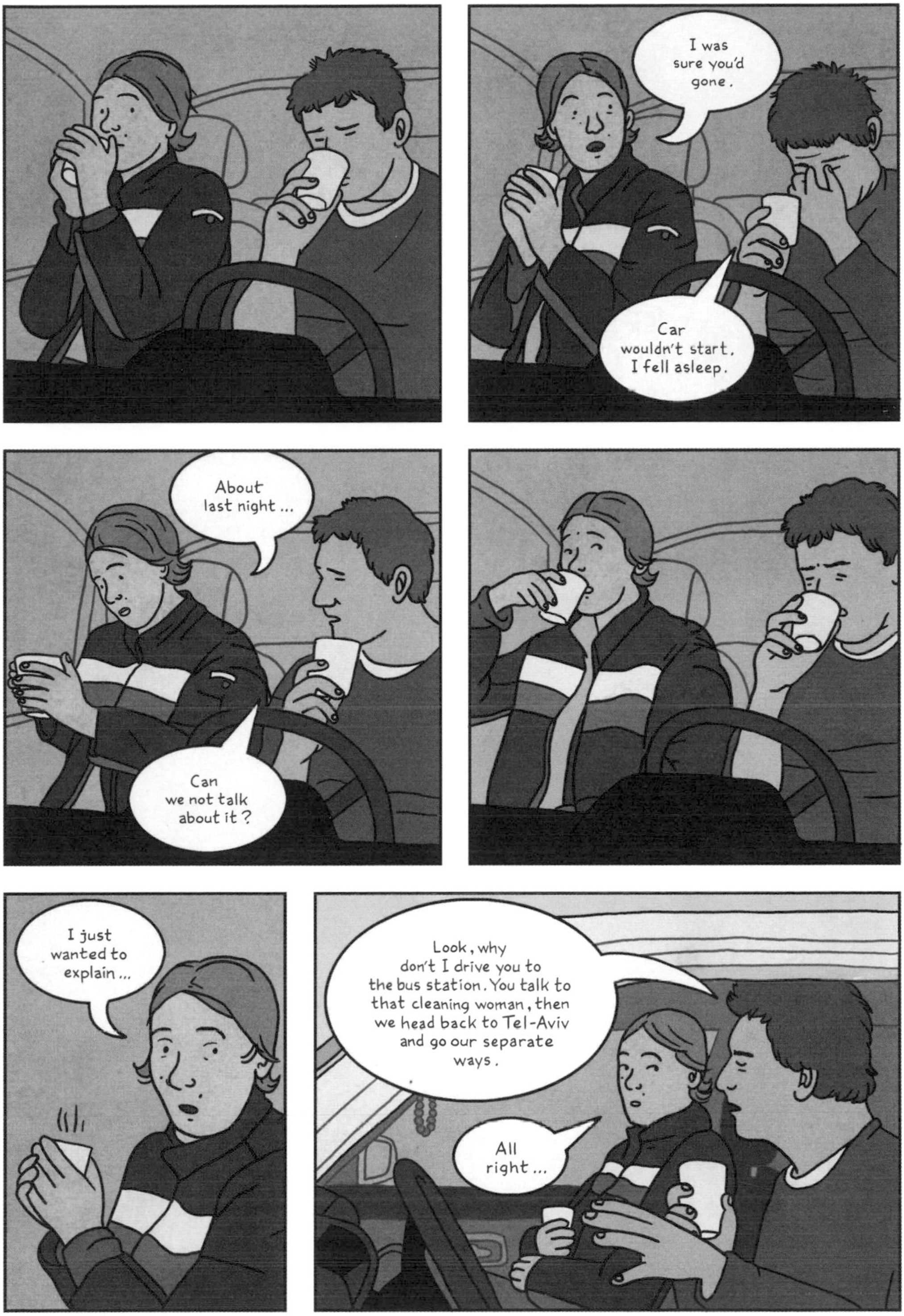
I was sure you'd gone.
Car wouldn't start. I fell asleep.
About last night ...
Can we not talk about it?
I just wanted to explain ...
Look, why don't I drive you to the bus station. You talk to that cleaning woman, then we head back to Tel-Aviv and go our separate ways.
All right ...

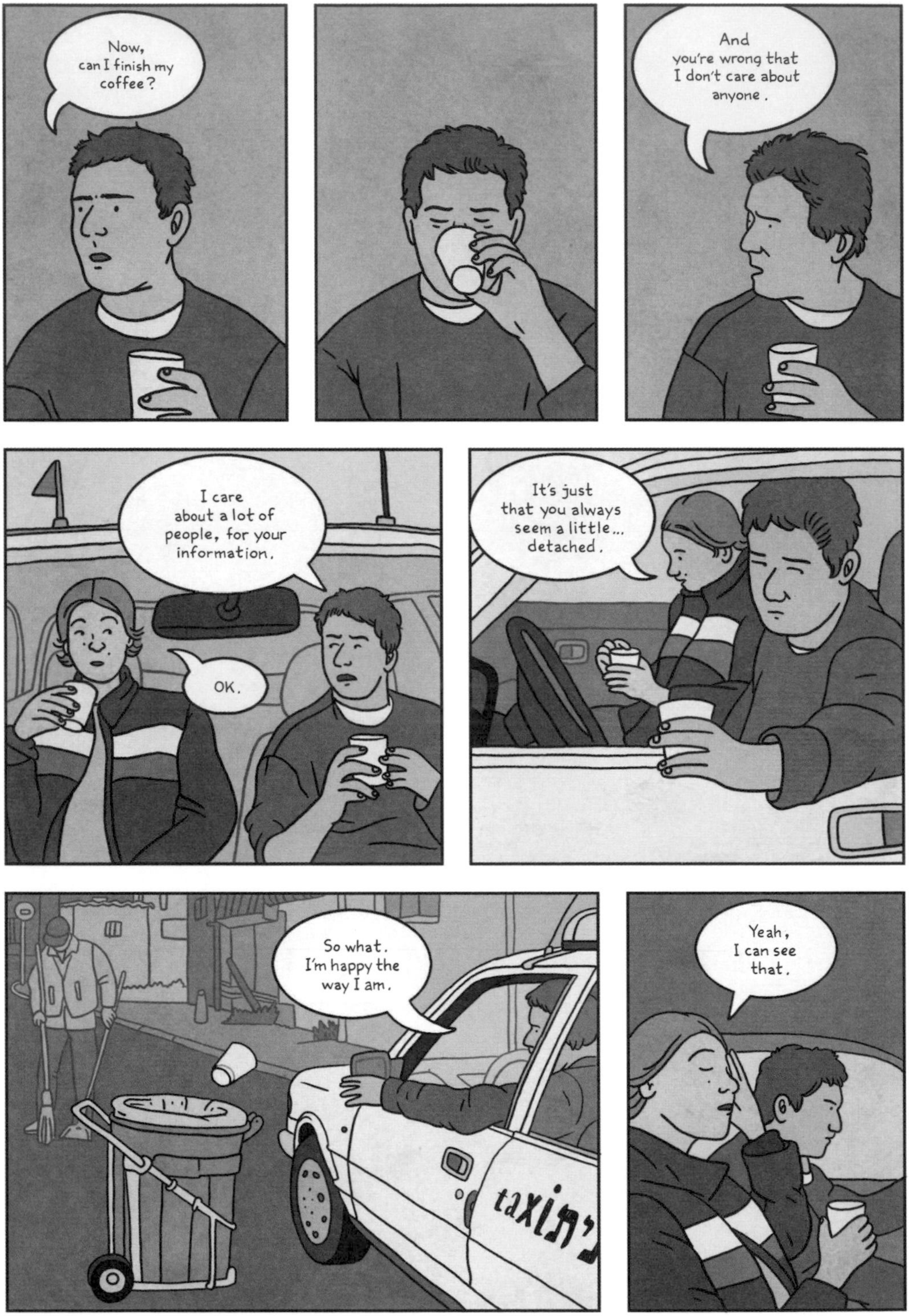
Now, can I finish my coffee?
And you're wrong that I don't care about anyone.
I care about a lot of people, for your information.
OK.
It's just that you always seem a little... detached.
So what. I'm happy the way I am.
taxi
Yeah, I can see that.

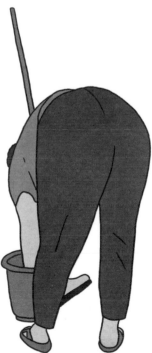

There she is!

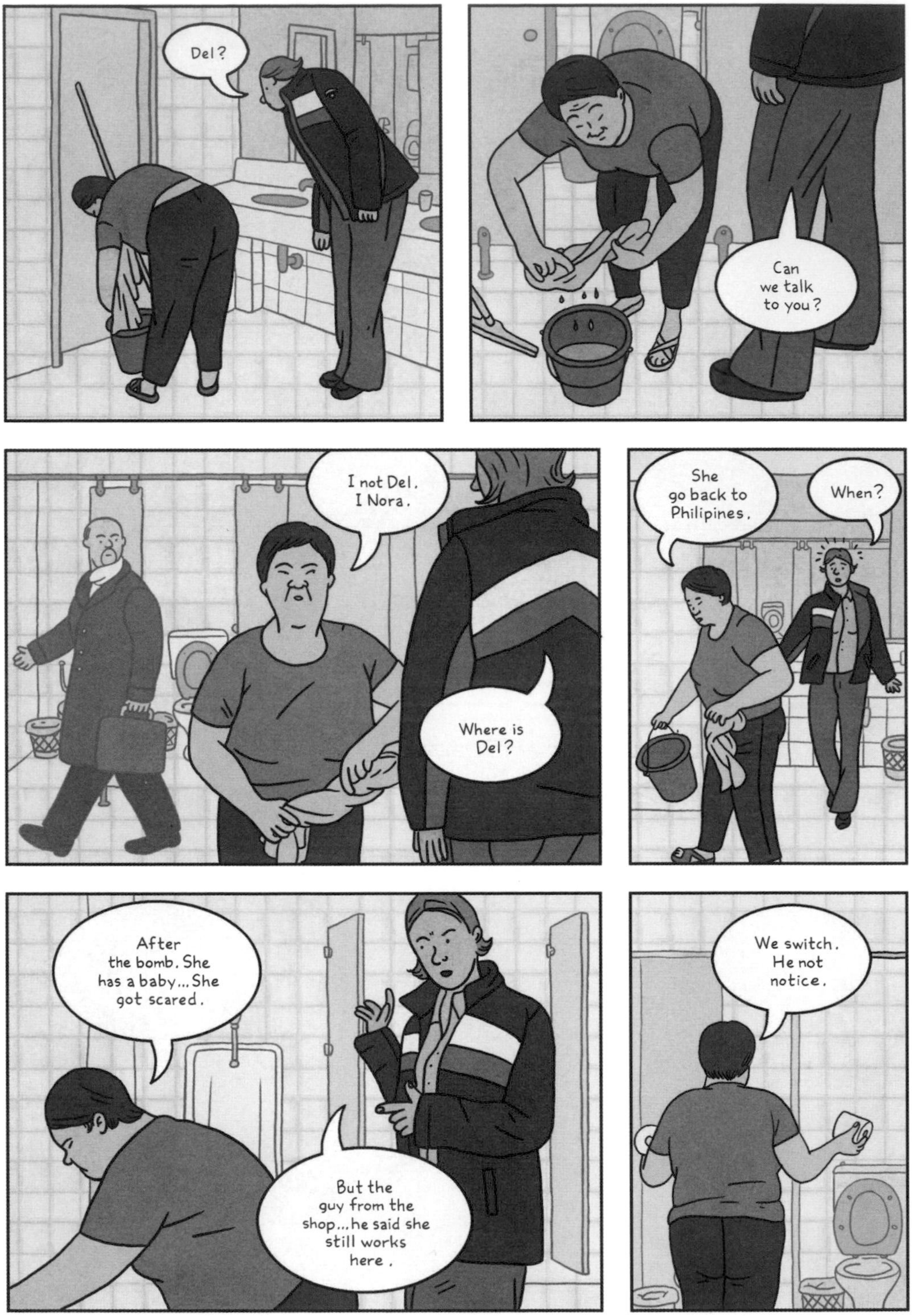

Del?
Can we talk to you?
I not Del. I Nora.
Where is Del?
She go back to Philipines.
When?
After the bomb. She has a baby... She got scared.
But the guy from the shop... he said she still works here.
We switch. He not notice.

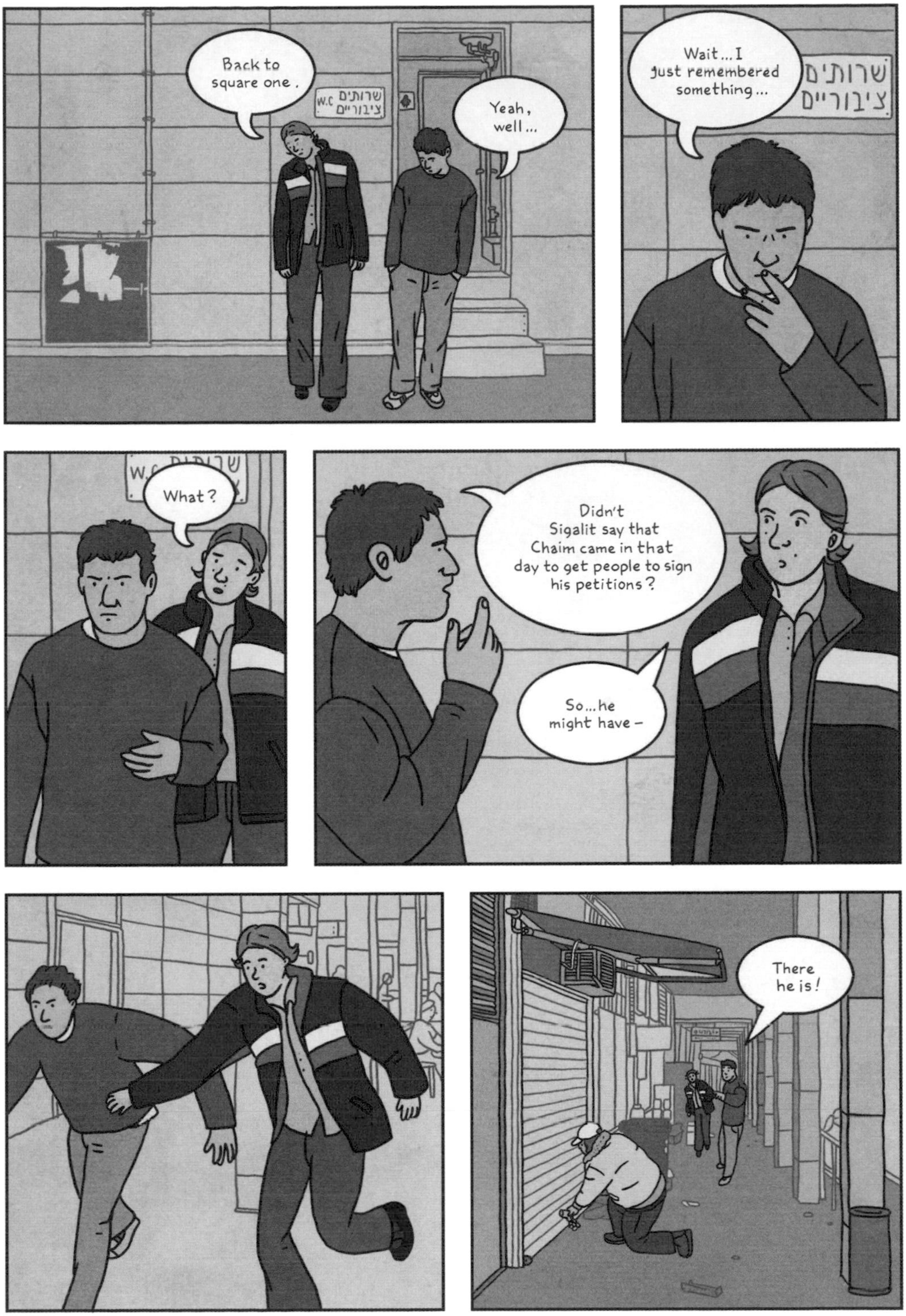
Back to square one.
W.C שרותים ציבוריים
Yeah, well...
Wait... I just remembered something...
שרותים ציבוריים
What?
Didn't Sigalit say that Chaim came in that day to get people to sign his petitions?
So... he might have –
There he is!

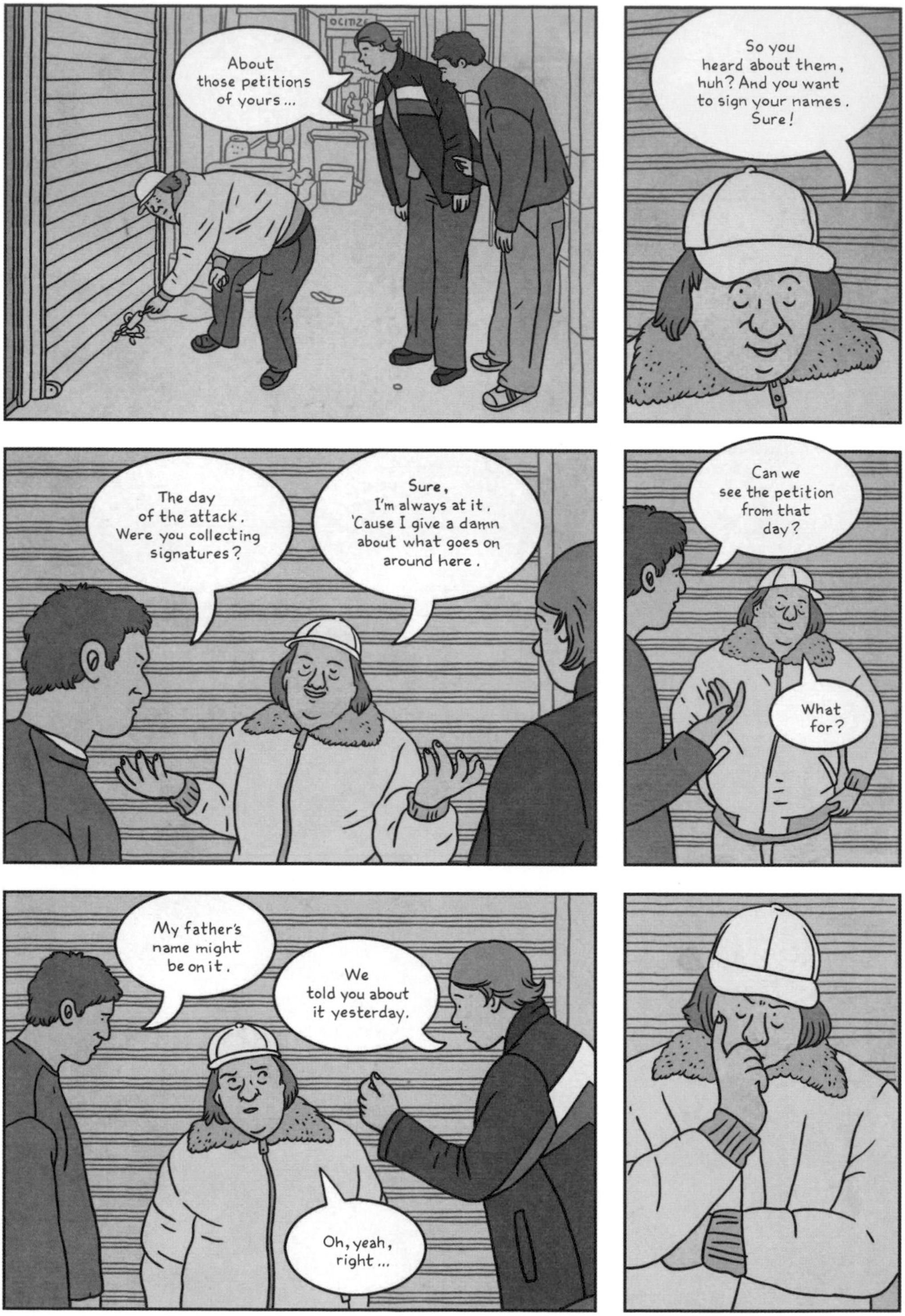
About those petitions of yours ...
So you heard about them, huh? And you want to sign your names. Sure!
The day of the attack. Were you collecting signatures?
Sure, I'm always at it. 'Cause I give a damn about what goes on around here.
Can we see the petition from that day?
What for?
My father's name might be on it.
We told you about it yesterday.
Oh, yeah, right ...

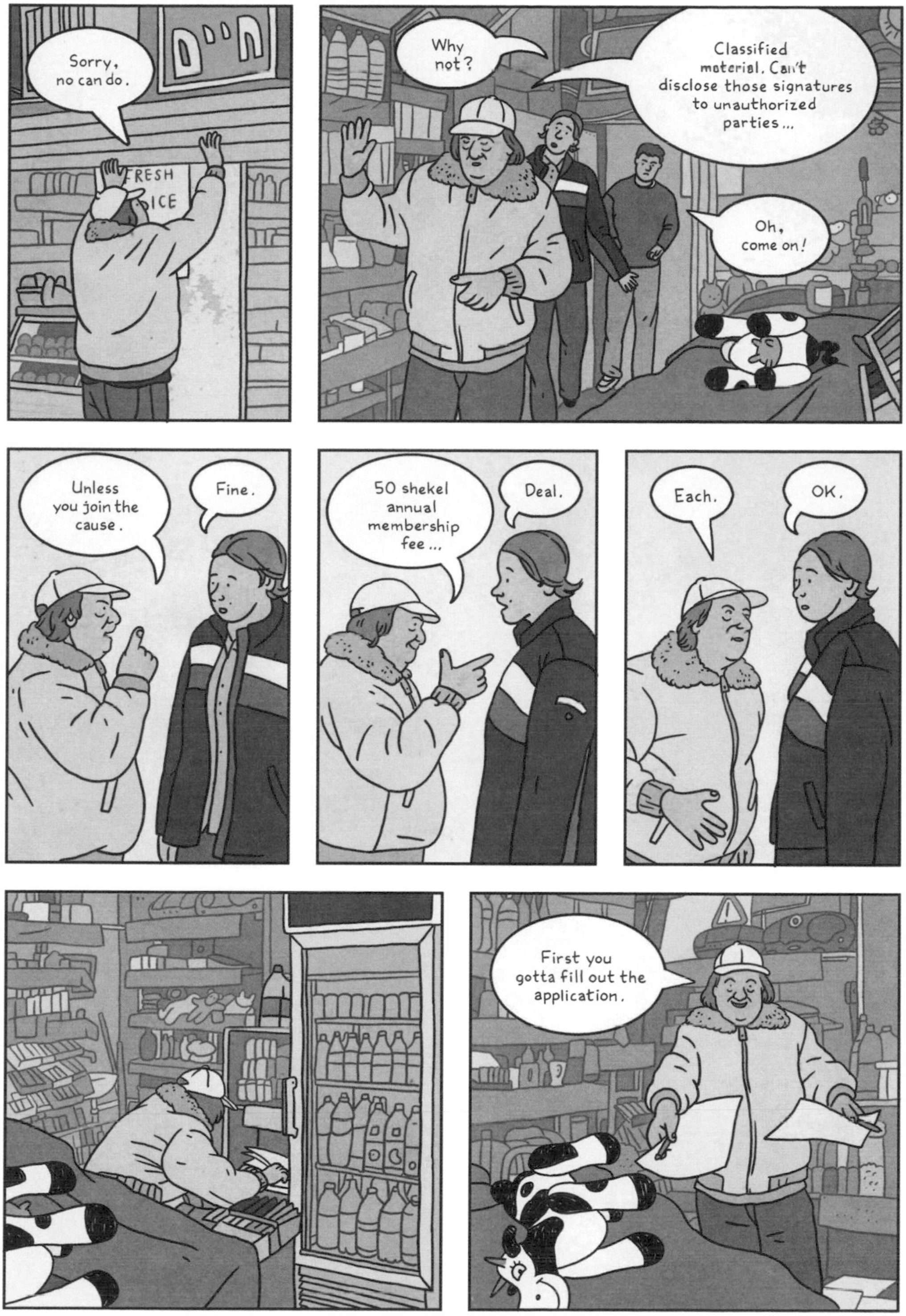

Sorry, no can do.
FRESH ICE
Why not?
Classified material. Can't disclose those signatures to unauthorized parties...
Oh, come on!
Unless you join the cause.
Fine.
50 shekel annual membership fee...
Deal.
Each.
OK.
First you gotta fill out the application.

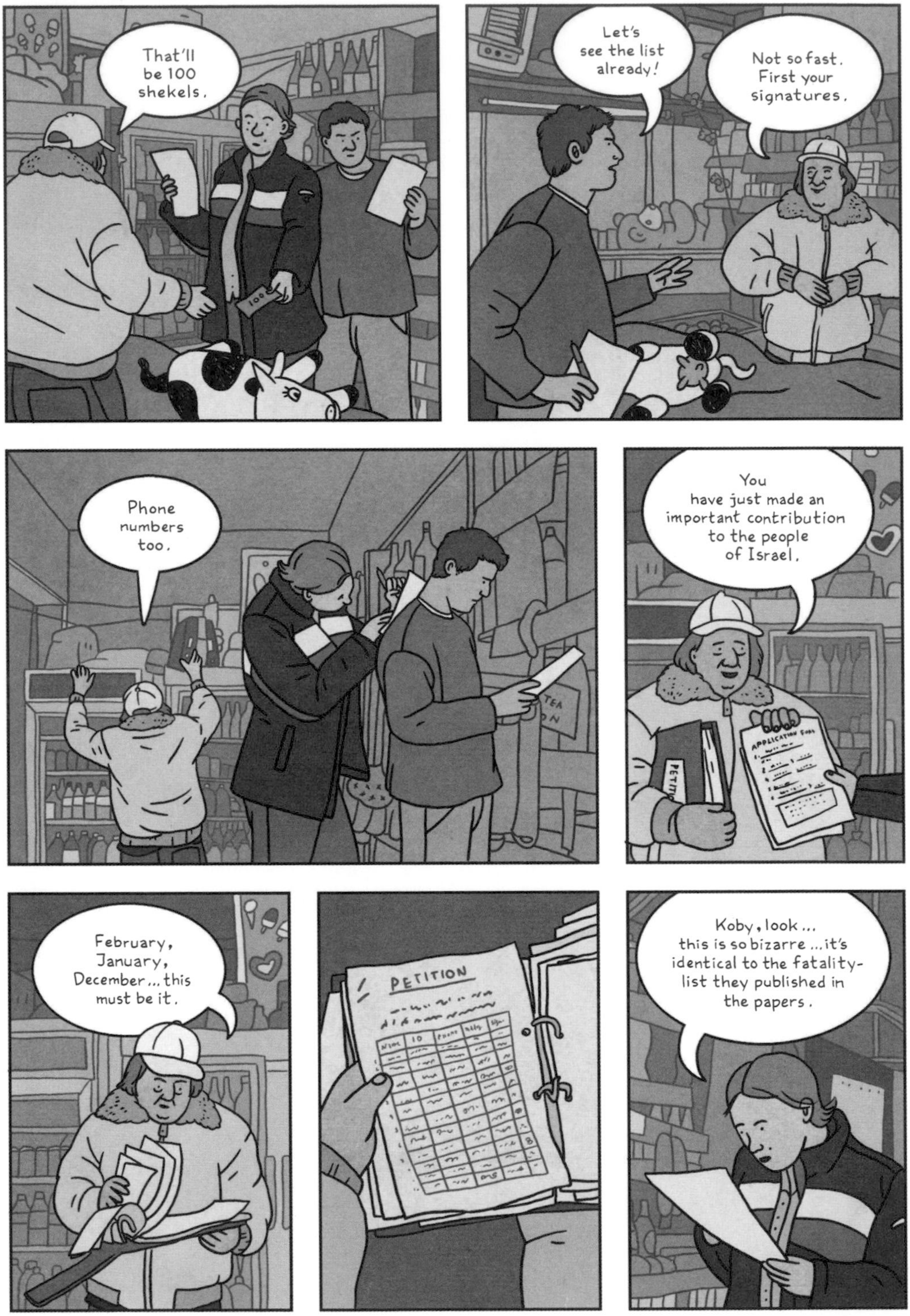
That'll be 100 shekels.
Let's see the list already!
Not so fast. First your signatures.
Phone numbers too.
You have just made an important contribution to the people of Israel.
APPLICATION FORM
PETITION
February, January, December... this must be it.
PETITION
Koby, look... this is so bizarre... it's identical to the fatality-list they published in the papers.

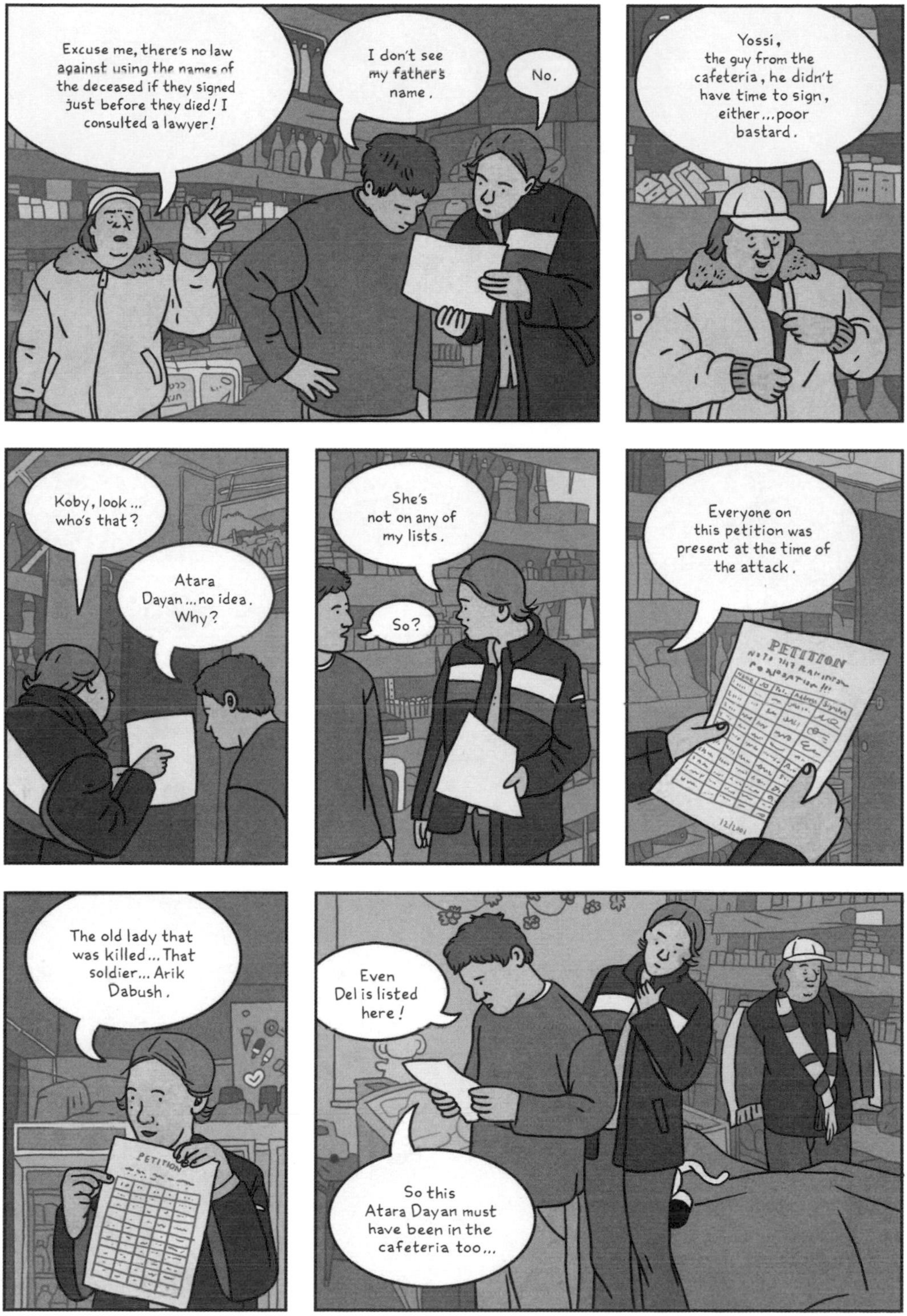
Excuse me, there's no law against using the names of the deceased if they signed just before they died! I consulted a lawyer!
I don't see my father's name.
No.
Yossi, the guy from the cafeteria, he didn't have time to sign, either...poor bastard.
Koby, look... who's that?
Atara Dayan...no idea. Why?
She's not on any of my lists.
So?
Everyone on this petition was present at the time of the attack.
PETITION
12/2001
The old lady that was killed... That soldier... Arik Dabush.
PETITION
Even Del is listed here!
So this Atara Dayan must have been in the cafeteria too...

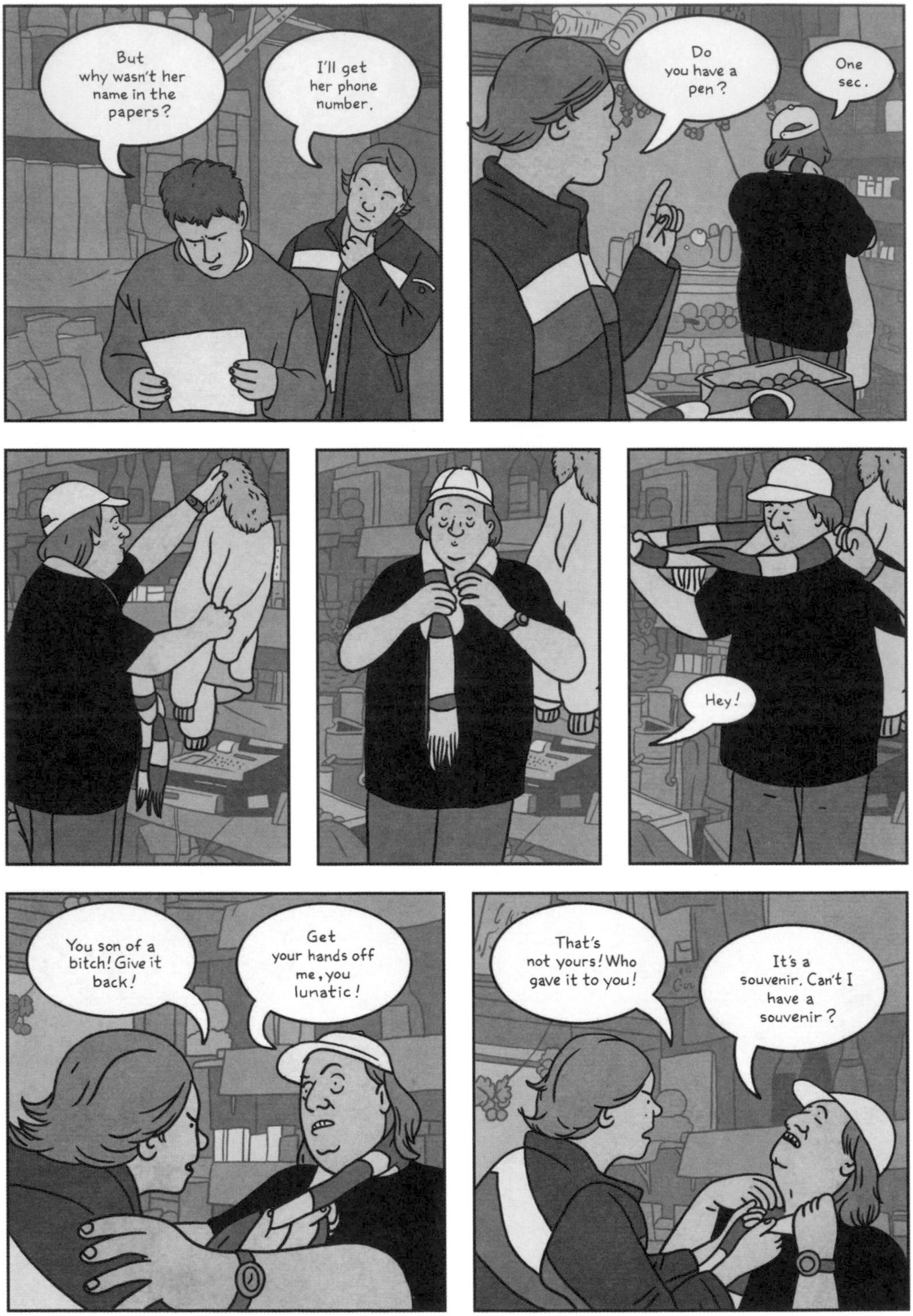

But why wasn't her name in the papers?
I'll get her phone number.
Do you have a pen?
One sec.
Hey!
You son of a bitch! Give it back!
Get your hands off me, you lunatic!
That's not yours! Who gave it to you!
It's a souvenir. Can't I have a souvenir?

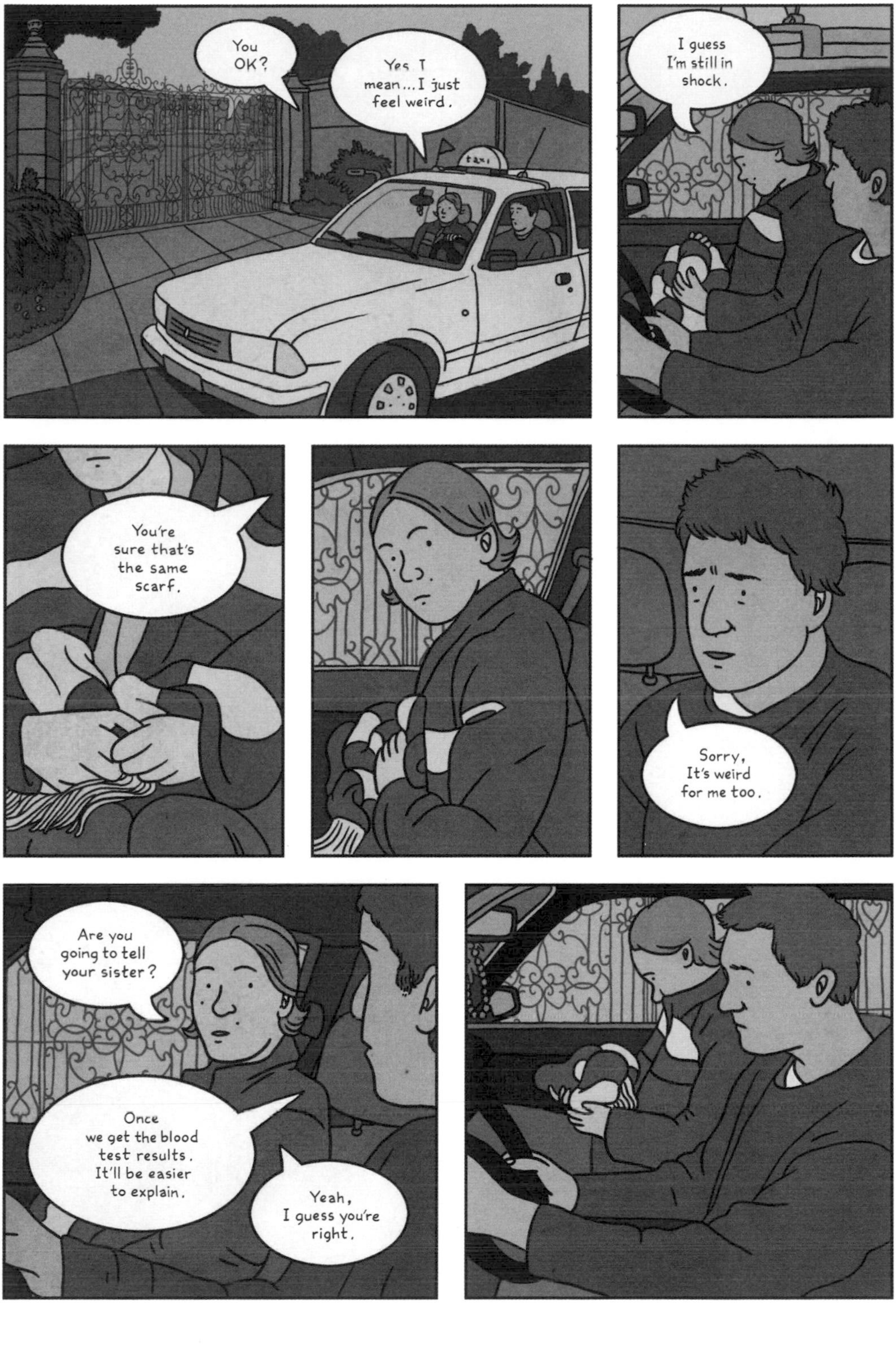
You OK?
Yes. I mean...I just feel weird.
I guess I'm still in shock.
You're sure that's the same scarf.
Sorry, It's weird for me too.
Are you going to tell your sister?
Once we get the blood test results. It'll be easier to explain.
Yeah, I guess you're right.

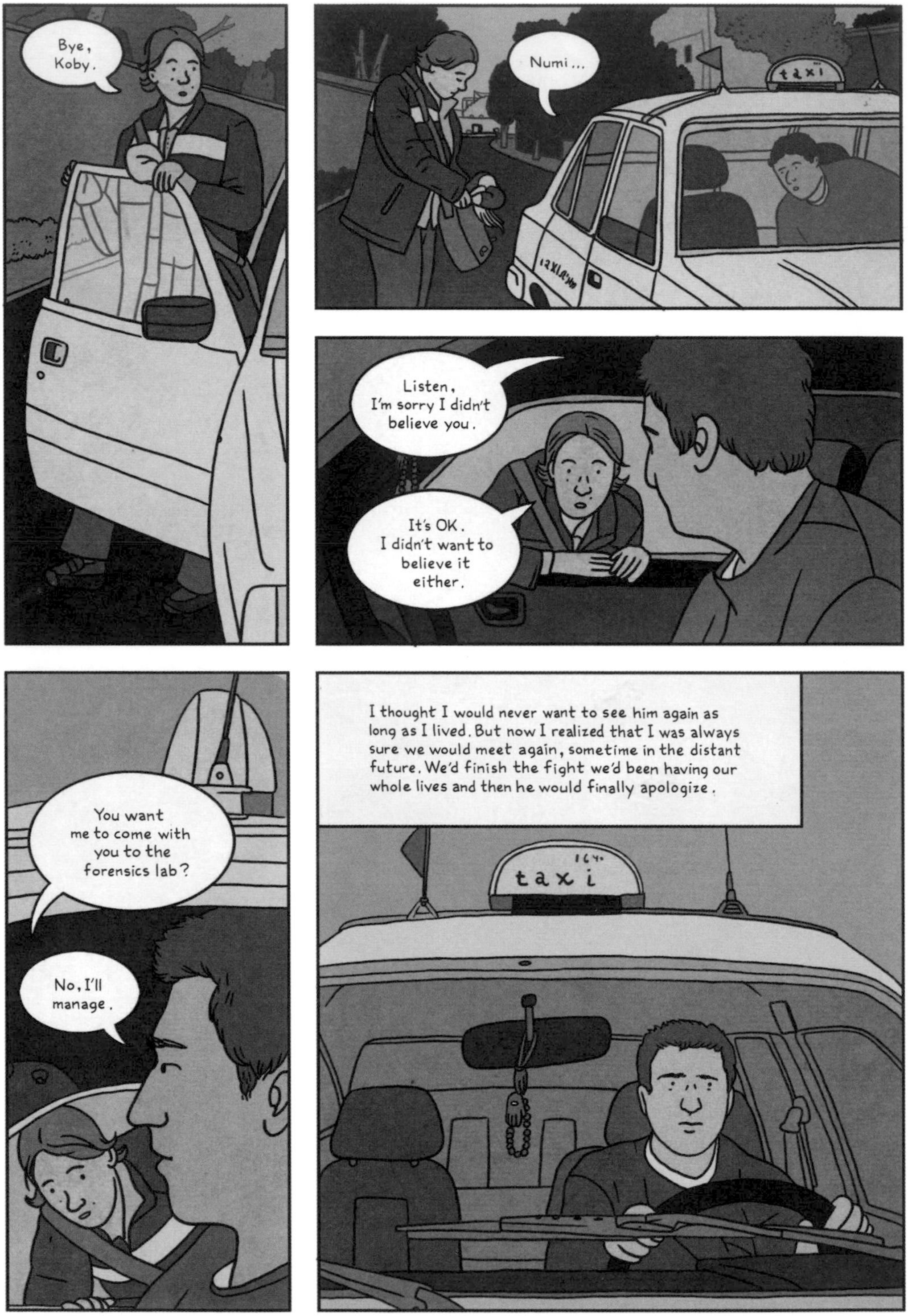
Bye, Koby.
Numi...
Listen, I'm sorry I didn't believe you.
It's OK. I didn't want to believe it either.
You want me to come with you to the forensics lab?
No, I'll manage.
I thought I would never want to see him again as long as I lived. But now I realized that I was always sure we would meet again, sometime in the distant future. We'd finish the fight we'd been having our whole lives and then he would finally apologize.
taxi

chapter three
riding the waves

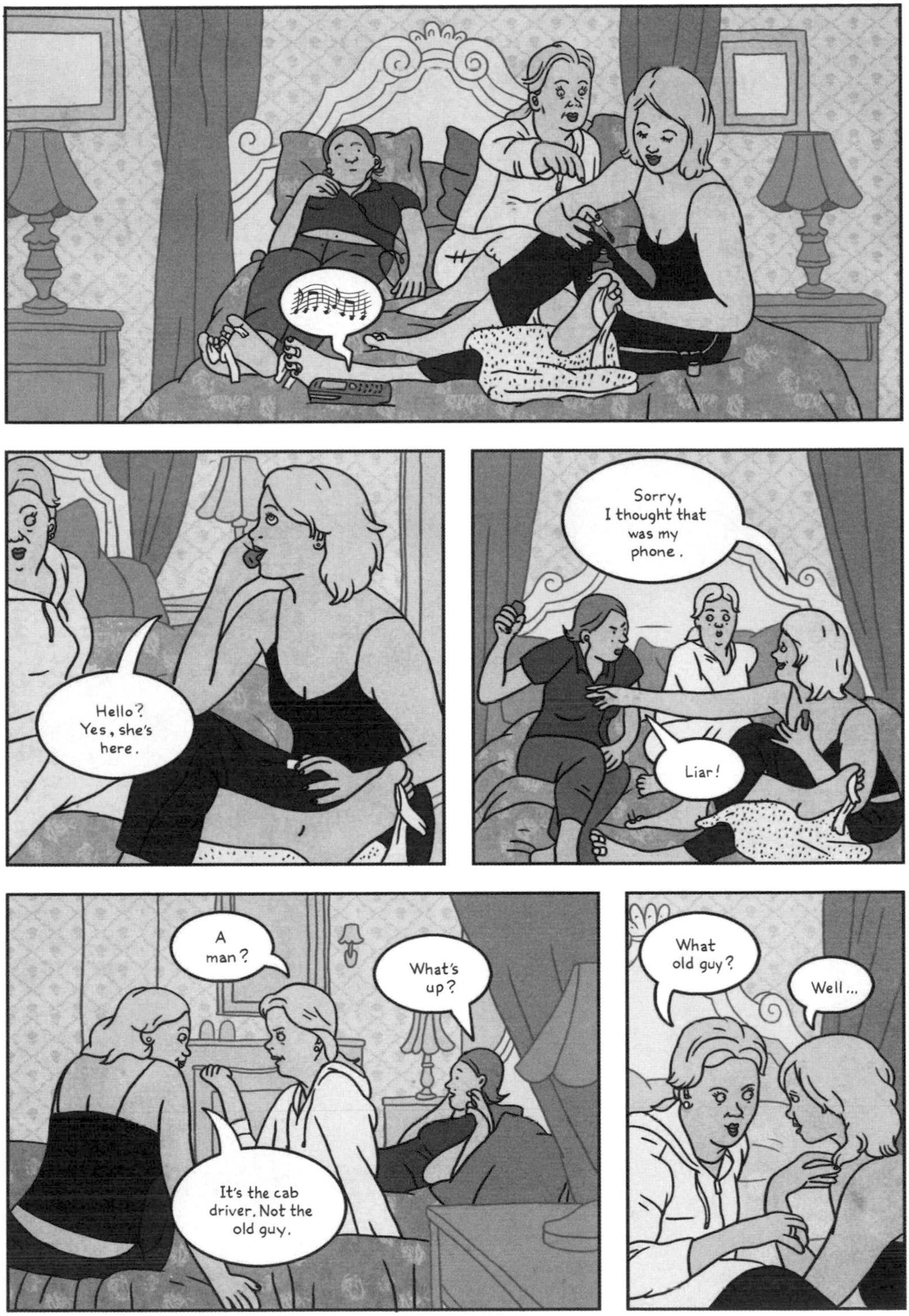
Hello? Yes, she's here.
Sorry, I thought that was my phone.
Liar!
A man?
What's up?
It's the cab driver. Not the old guy.
What old guy?
Well...

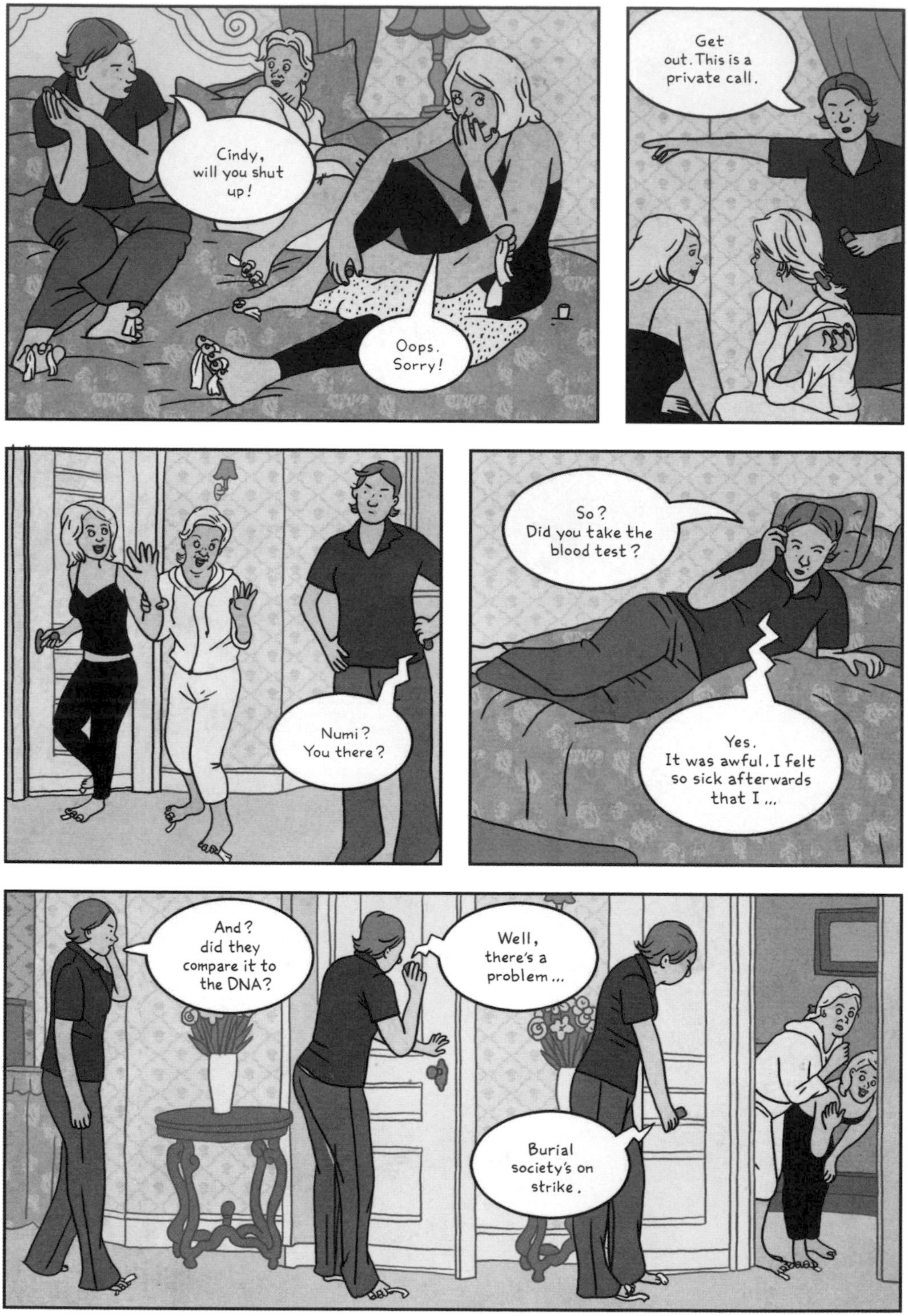
Cindy, will you shut up!
Oops. Sorry!
Get out. This is a private call.
Numi? You there?
So? Did you take the blood test?
Yes. It was awful. I felt so sick afterwards that I...
And? did they compare it to the DNA?
Well, there's a problem...
Burial society's on strike.

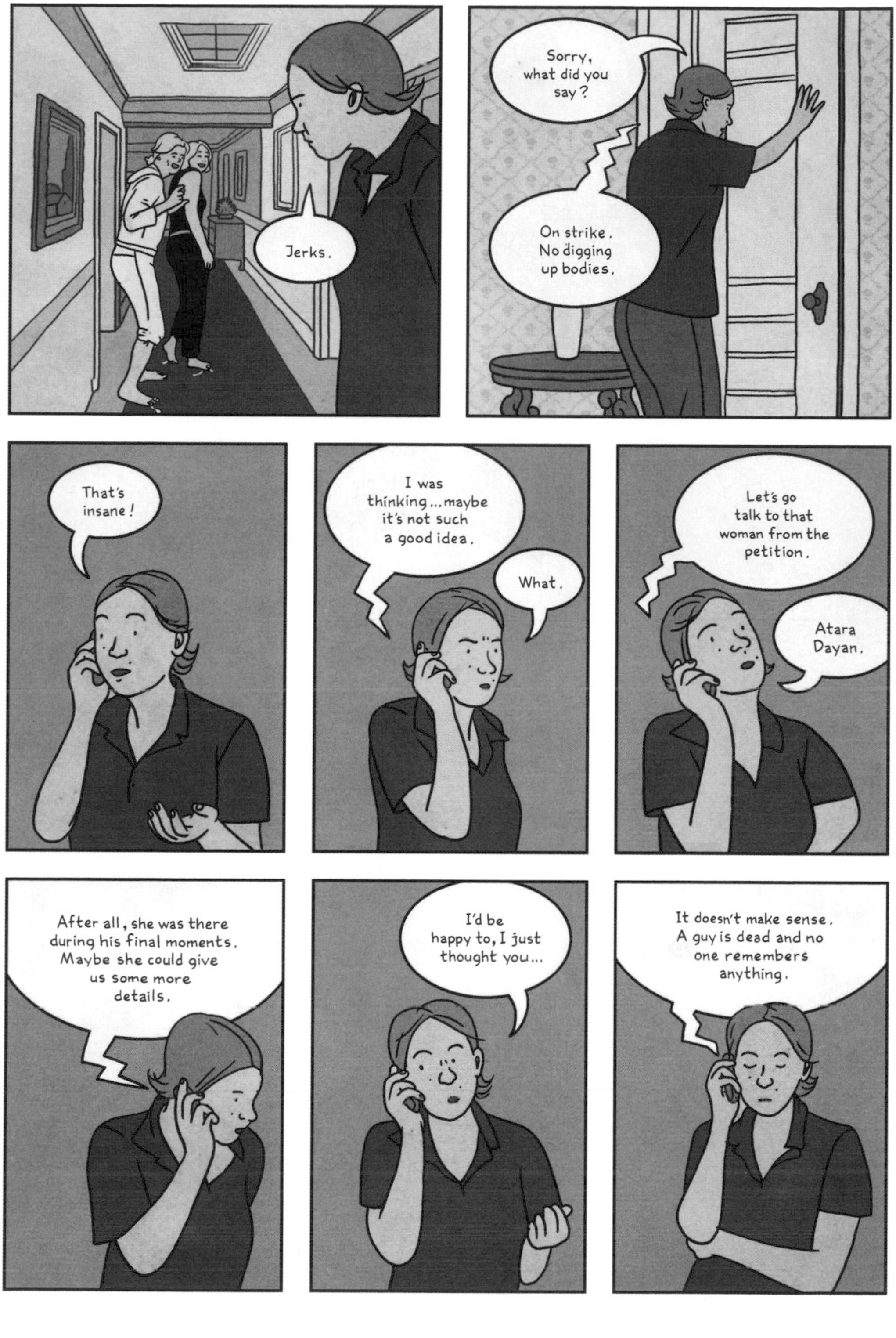
Jerks.
Sorry, what did you say?
On strike. No digging up bodies.
That's insane!
I was thinking... maybe it's not such a good idea.
What.
Let's go talk to that woman from the petition.
Atara Dayan.
After all, she was there during his final moments. Maybe she could give us some more details.
I'd be happy to, I just thought you...
It doesn't make sense. A guy is dead and no one remembers anything.

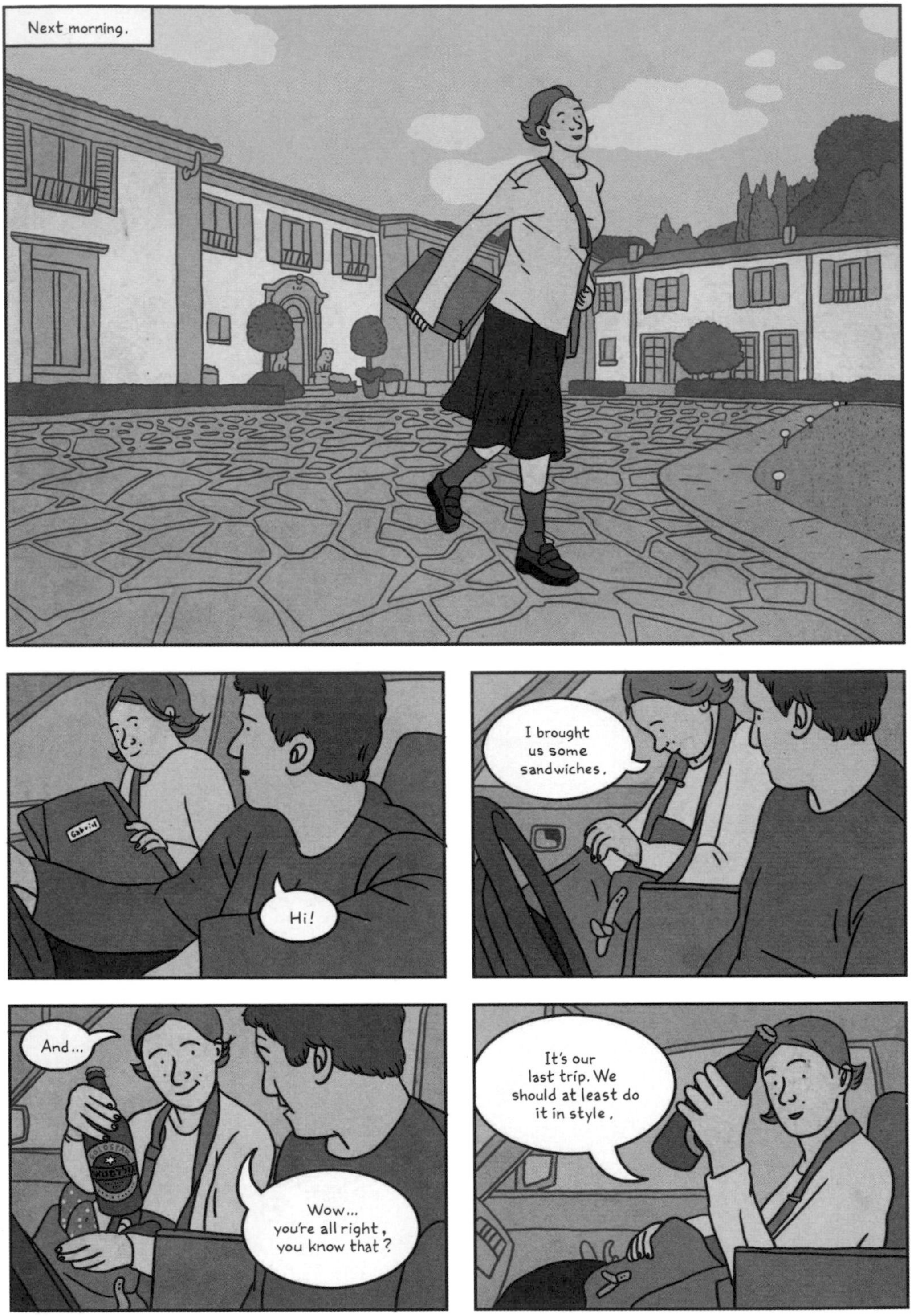
Next morning.
Hi!
I brought us some sandwiches.
And...
Wow... you're all right, you know that?
It's our last trip. We should at least do it in style.

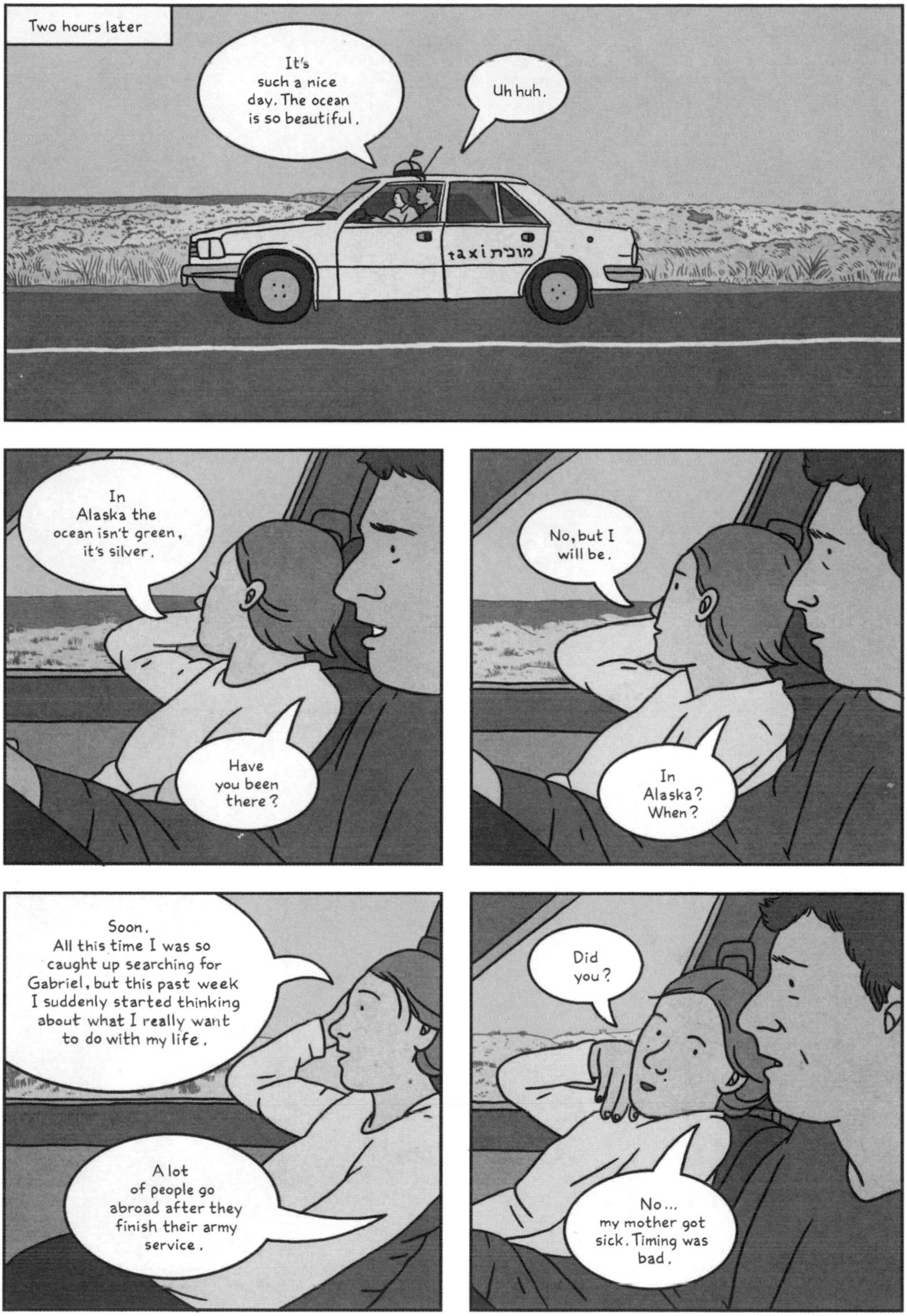
Two hours later
It's such a nice day. The ocean is so beautiful.
Uh huh.
taxi מונית
In Alaska the ocean isn't green, it's silver.
Have you been there?
No, but I will be.
In Alaska? When?
Soon. All this time I was so caught up searching for Gabriel, but this past week I suddenly started thinking about what I really want to do with my life.
A lot of people go abroad after they finish their army service.
Did you?
No... my mother got sick. Timing was bad.

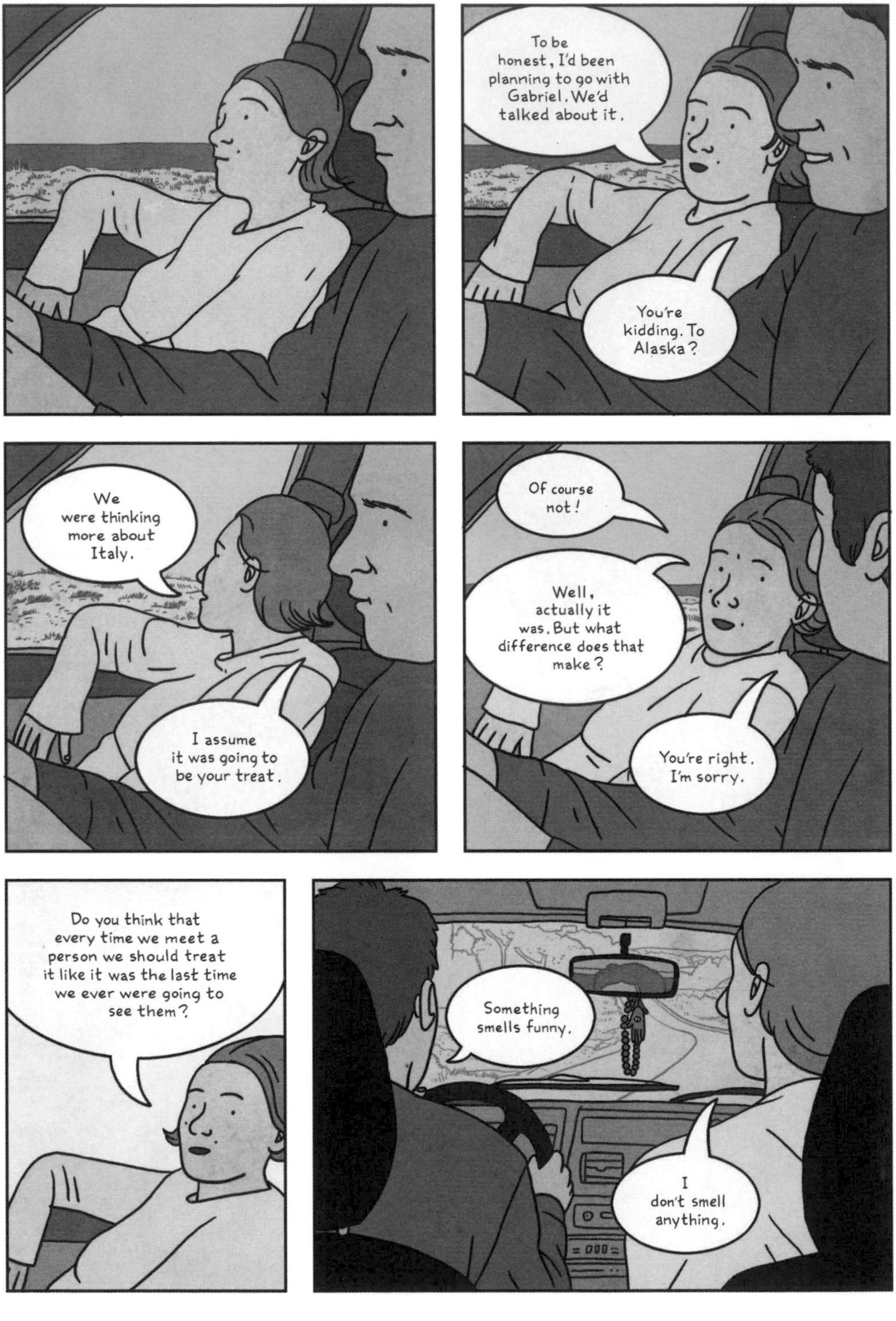
To be honest, I'd been planning to go with Gabriel. We'd talked about it.
You're kidding. To Alaska?
We were thinking more about Italy.
I assume it was going to be your treat.
Of course not!
Well, actually it was. But what difference does that make?
You're right. I'm sorry.
Do you think that every time we meet a person we should treat it like it was the last time we ever were going to see them?
Something smells funny.
I don't smell anything.

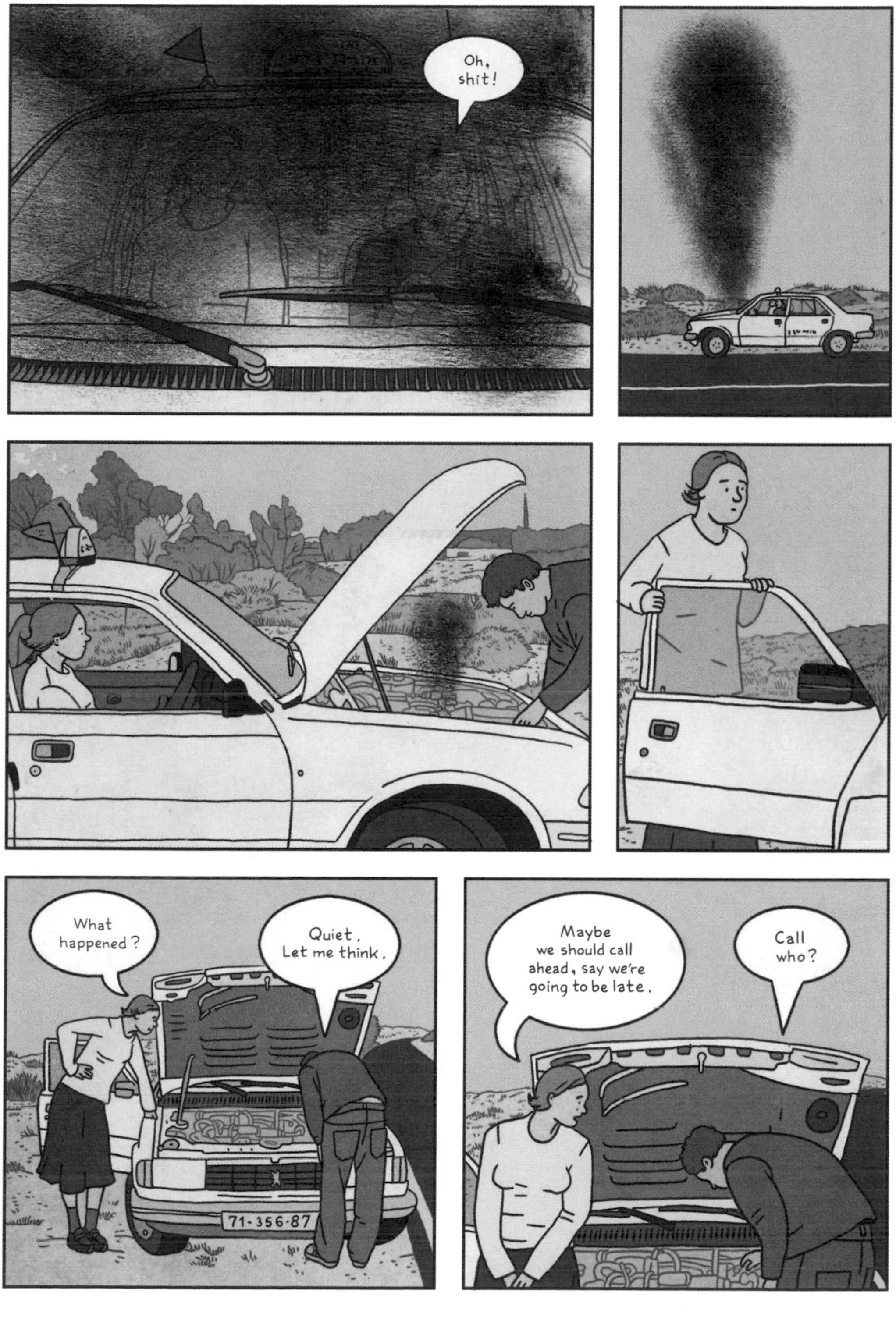
Oh, shit!
What happened?
Quiet. Let me think.
Maybe we should call ahead, say we're going to be late.
Call who?
71-356-87

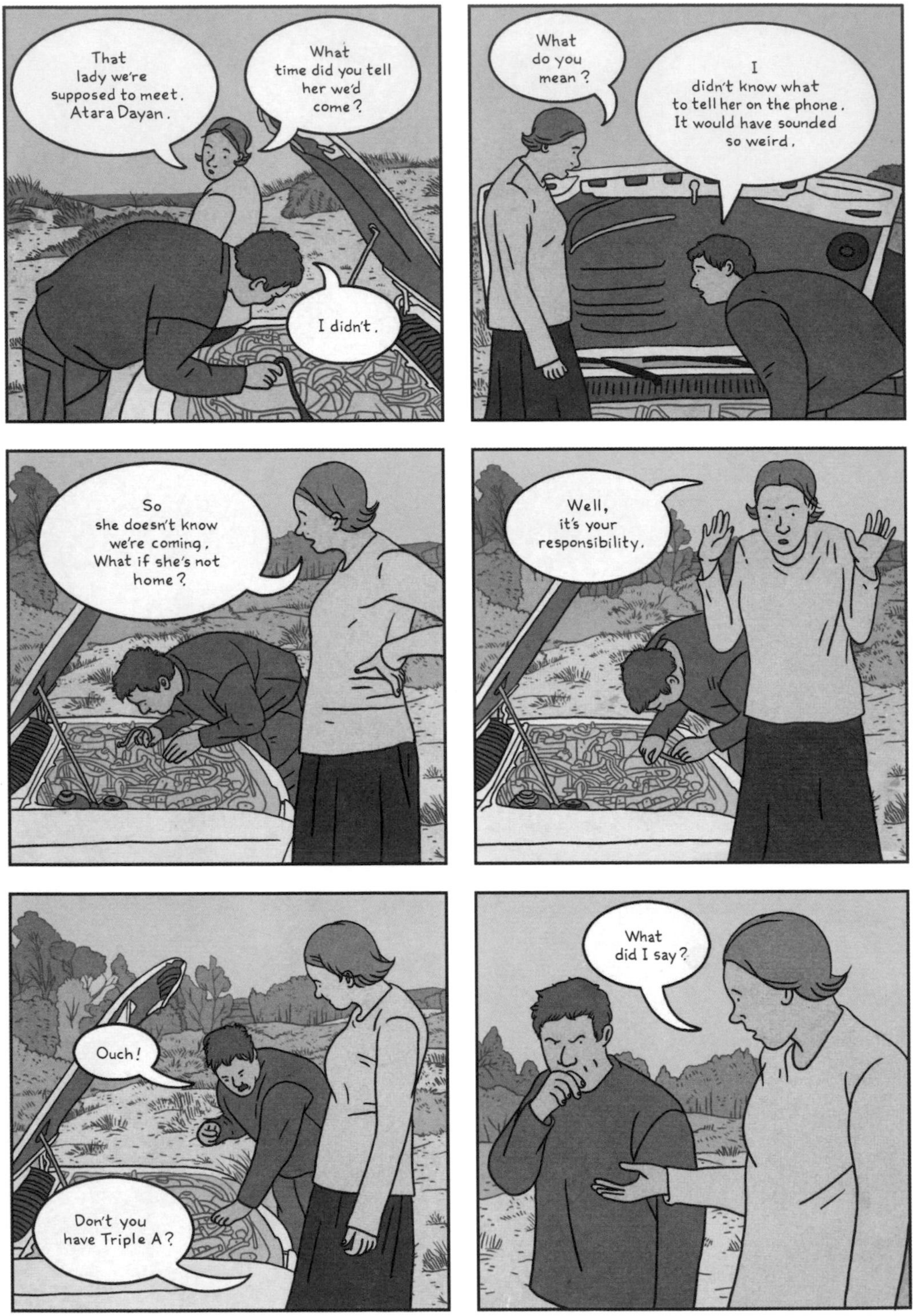
That lady we're supposed to meet. Atara Dayan.
What time did you tell her we'd come?
I didn't.
What do you mean?
I didn't know what to tell her on the phone. It would have sounded so weird.
So she doesn't know we're coming. What if she's not home?
Well, it's your responsibility.
Ouch!
Don't you have Triple A?
What did I say?

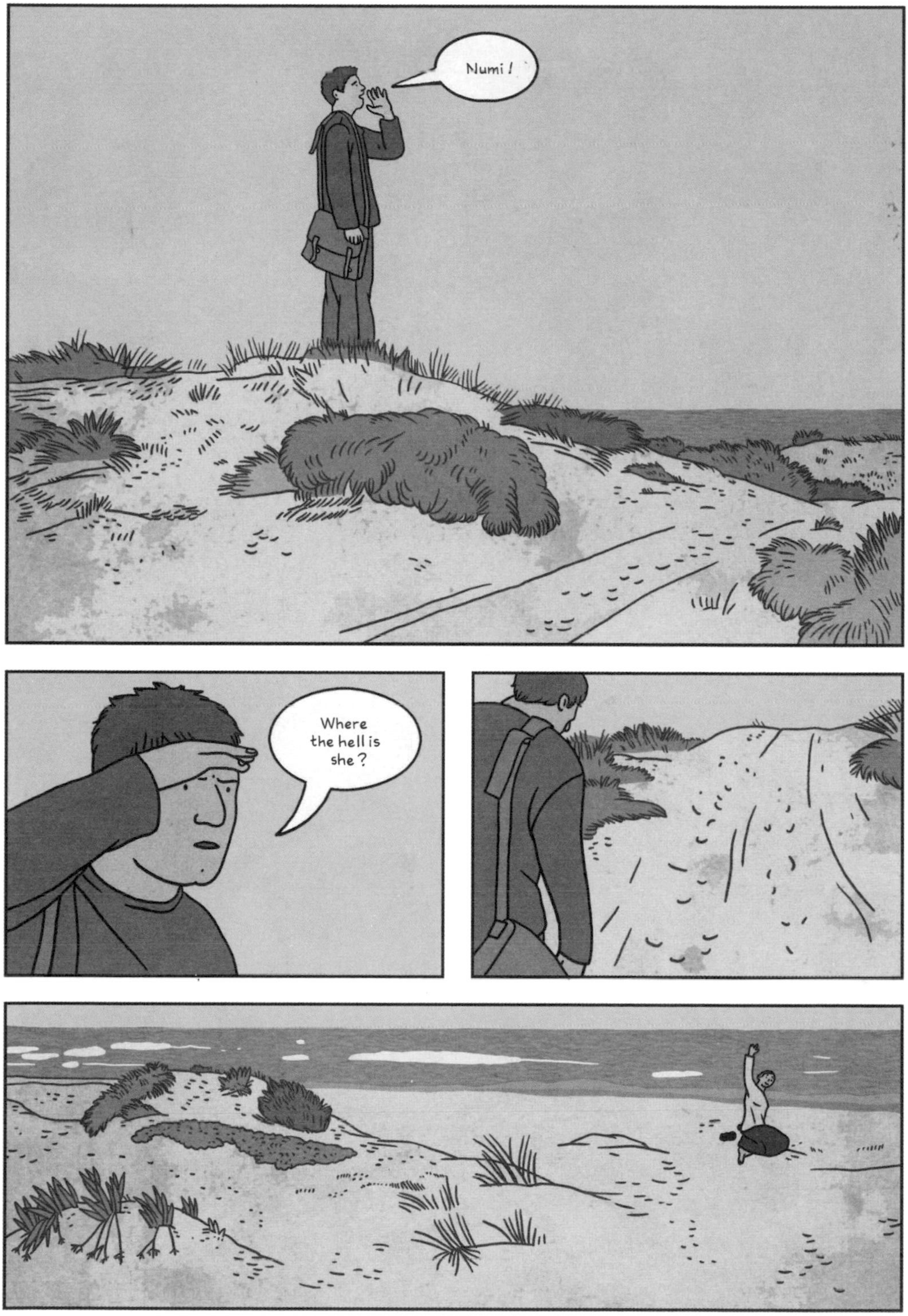
Numi!
Where the hell is she?

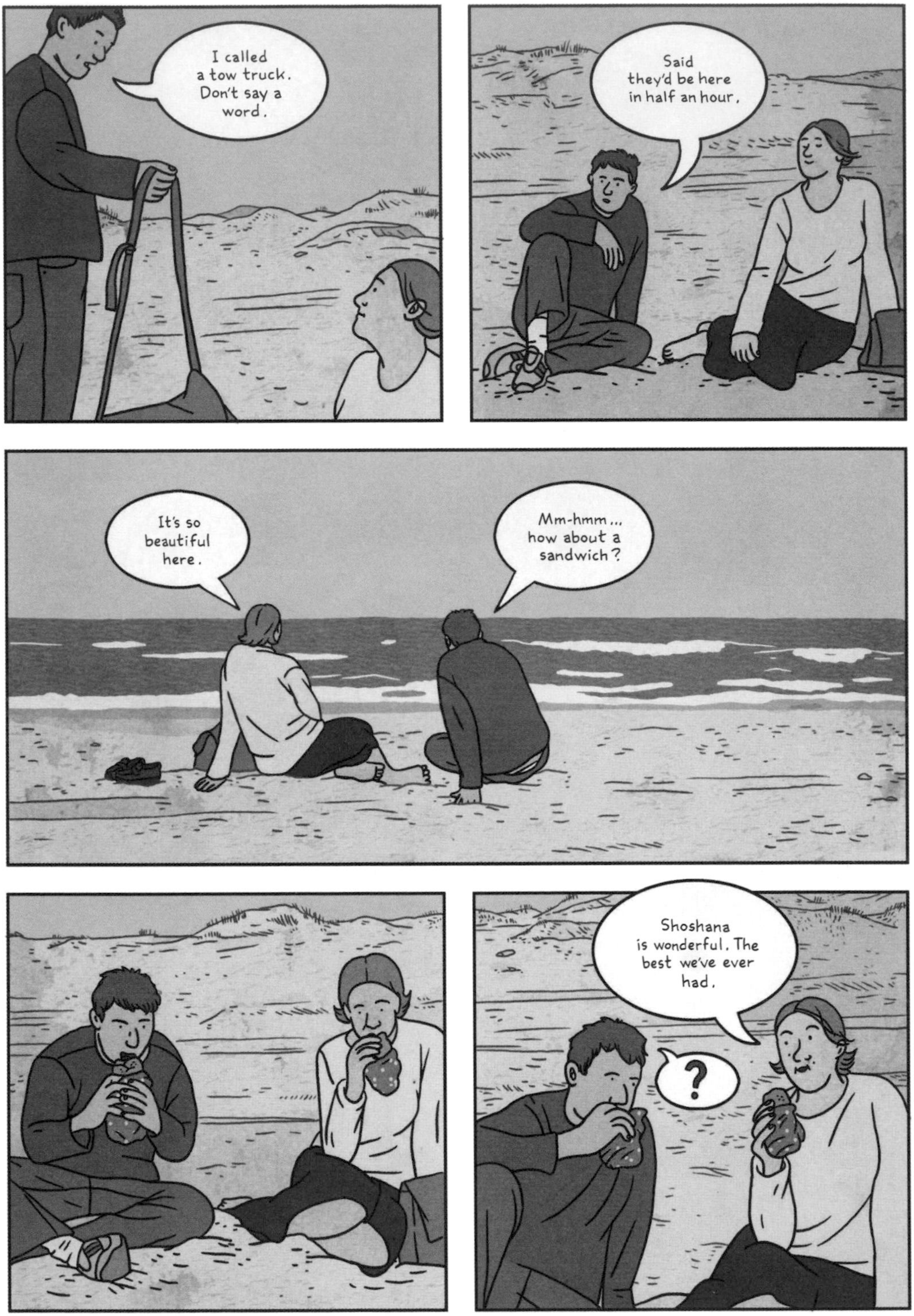
I called a tow truck. Don't say a word.
Said they'd be here in half an hour.
It's so beautiful here.
Mm-hmm... how about a sandwich?
Shoshana is wonderful. The best we've ever had.
?

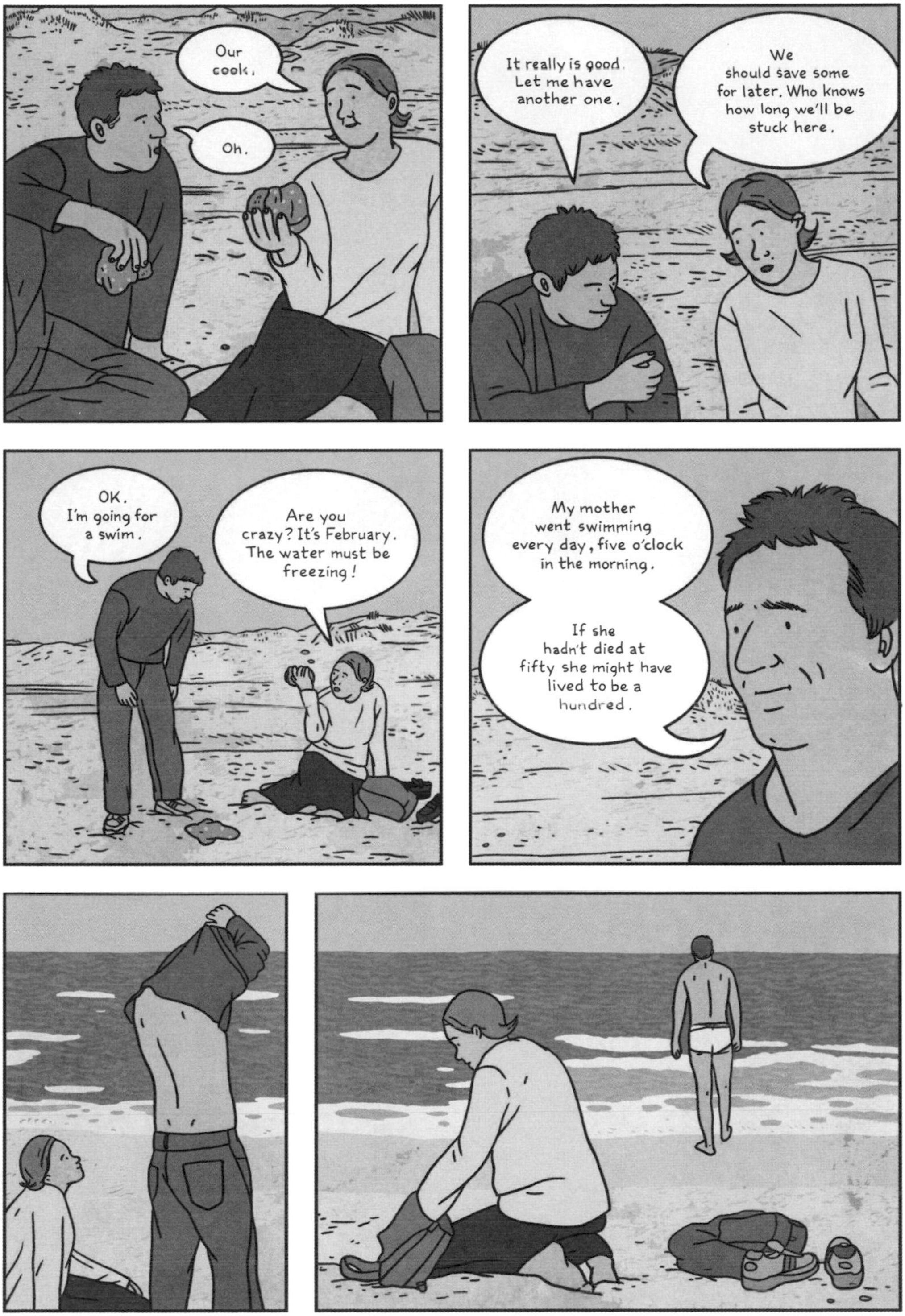
Our cook.
Oh.
It really is good. Let me have another one.
We should save some for later. Who knows how long we'll be stuck here.
OK. I'm going for a swim.
Are you crazy? It's February. The water must be freezing!
My mother went swimming every day, five o'clock in the morning.
If she hadn't died at fifty she might have lived to be a hundred.

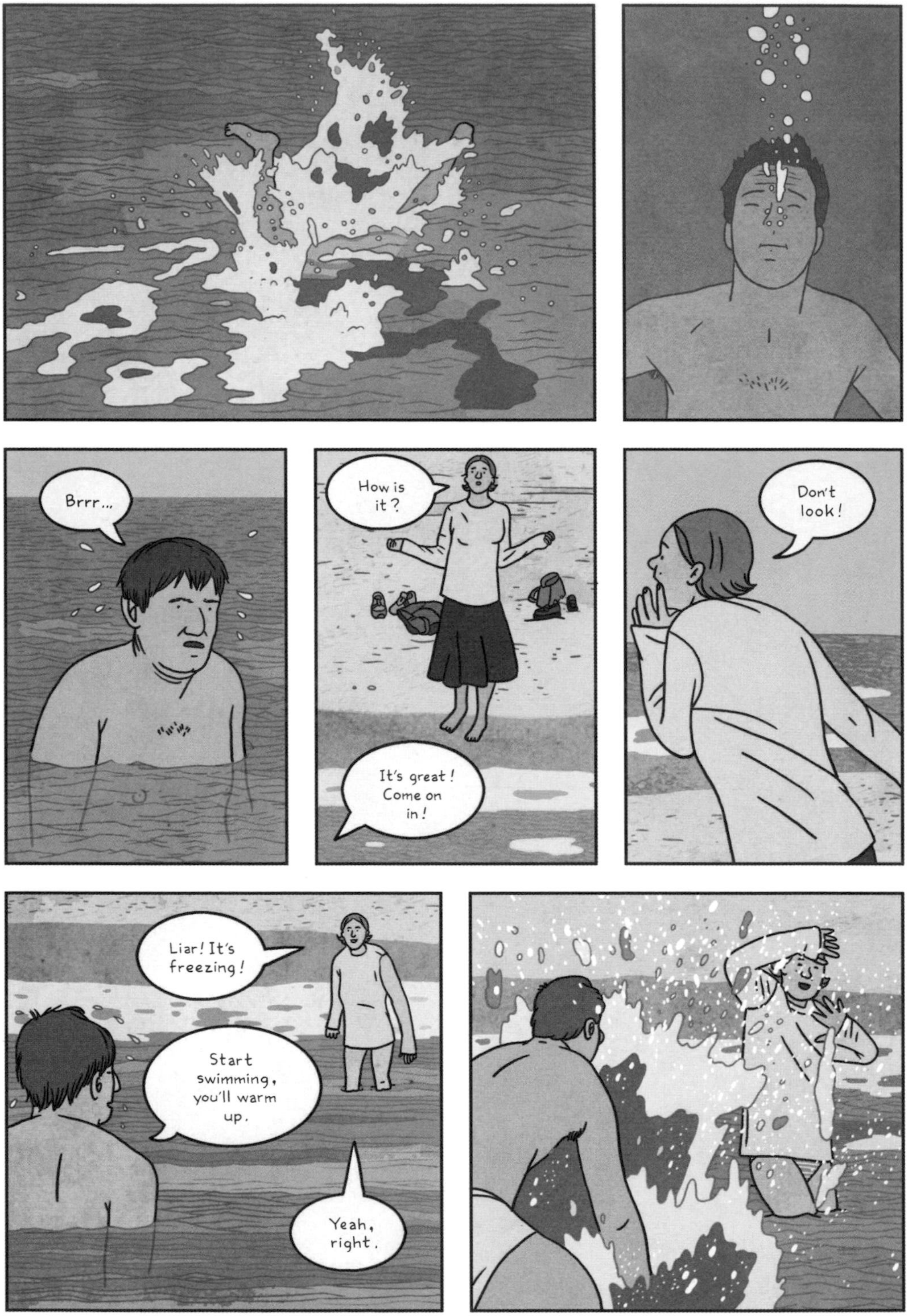
Brrr...
How is it?
It's great! Come on in!
Don't look!
Liar! It's freezing!
Start swimming, you'll warm up.
Yeah, right.

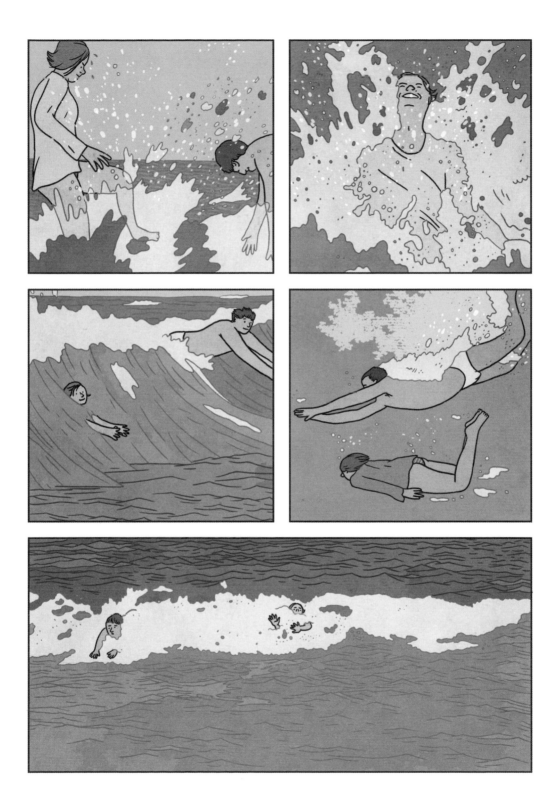

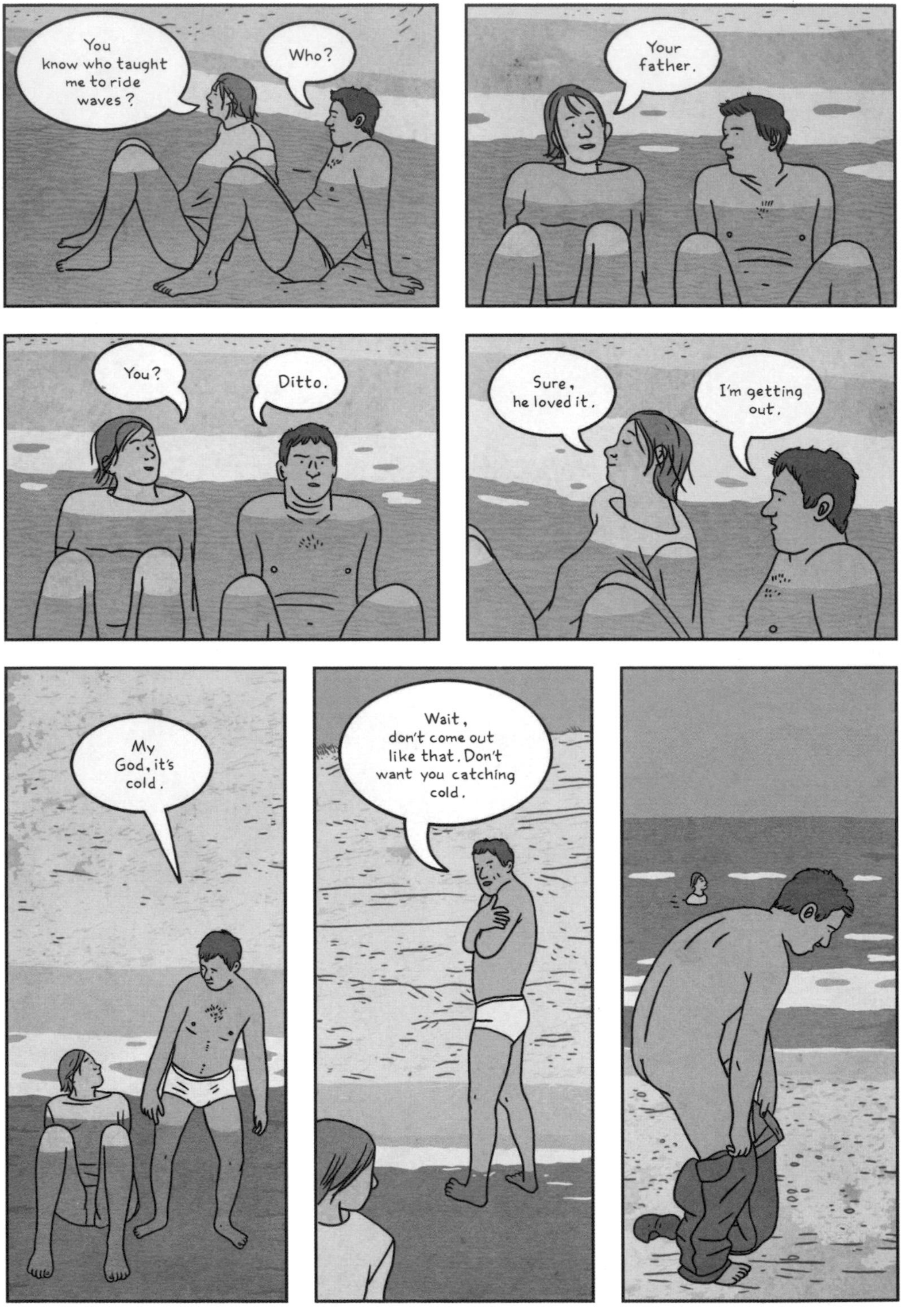
You know who taught me to ride waves?
Who?
Your father.
You?
Ditto.
Sure, he loved it.
I'm getting out.
My God, it's cold.
Wait, don't come out like that. Don't want you catching cold.

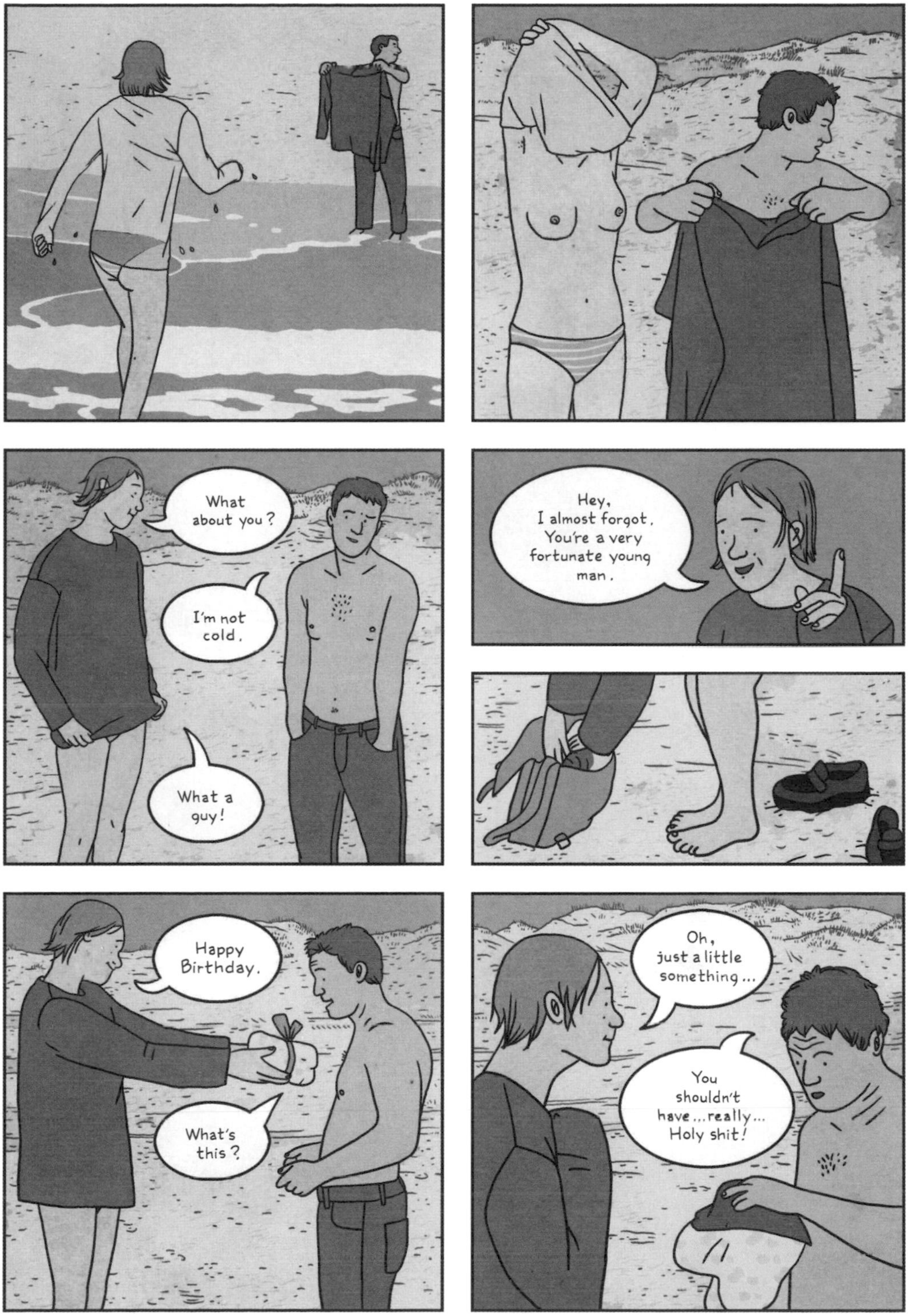

What about you?
I'm not cold.
What a guy!
Hey, I almost forgot. You're a very fortunate young man.
Happy Birthday.
What's this?
Oh, just a little something...
You shouldn't have...really... Holy shit!

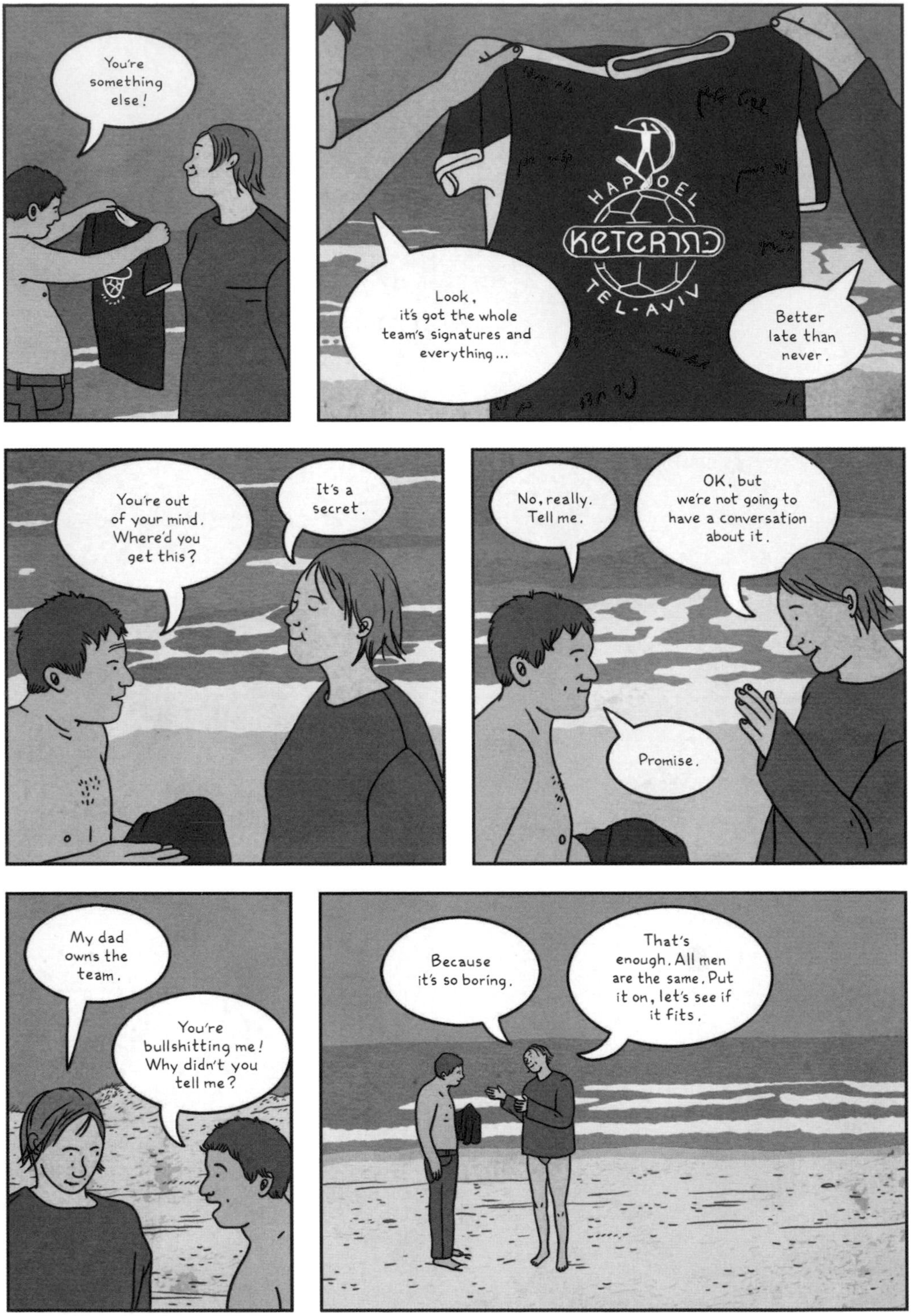
You're something else!
Look, it's got the whole team's signatures and everything...
HAPOEL
KETER
TEL-AVIV
Better late than never.
You're out of your mind. Where'd you get this?
It's a secret.
No, really. Tell me.
OK, but we're not going to have a conversation about it.
Promise.
My dad owns the team.
You're bullshitting me! Why didn't you tell me?
Because it's so boring.
That's enough. All men are the same. Put it on, let's see if it fits.

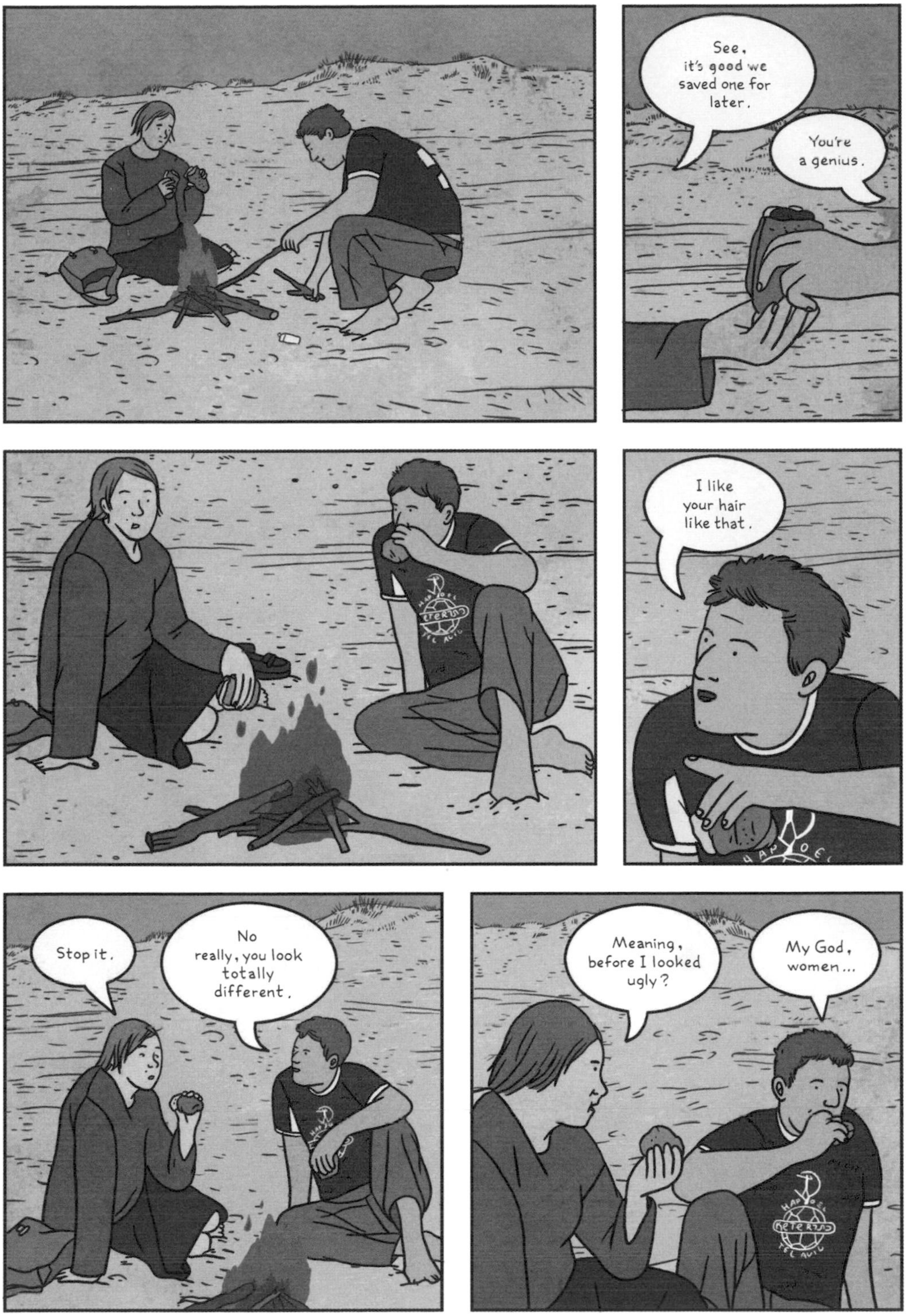
See, it's good we saved one for later.
You're a genius.
I like your hair like that.
Stop it.
No really, you look totally different.
Meaning, before I looked ugly?
My God, women...

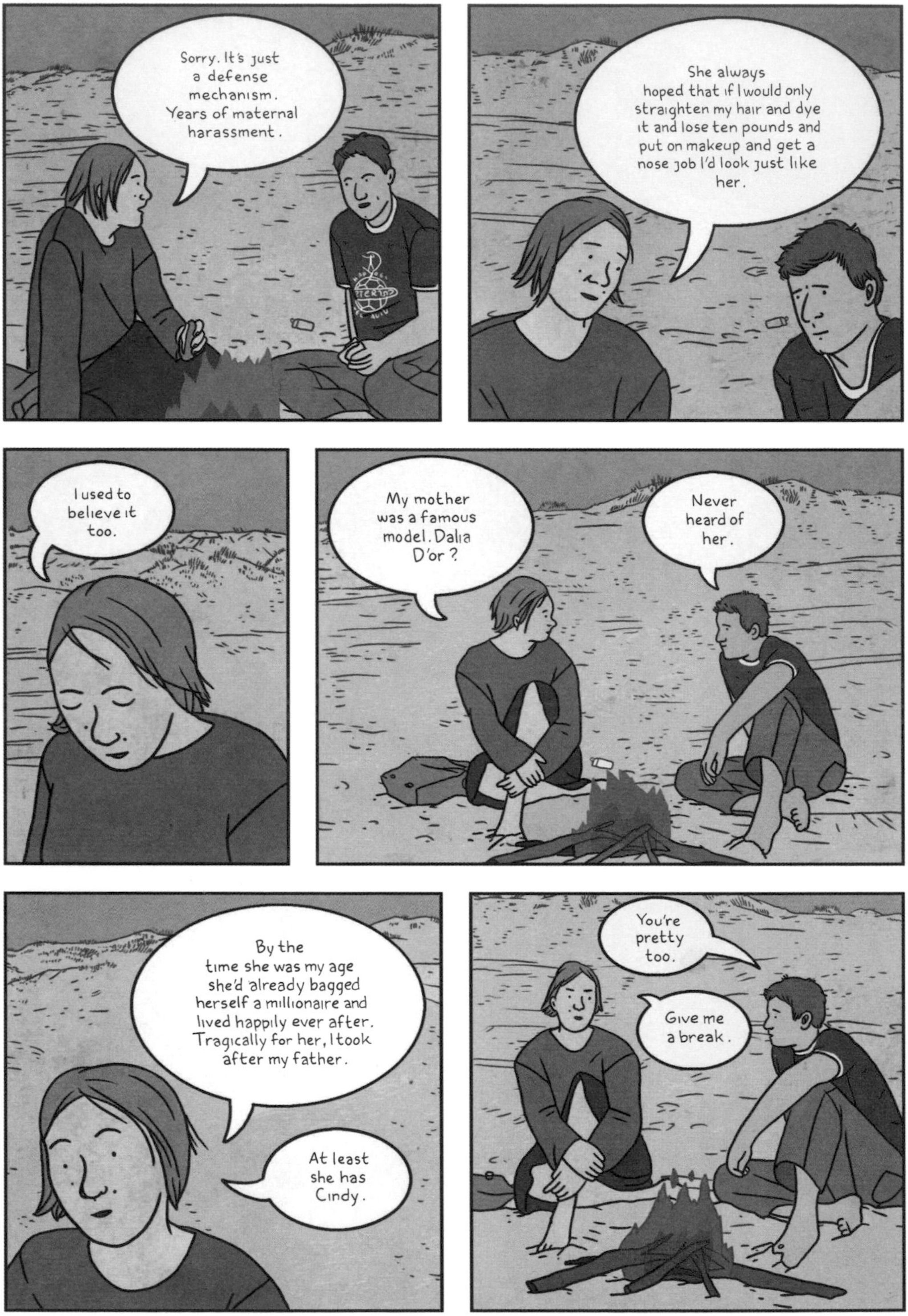
Sorry. It's just a defense mechanism. Years of maternal harassment.
She always hoped that if I would only straighten my hair and dye it and lose ten pounds and put on makeup and get a nose job I'd look just like her.
I used to believe it too.
My mother was a famous model. Dalia D'or?
Never heard of her.
By the time she was my age she'd already bagged herself a millionaire and lived happily ever after. Tragically for her, I took after my father.
At least she has Cindy.
You're pretty too.
Give me a break.

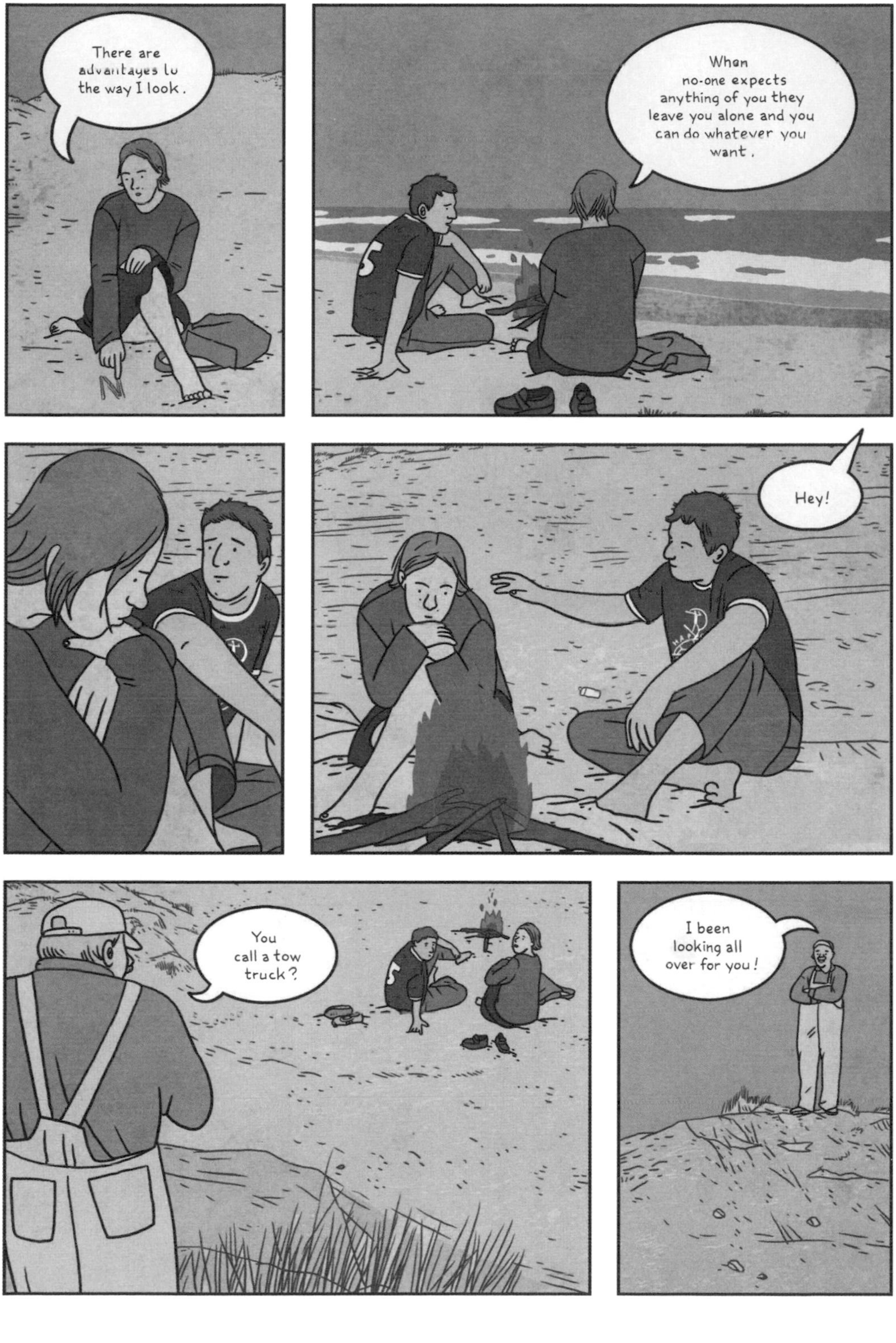
There are advantages to the way I look.
When no-one expects anything of you they leave you alone and you can do whatever you want.
Hey!
You call a tow truck?
I been looking all over for you!

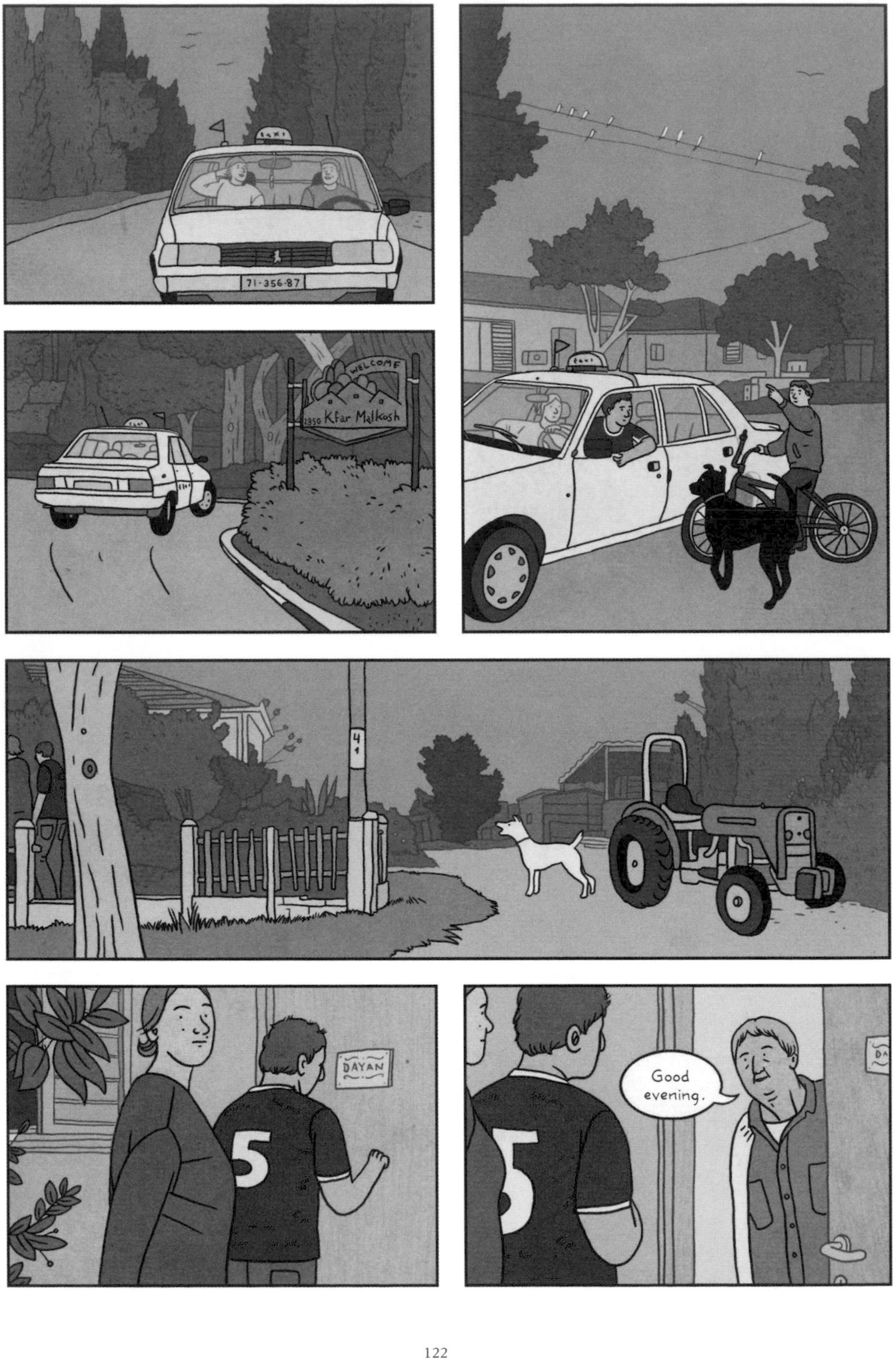
71-356-87
WELCOME
1950 Kfar Malkosh
41
DAYAN
Good evening.

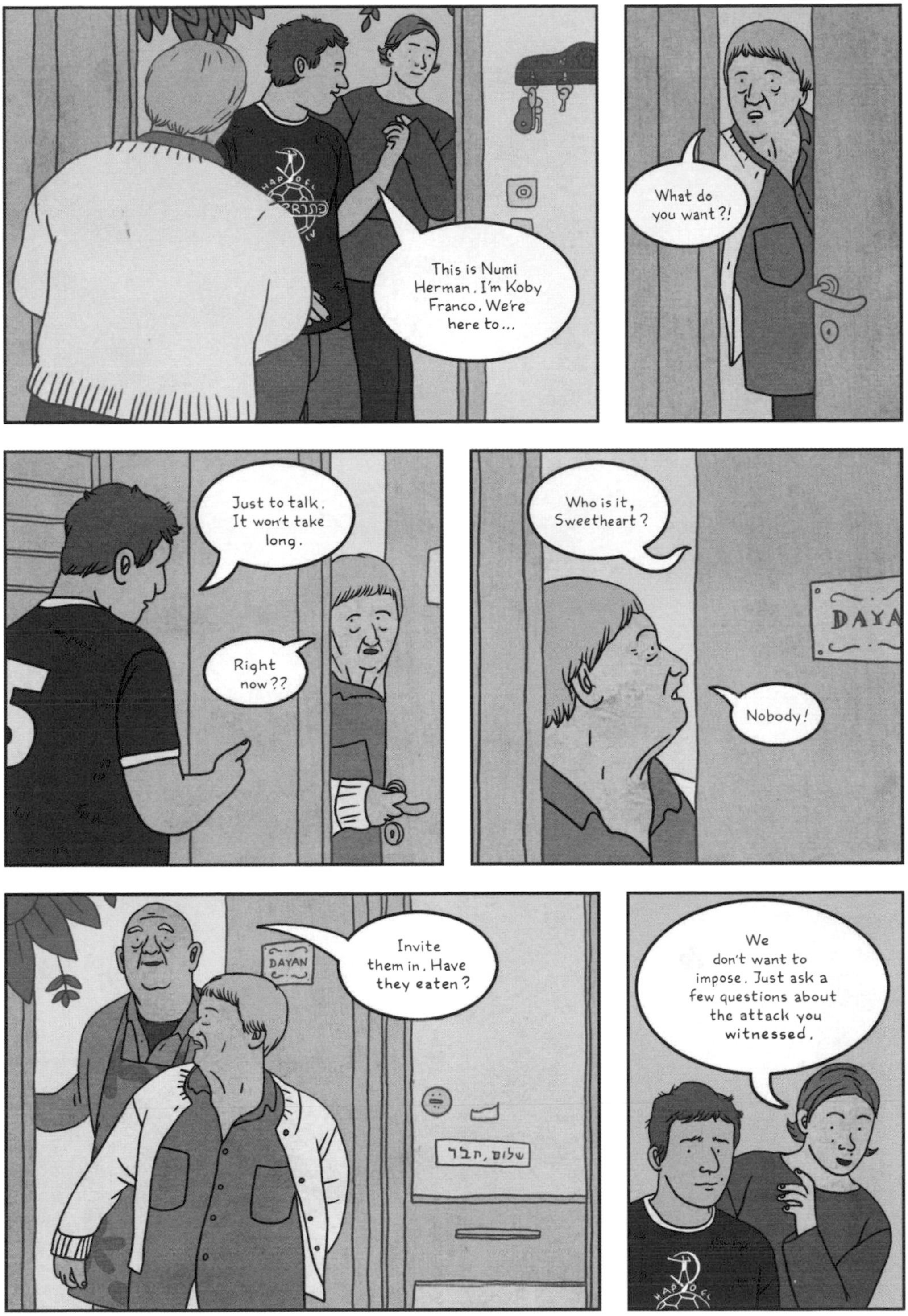
This is Numi Herman. I'm Koby Franco. We're here to...
What do you want?!
Just to talk. It won't take long.
Right now??
Who is it, Sweetheart?
DAYA
Nobody!
DAYAN
Invite them in. Have they eaten?
שלום, חבר
We don't want to impose. Just ask a few questions about the attack you witnessed.

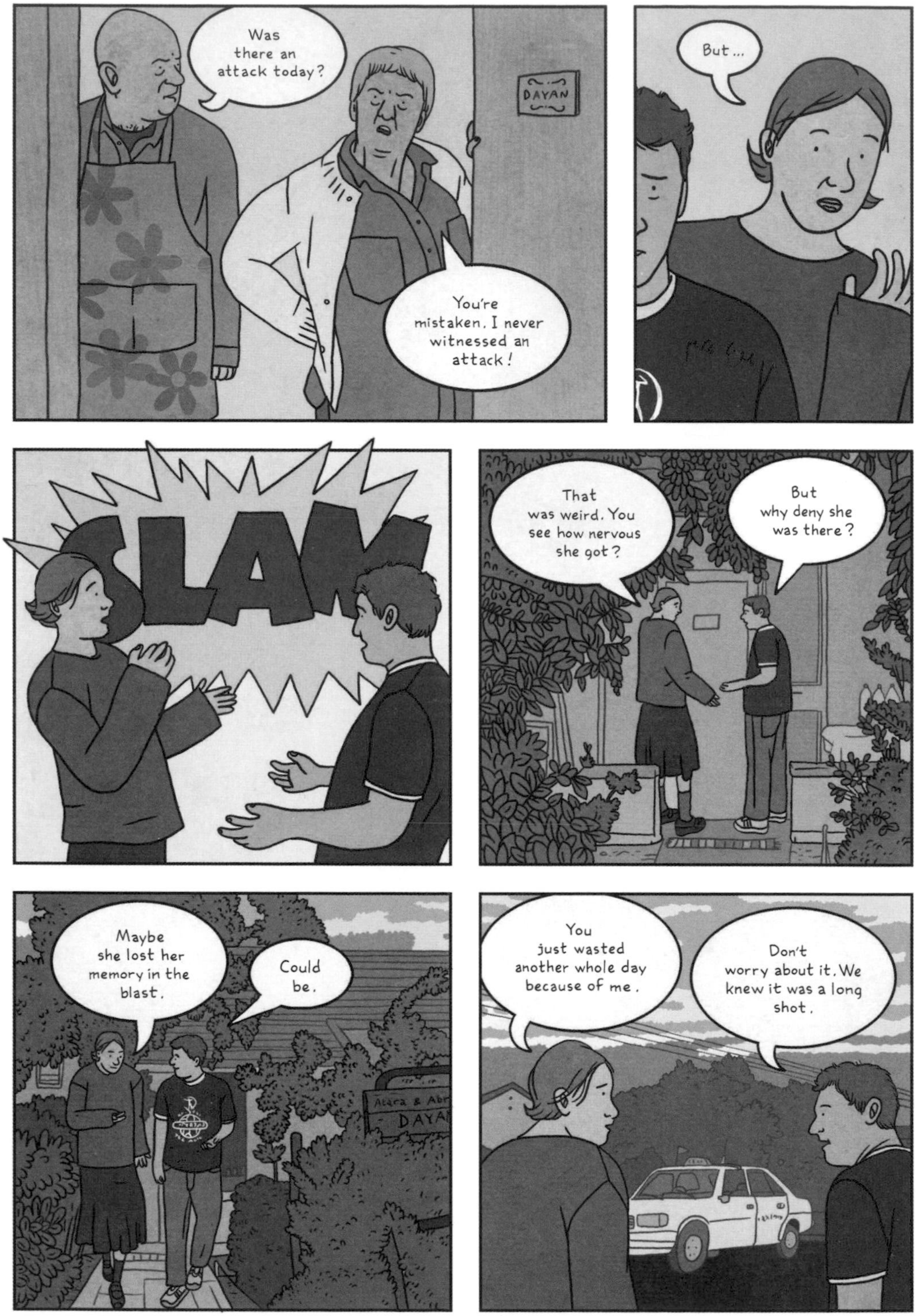
Was there an attack today?
DAYAN
You're mistaken. I never witnessed an attack!
But...
SLAM
That was weird. You see how nervous she got?
But why deny she was there?
Maybe she lost her memory in the blast.
Could be.
You just wasted another whole day because of me.
Don't worry about it. We knew it was a long shot.

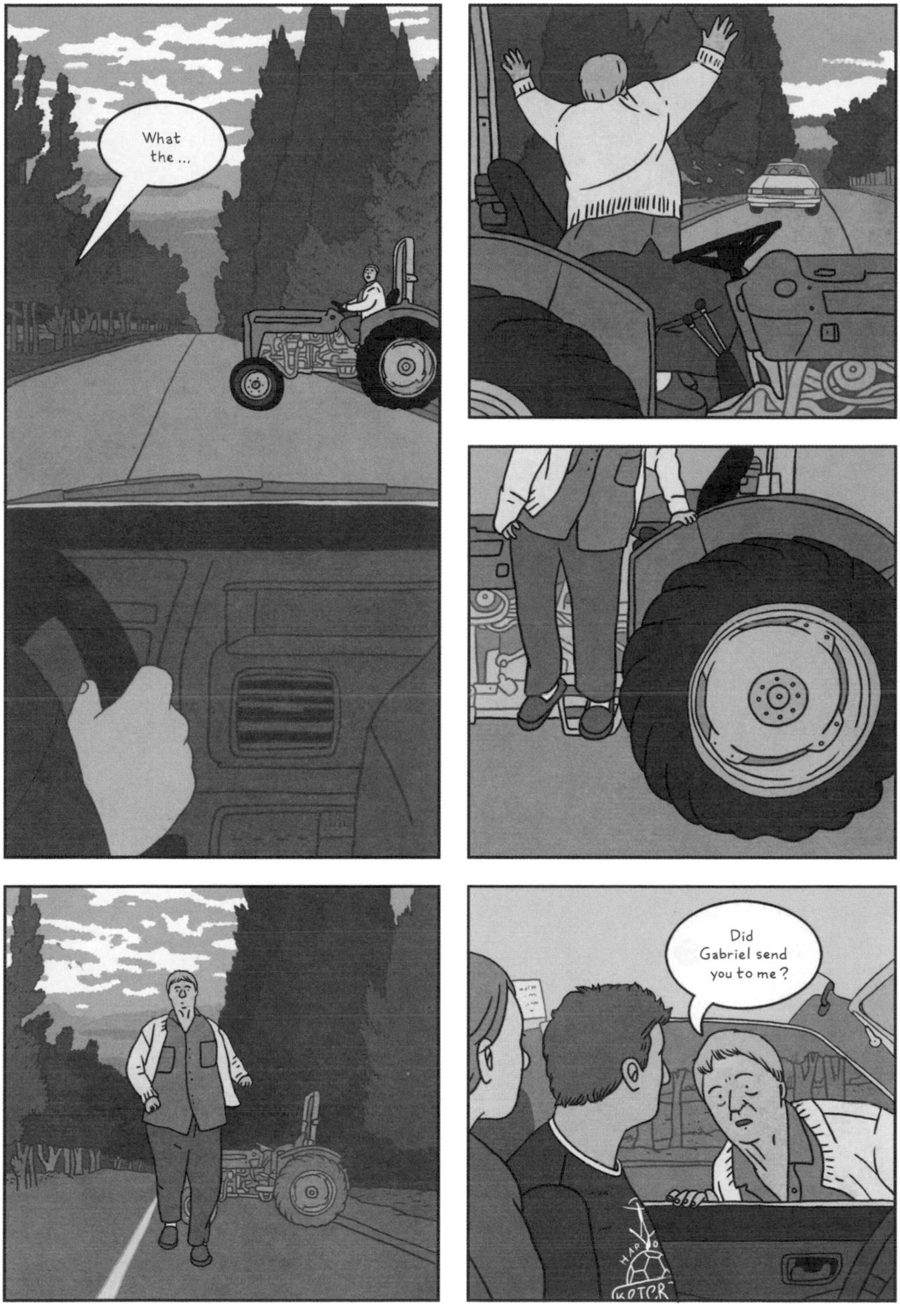
What the ...
Did Gabriel send you to me?

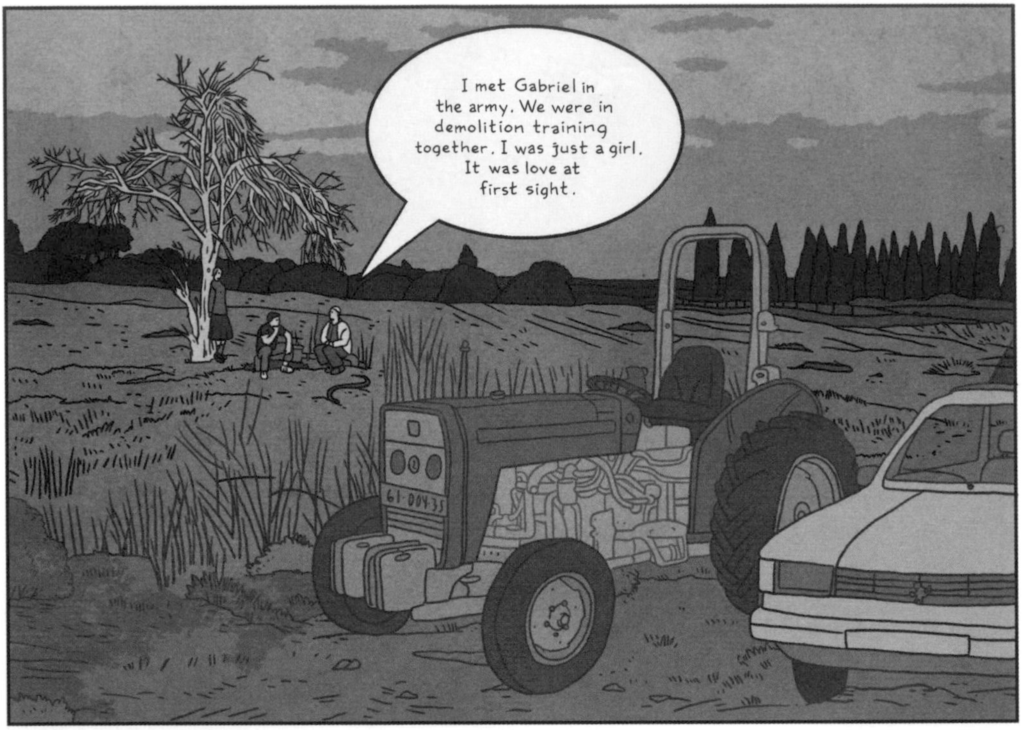
I met Gabriel in the army. We were in demolition training together. I was just a girl. It was love at first sight.
61-004-35

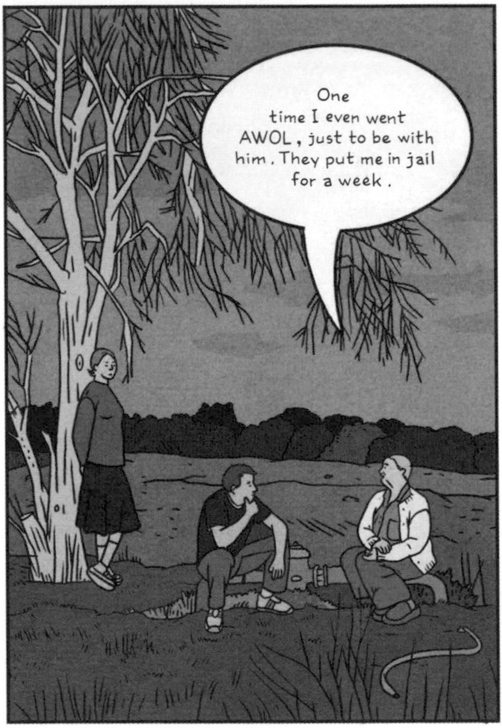
One time I even went AWOL, just to be with him. They put me in jail for a week.

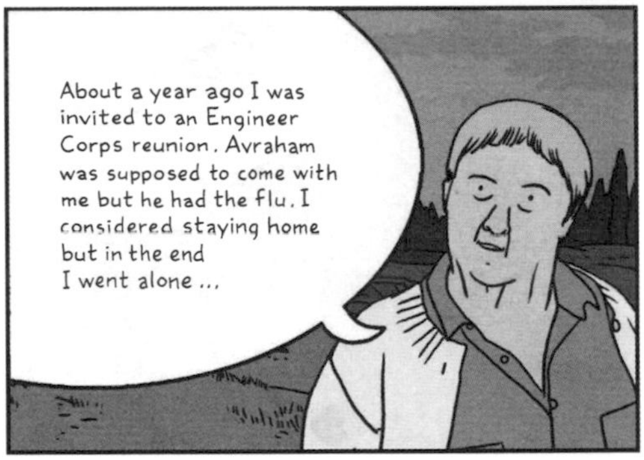
About a year ago I was invited to an Engineer Corps reunion. Avraham was supposed to come with me but he had the flu. I considered staying home but in the end I went alone...

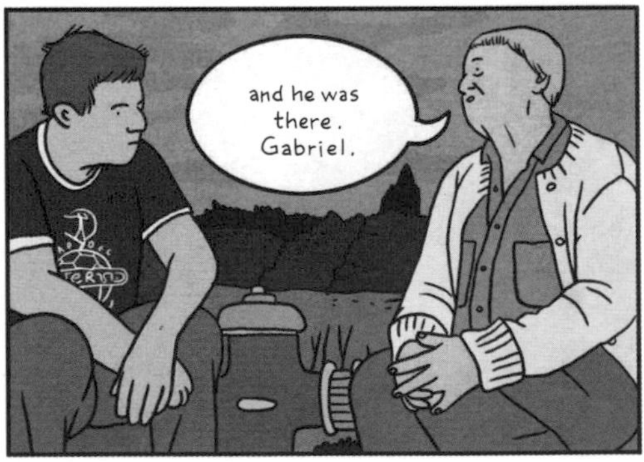
and he was there. Gabriel.

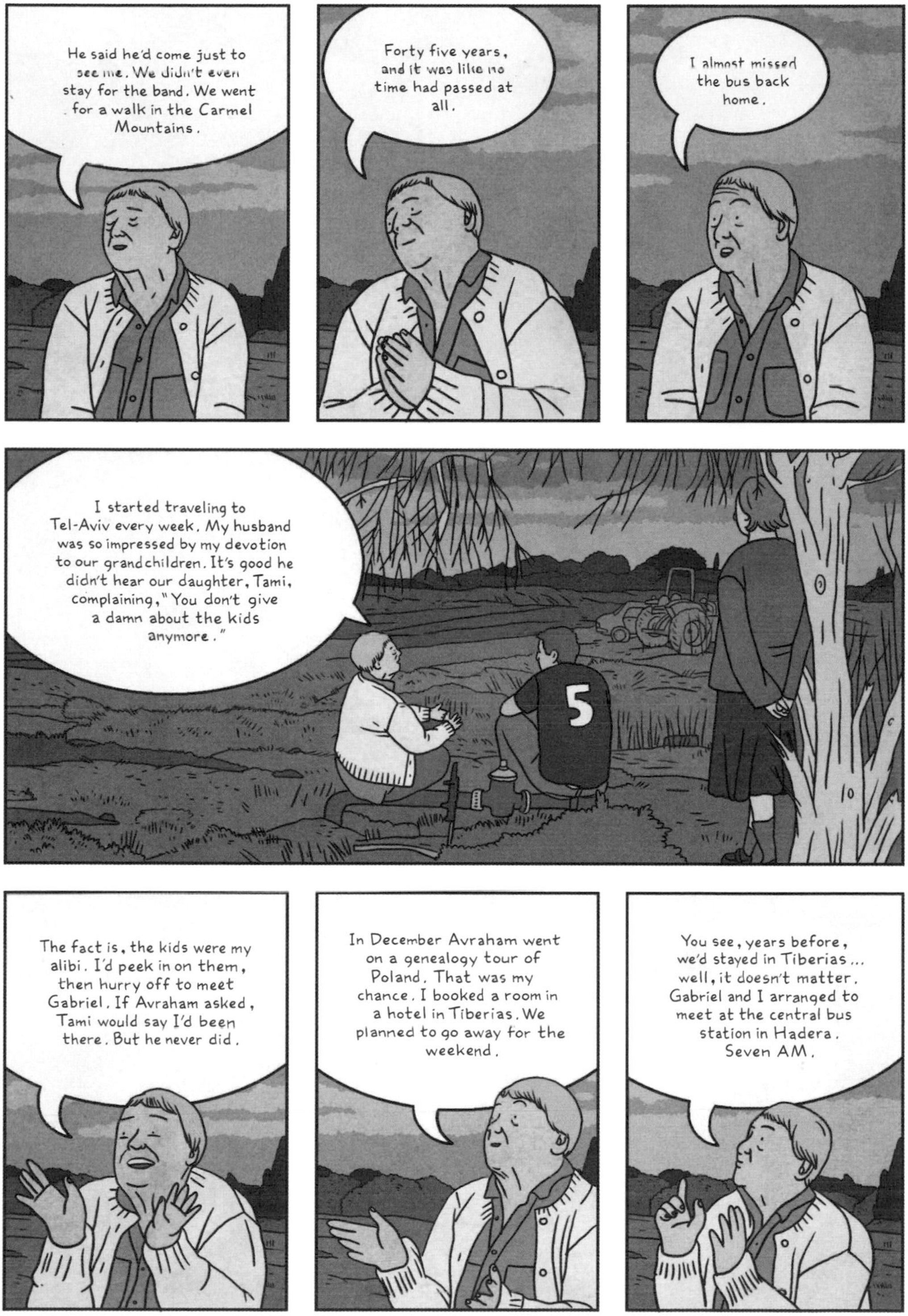
He said he'd come just to see me. We didn't even stay for the band. We went for a walk in the Carmel Mountains.
Forty five years, and it was like no time had passed at all.
I almost missed the bus back home.
I started traveling to Tel-Aviv every week. My husband was so impressed by my devotion to our grandchildren. It's good he didn't hear our daughter, Tami, complaining, "You don't give a damn about the kids anymore."
5
The fact is, the kids were my alibi. I'd peek in on them, then hurry off to meet Gabriel. If Avraham asked, Tami would say I'd been there. But he never did.
In December Avraham went on a genealogy tour of Poland. That was my chance. I booked a room in a hotel in Tiberias. We planned to go away for the weekend.
You see, years before, we'd stayed in Tiberias... well, it doesn't matter. Gabriel and I arranged to meet at the central bus station in Hadera. Seven AM.

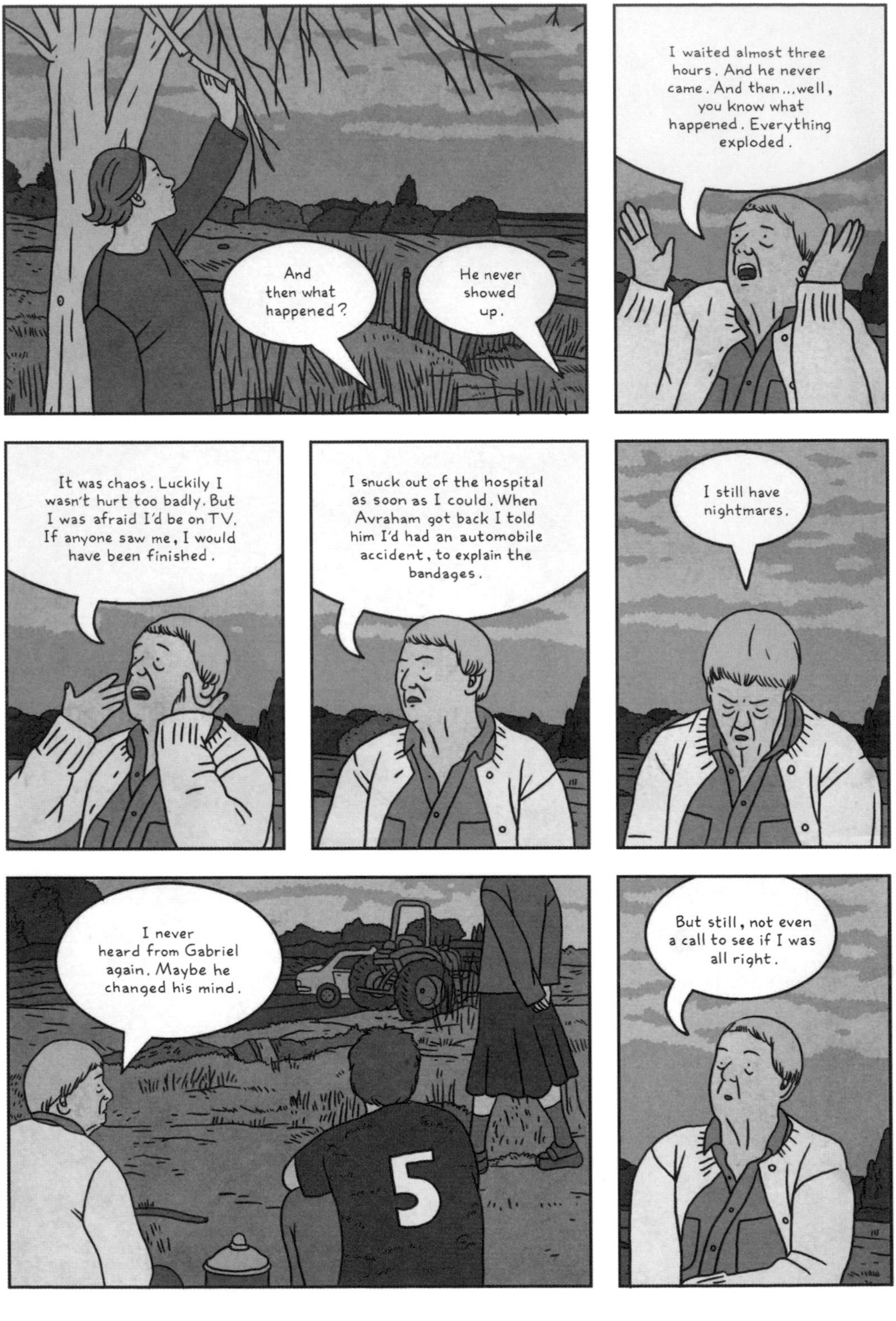
And then what happened?
He never showed up.
I waited almost three hours. And he never came. And then...well, you know what happened. Everything exploded.
It was chaos. Luckily I wasn't hurt too badly. But I was afraid I'd be on TV. If anyone saw me, I would have been finished.
I snuck out of the hospital as soon as I could. When Avraham got back I told him I'd had an automobile accident, to explain the bandages.
I still have nightmares.
I never heard from Gabriel again. Maybe he changed his mind.
5
But still, not even a call to see if I was all right.

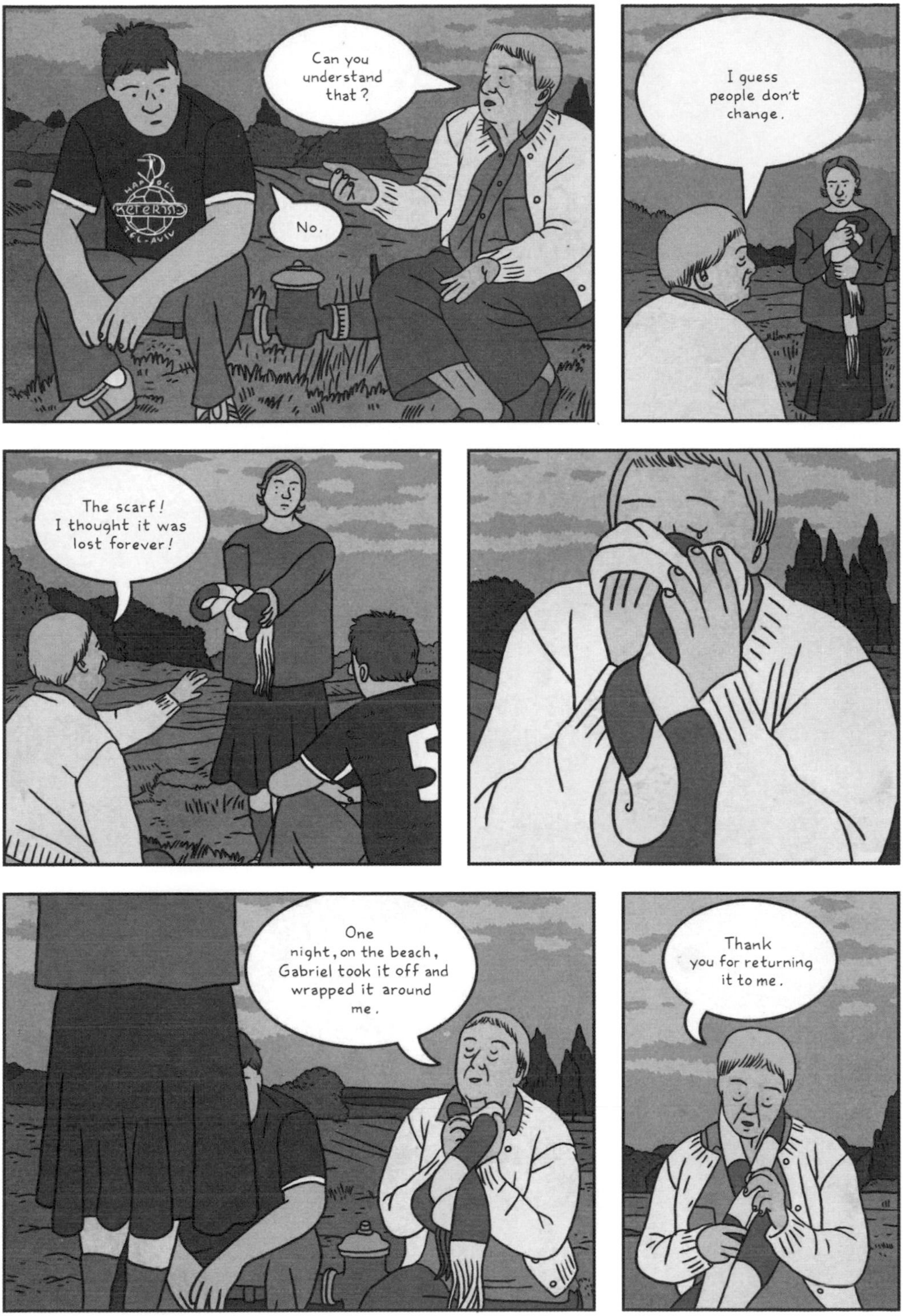
Can you understand that?
No.
I guess people don't change.
The scarf! I thought it was lost forever!
One night, on the beach, Gabriel took it off and wrapped it around me.
Thank you for returning it to me.

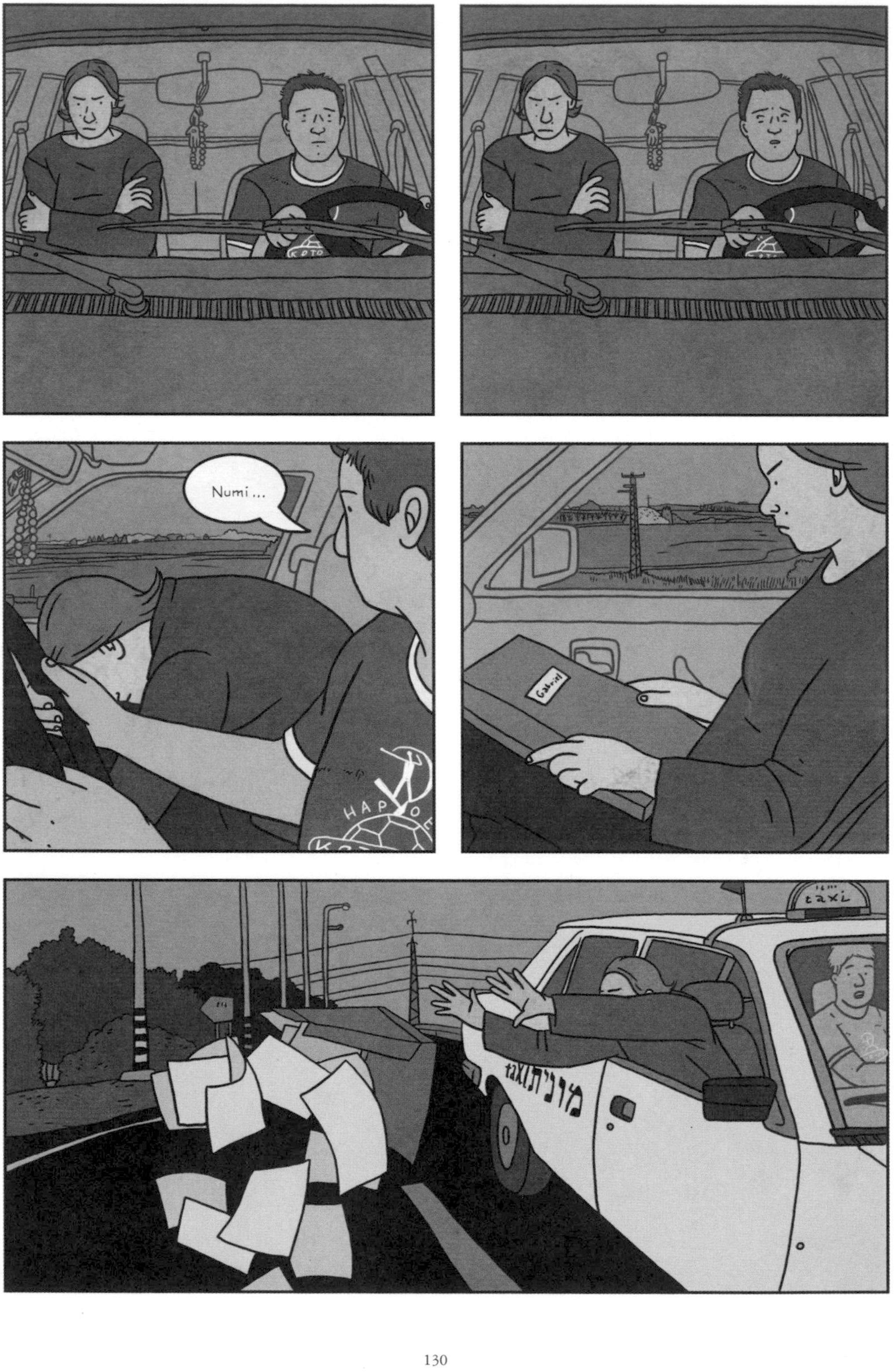
Numi ...
Gabriel
taxi

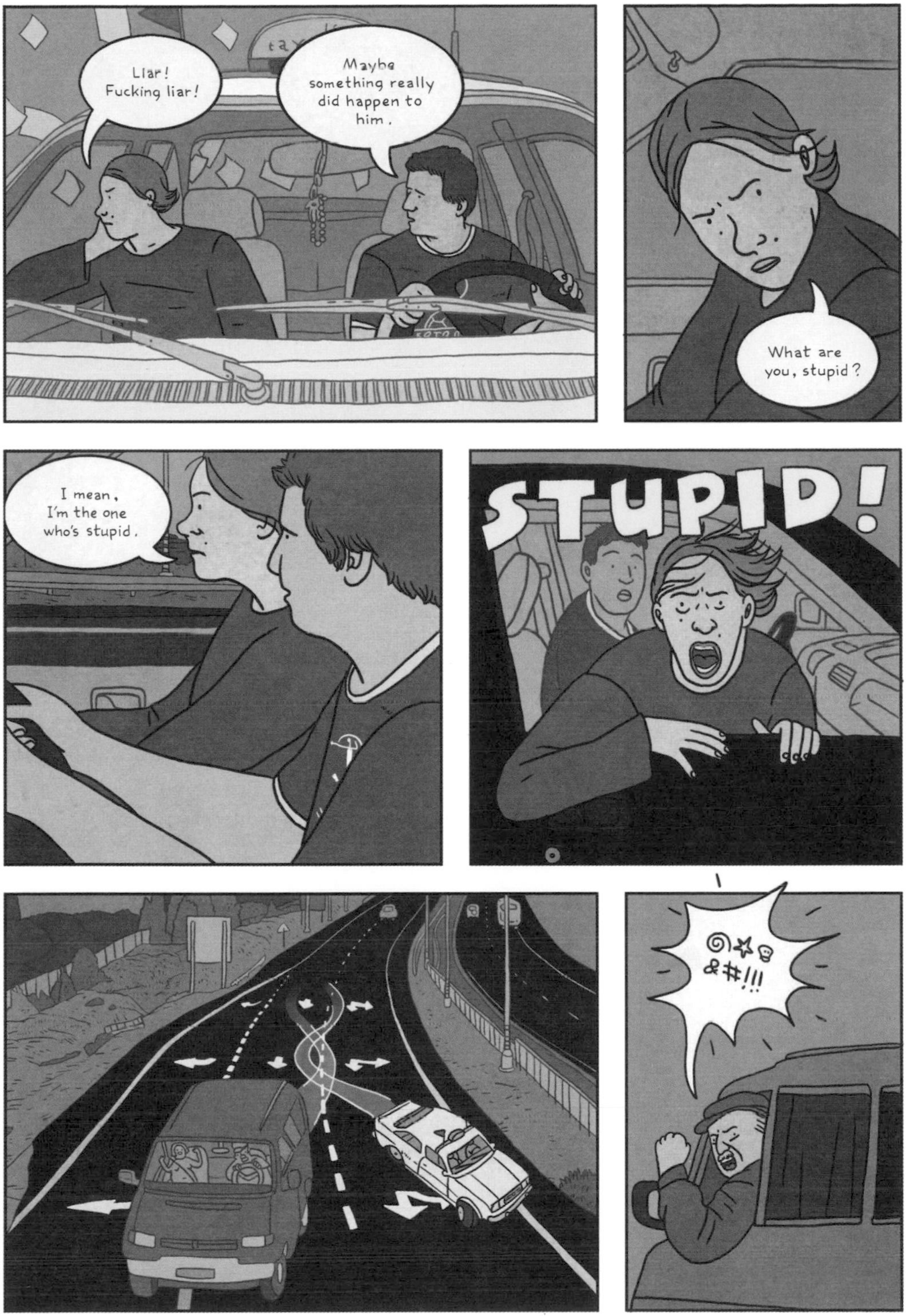
Liar! Fucking liar!
Maybe something really did happen to him.
What are you, stupid?
I mean, I'm the one who's stupid.
STUPID!
&#!!!

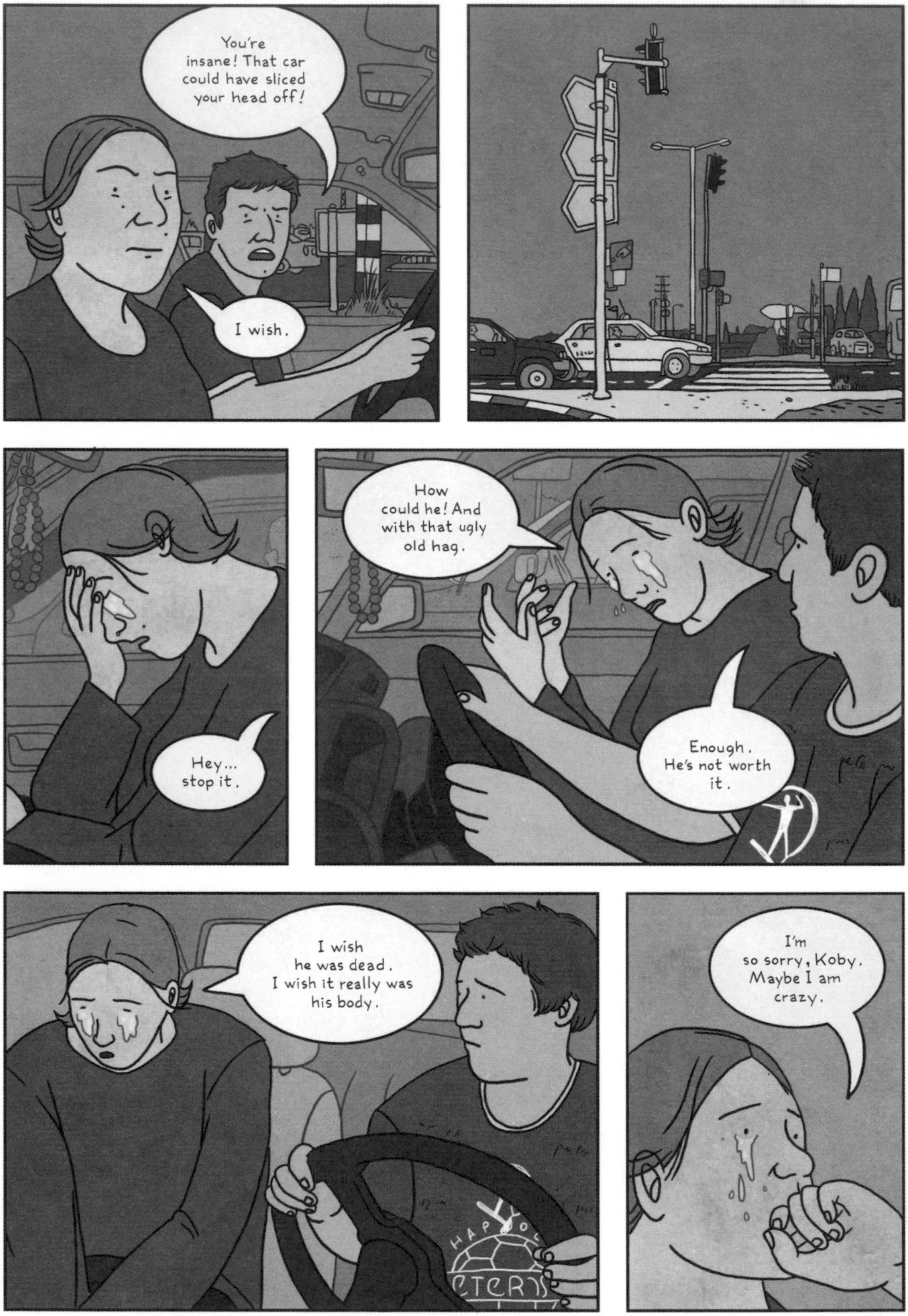
You're insane! That car could have sliced your head off!
I wish.
Hey... stop it.
How could he! And with that ugly old hag.
Enough. He's not worth it.
I wish he was dead. I wish it really was his body.
I'm so sorry, Koby. Maybe I am crazy.

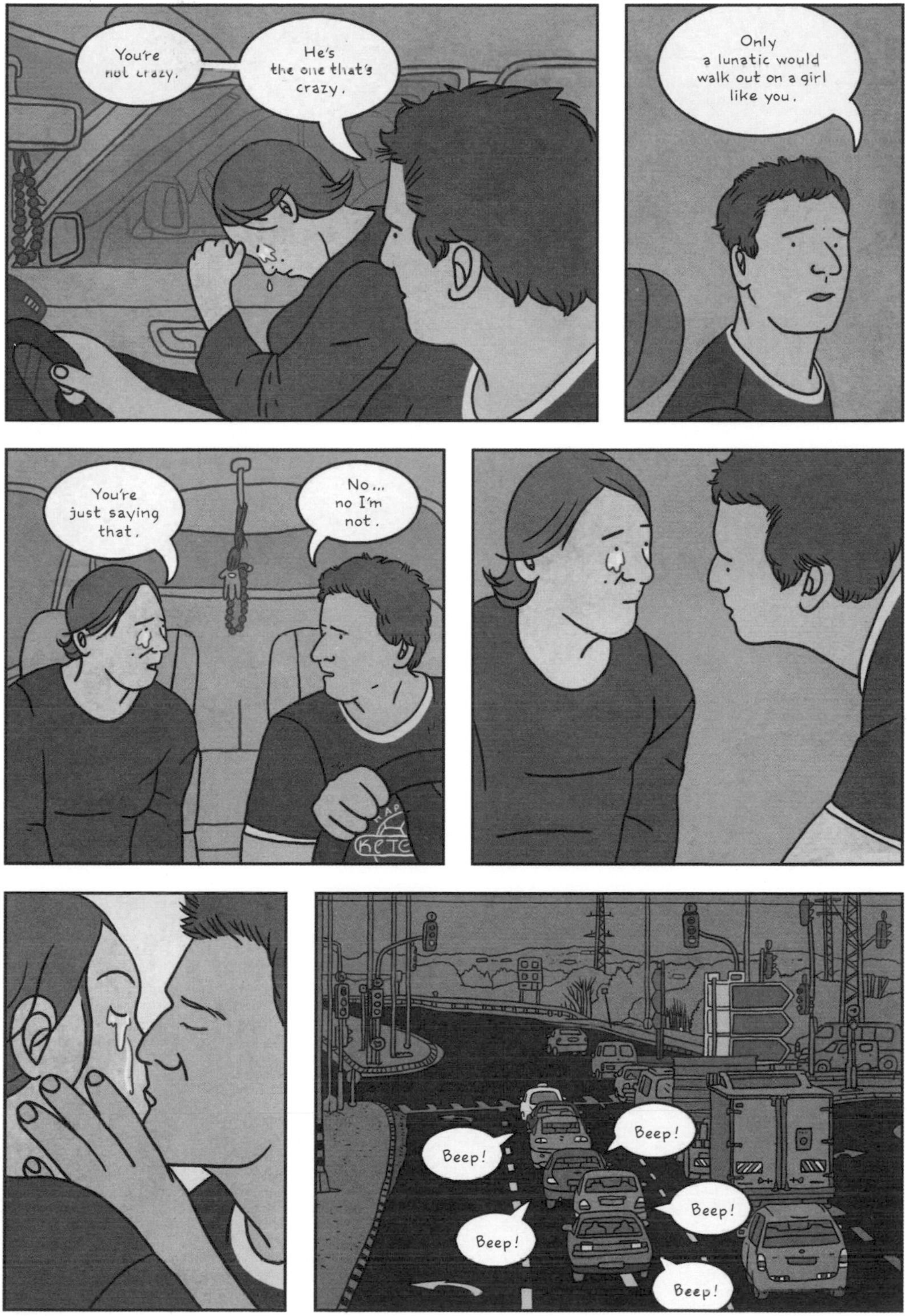
You're not crazy.
He's the one that's crazy.
Only a lunatic would walk out on a girl like you.
You're just saying that.
No... no I'm not.
Beep!
Beep!
Beep!
Beep!
Beep!

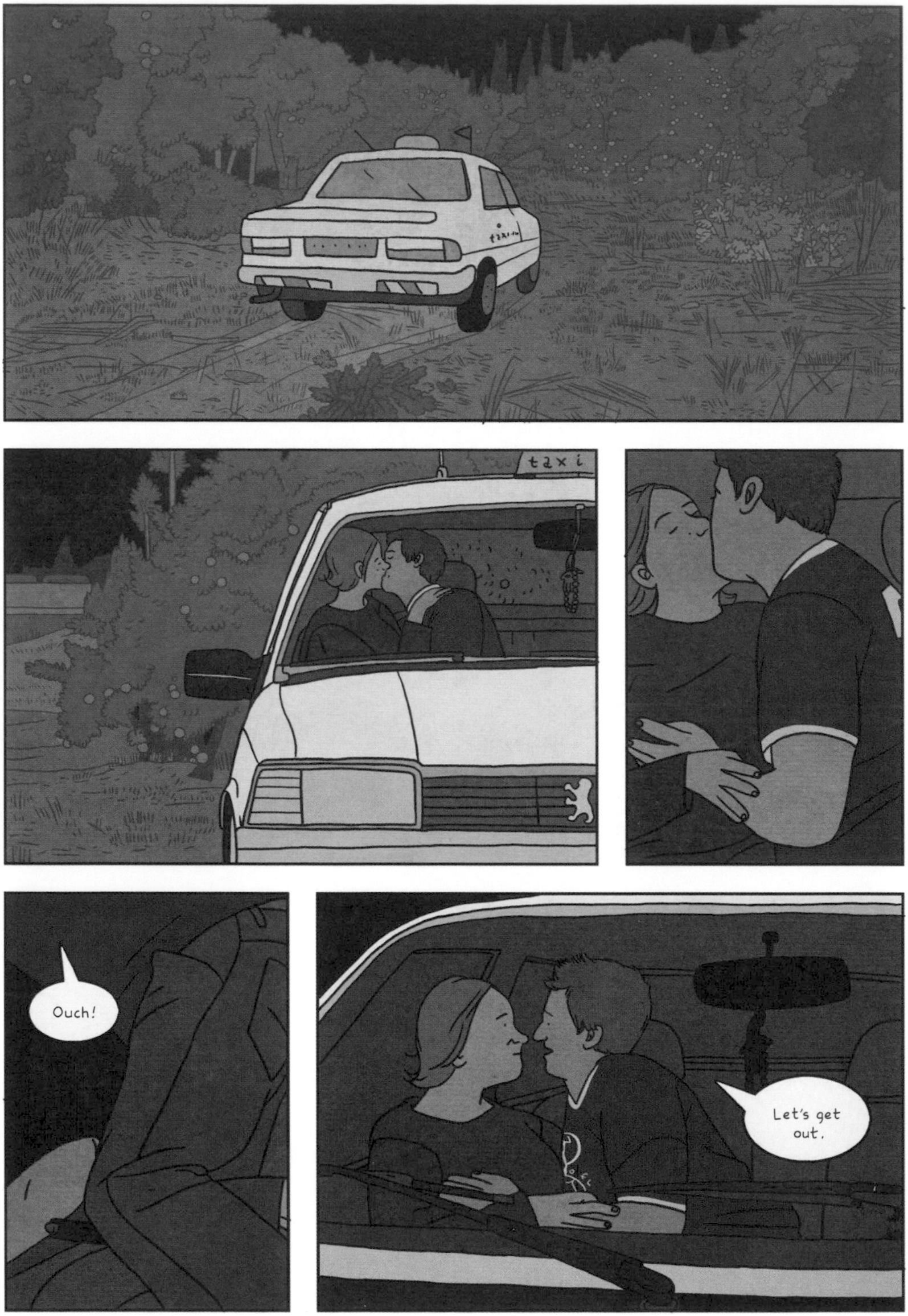
taxi
Ouch!
Let's get out.

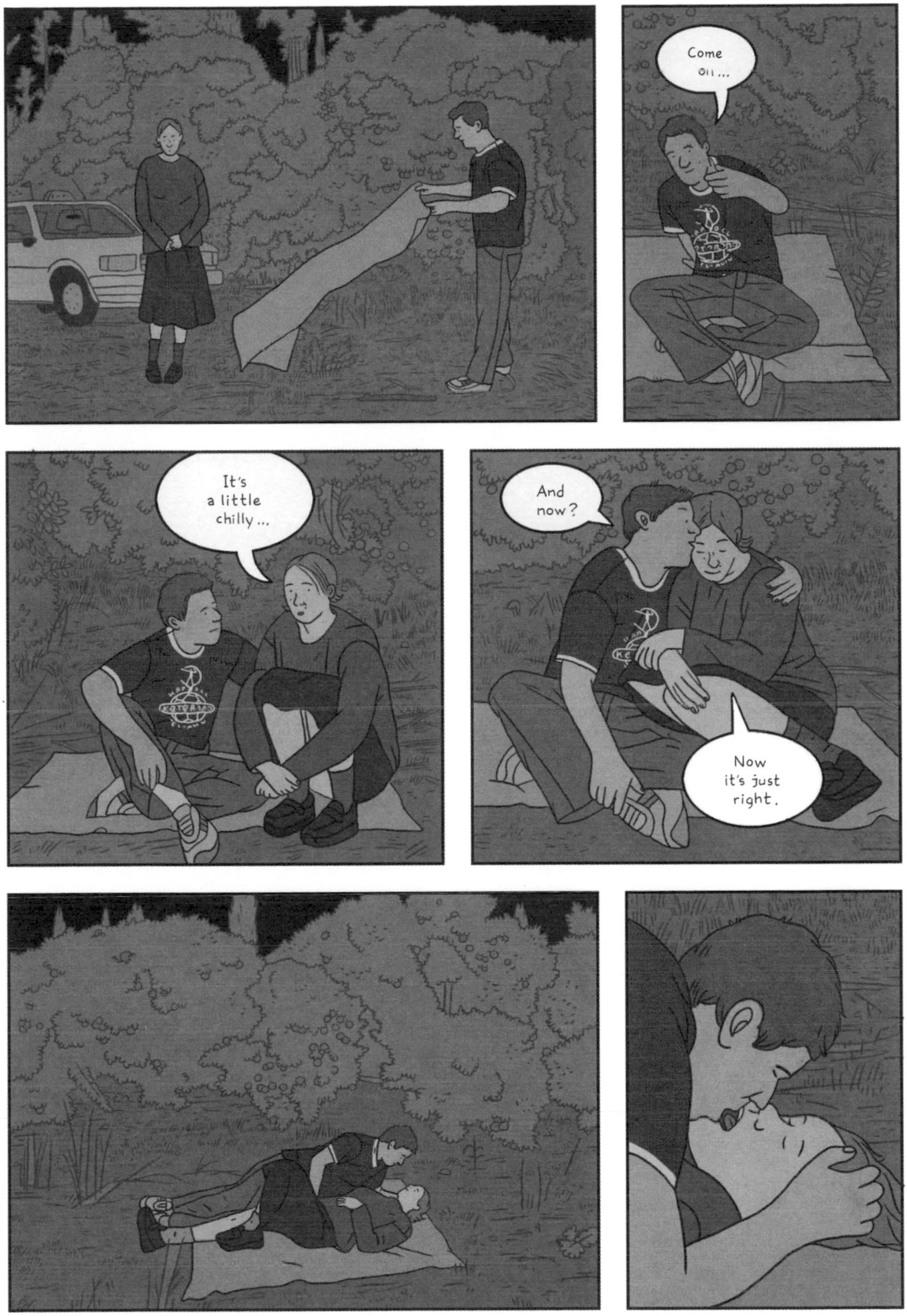
Come on...
It's a little chilly...
And now?
Now it's just right.

It's like being fifteen again... doing it with your clothes on.

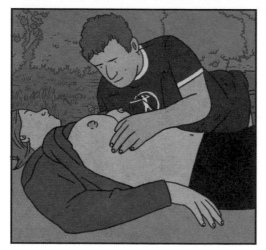

Stop... don't look.

You're salty.

Does it bother you?

No, actually it's nice.

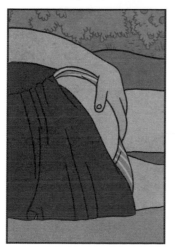

Let me... I'll do it.

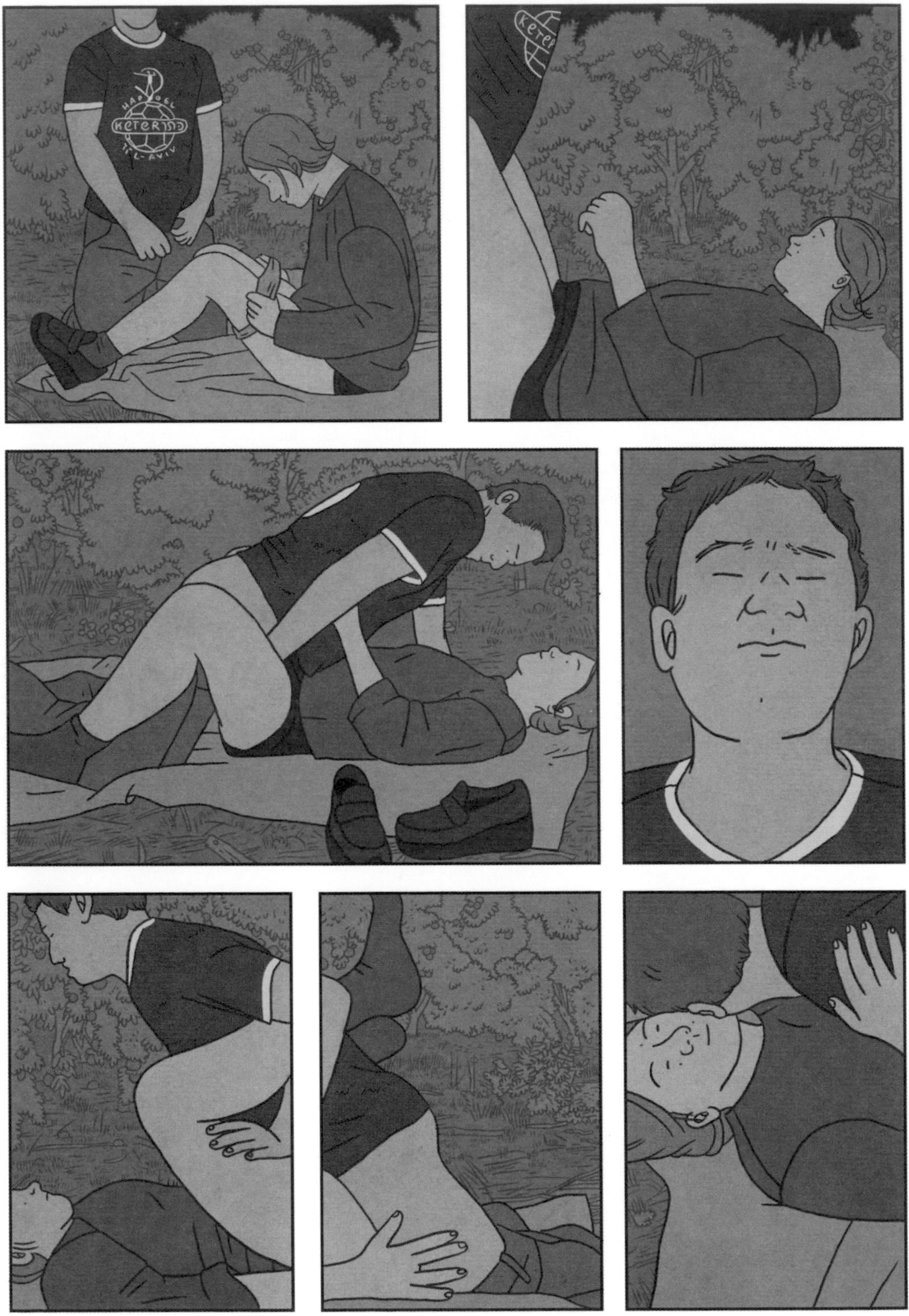

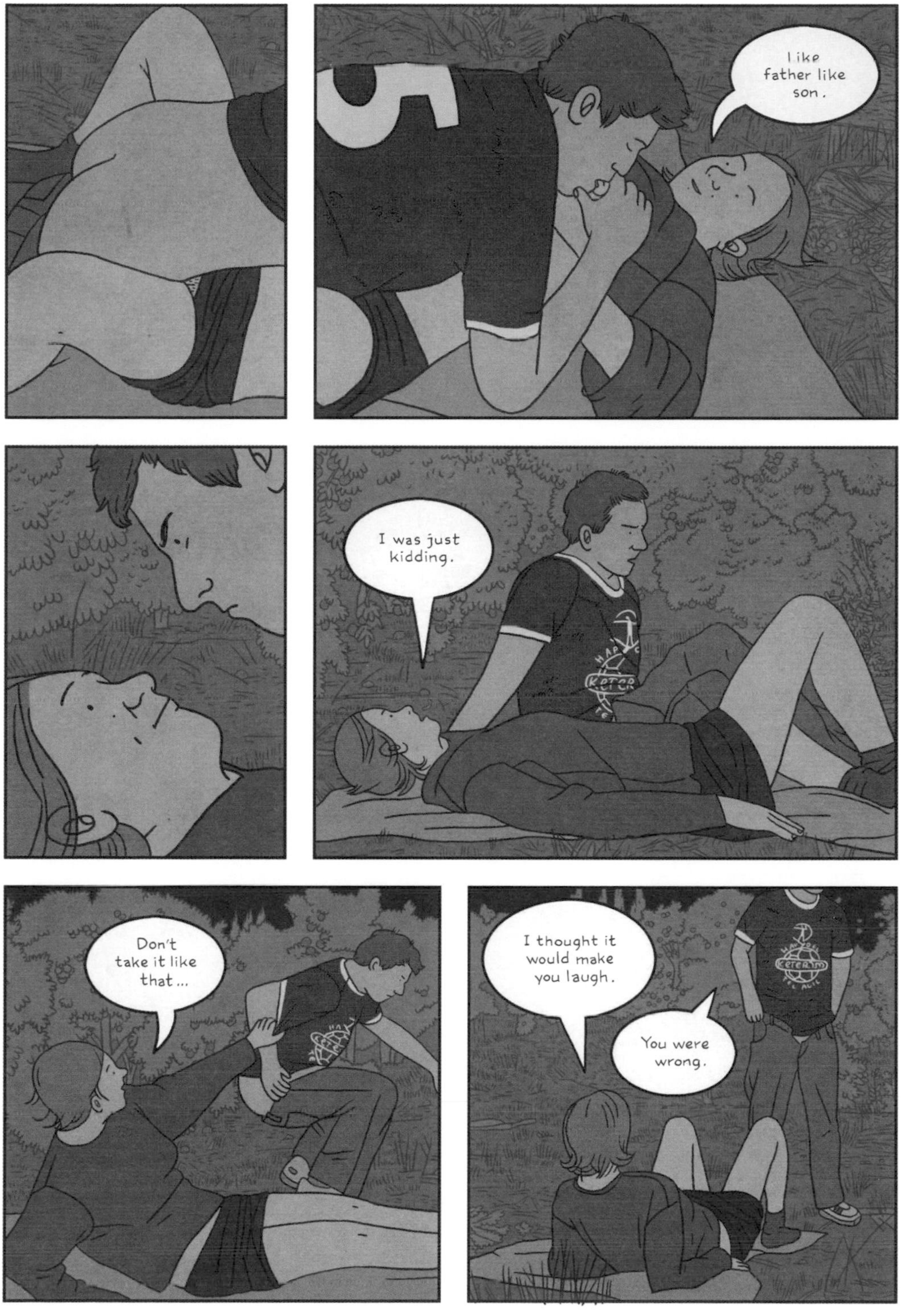
Like father like son.
I was just kidding.
Don't take it like that...
I thought it would make you laugh.
You were wrong.

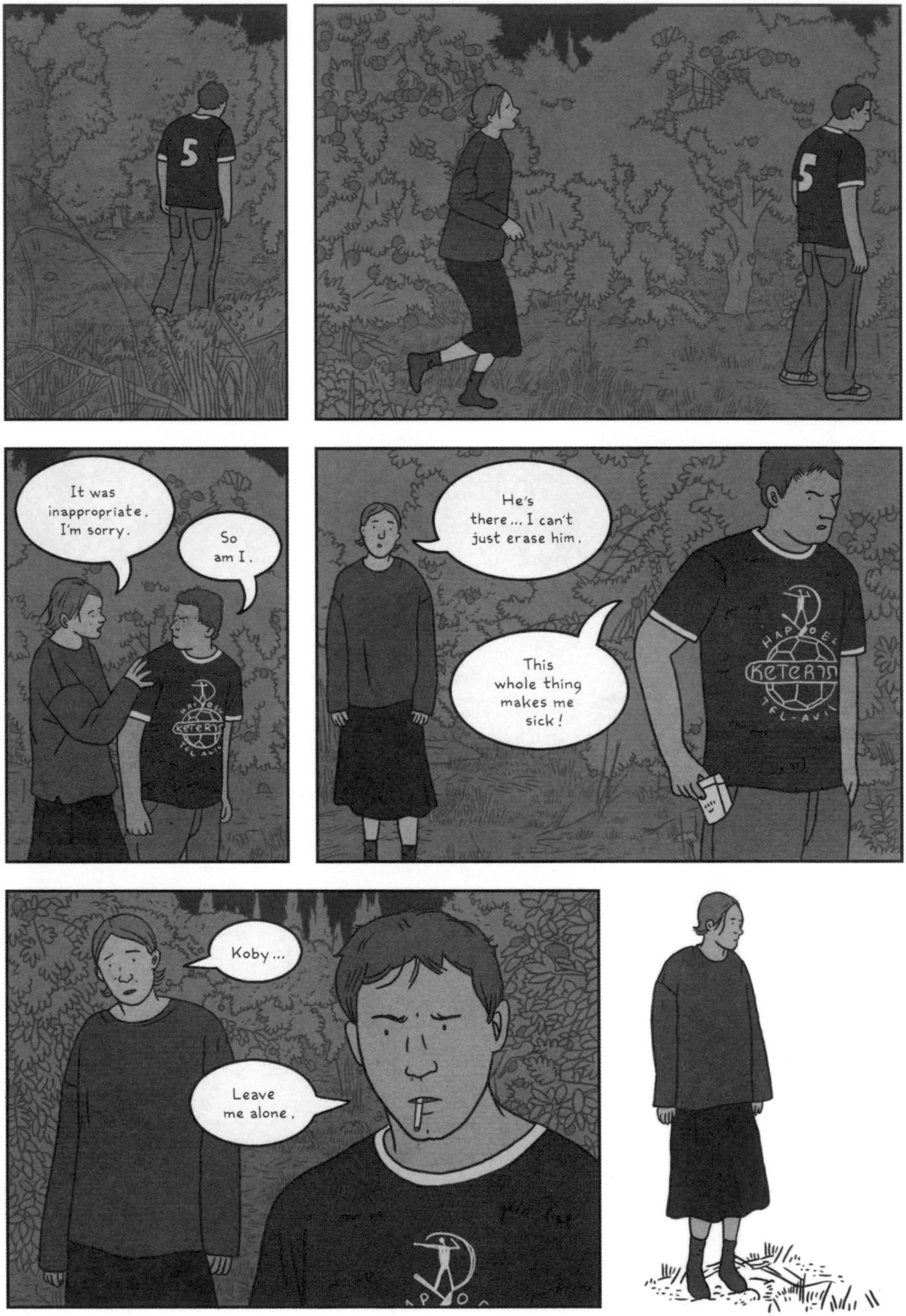
It was inappropriate. I'm sorry.
So am I.
He's there... I can't just erase him.
This whole thing makes me sick!
Koby...
Leave me alone.

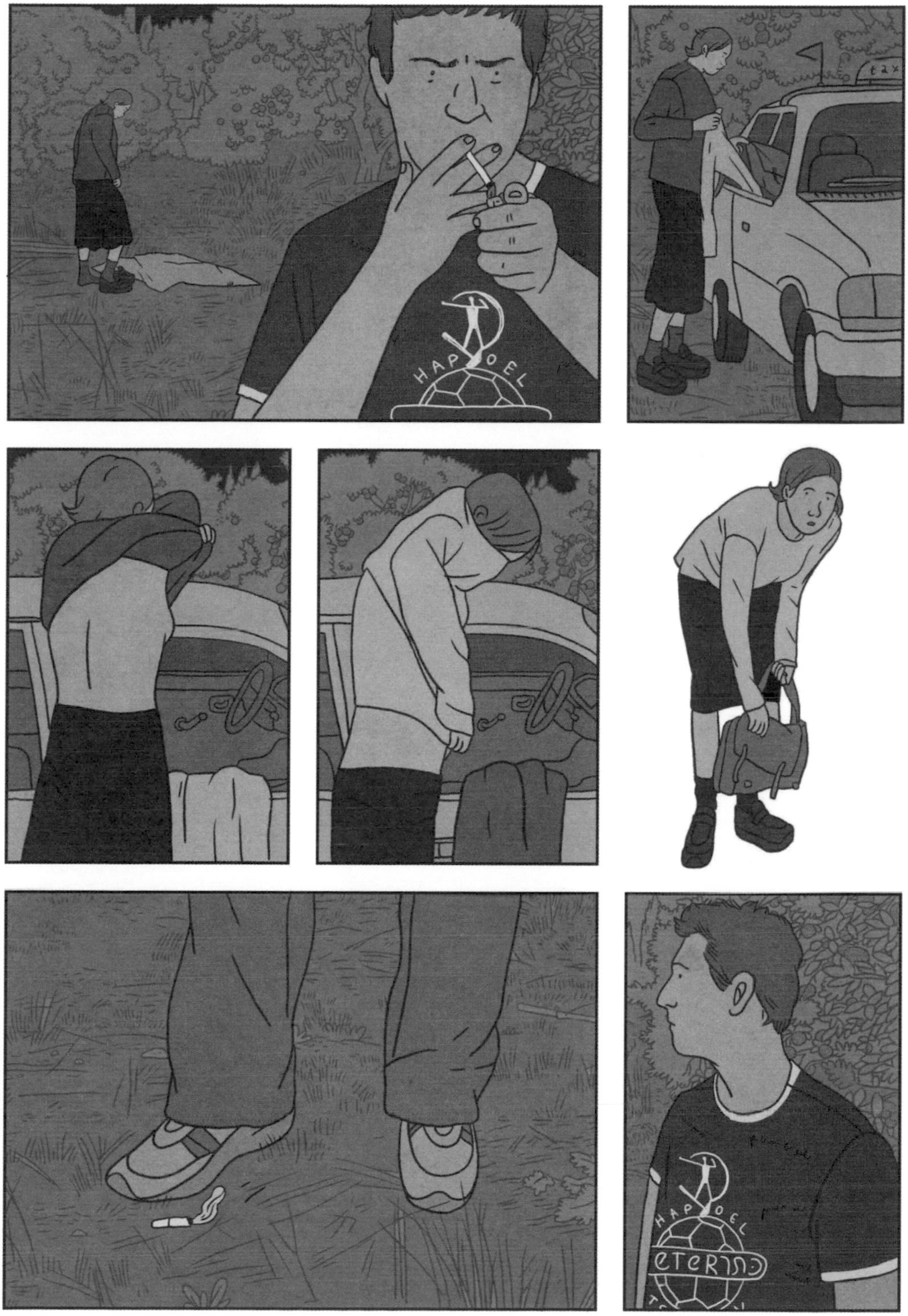
HAPOEL
taxi
HAPOEL
eternal

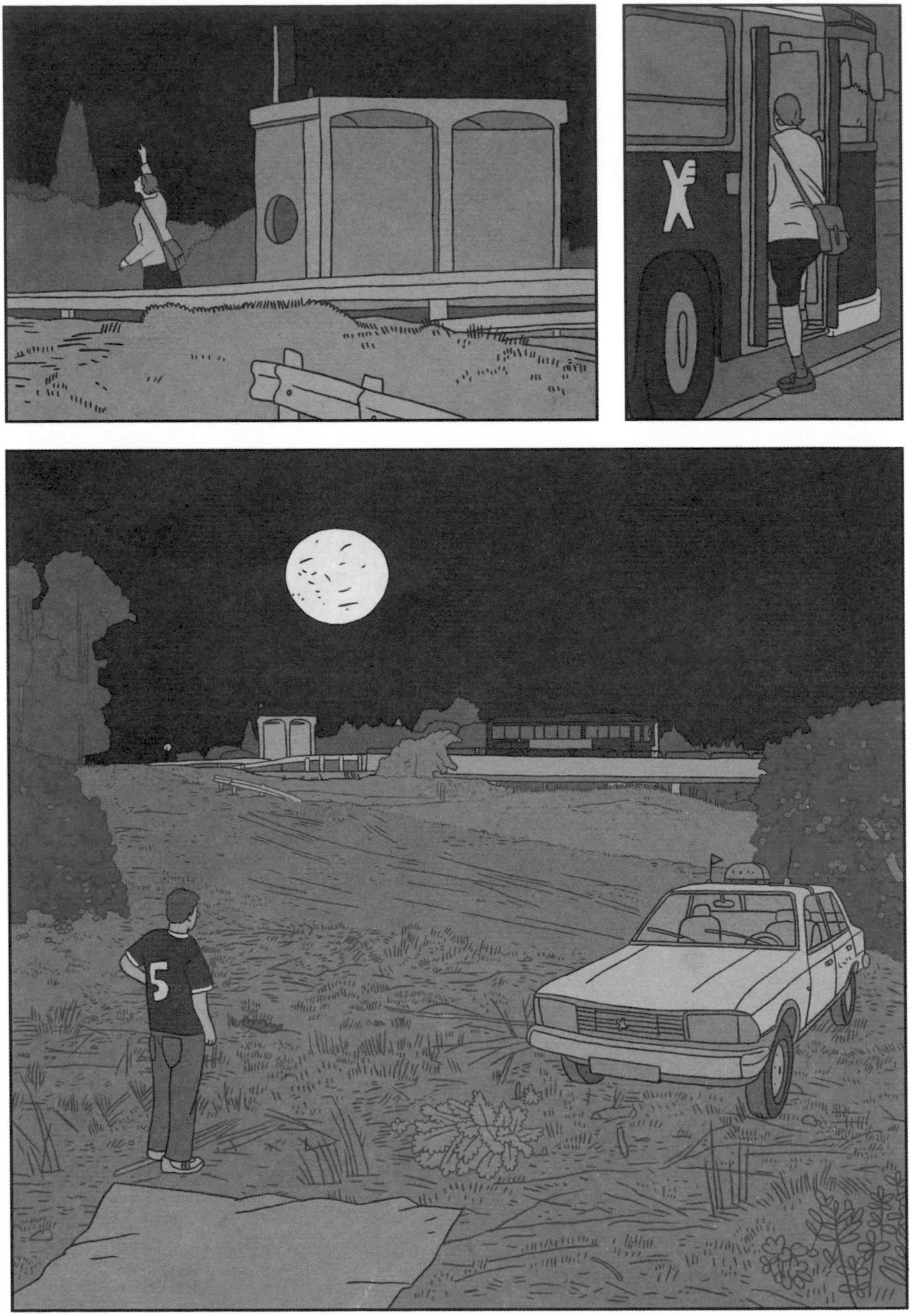

chapter four
resurrection

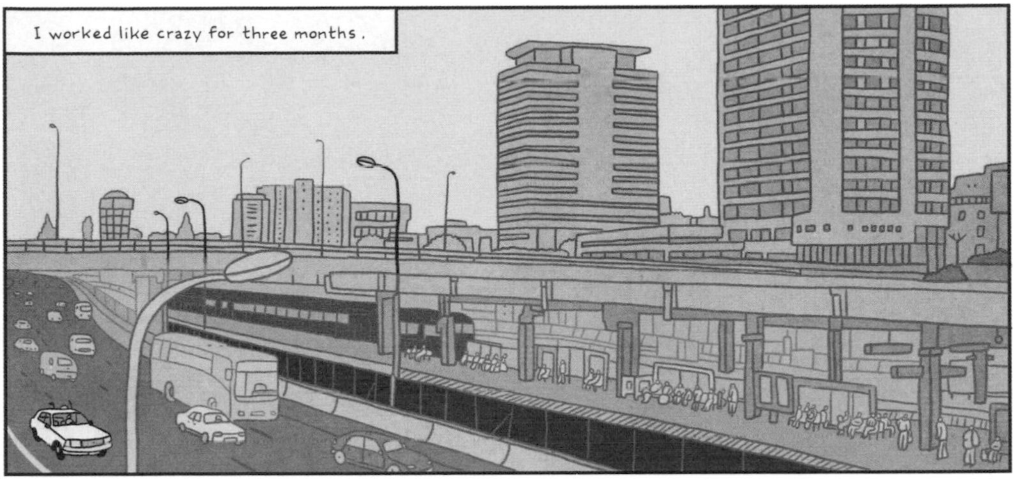
I worked like crazy for three months.

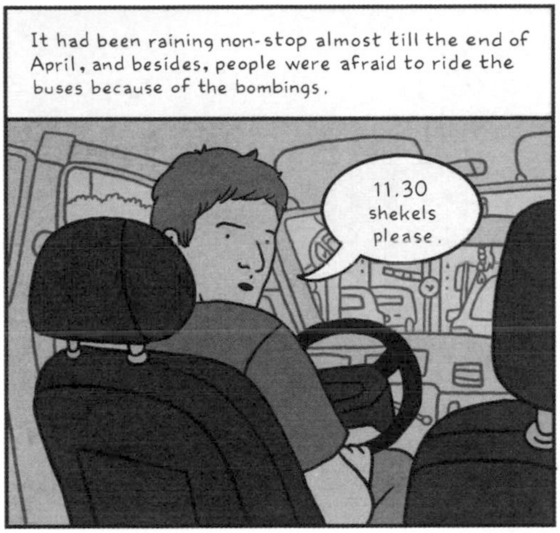
It had been raining non-stop almost till the end of April, and besides, people were afraid to ride the buses because of the bombings.
11.30 shekels please.

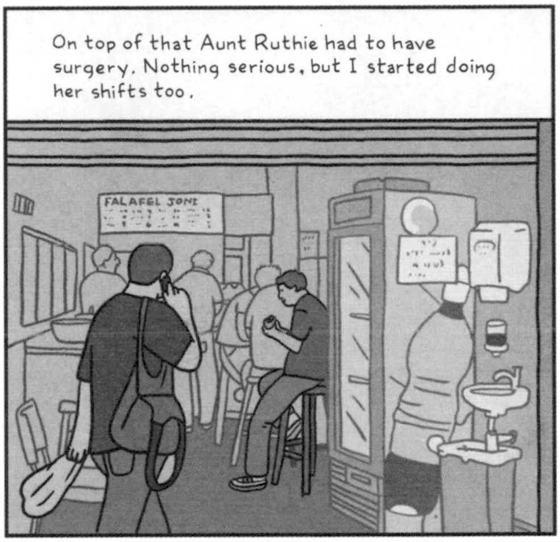
On top of that Aunt Ruthie had to have surgery. Nothing serious, but I started doing her shifts too.
FALAFEL JONI

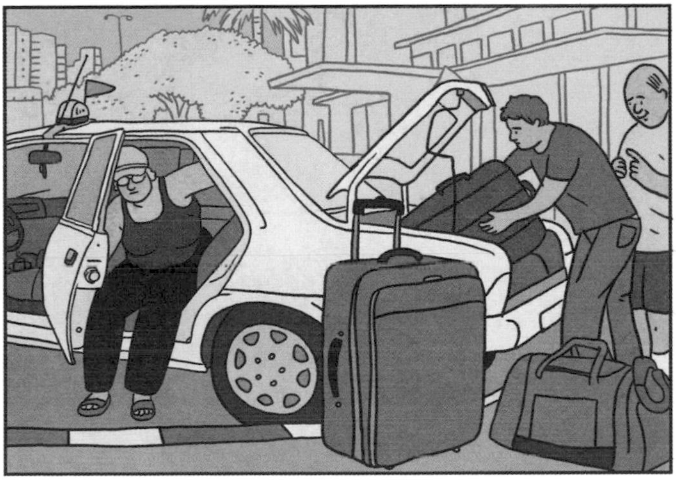

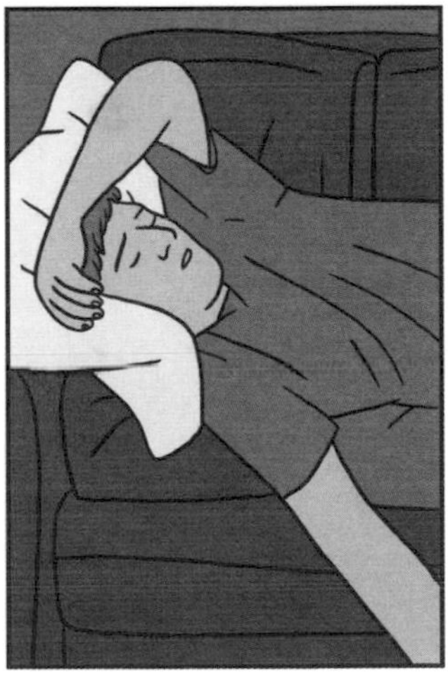

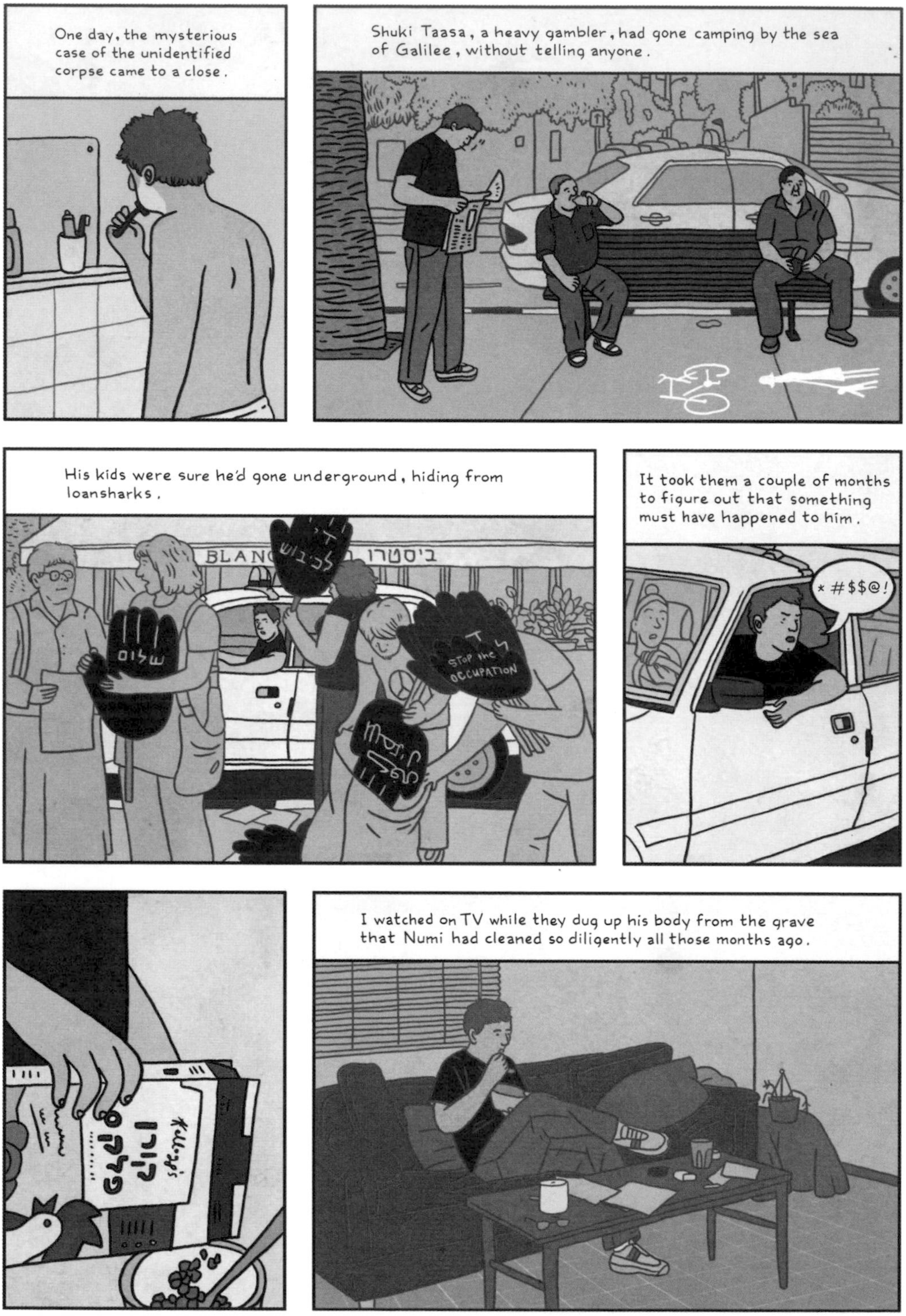

One day, the mysterious case of the unidentified corpse came to a close.
Shuki Taasa, a heavy gambler, had gone camping by the sea of Galilee, without telling anyone.
His kids were sure he'd gone underground, hiding from loansharks.
BLANC
ביסטרו
שלום
STOP the OCCUPATION
It took them a couple of months to figure out that something must have happened to him.
* #$$@!
Kellogg's
I watched on TV while they dug up his body from the grave that Numi had cleaned so diligently all those months ago.

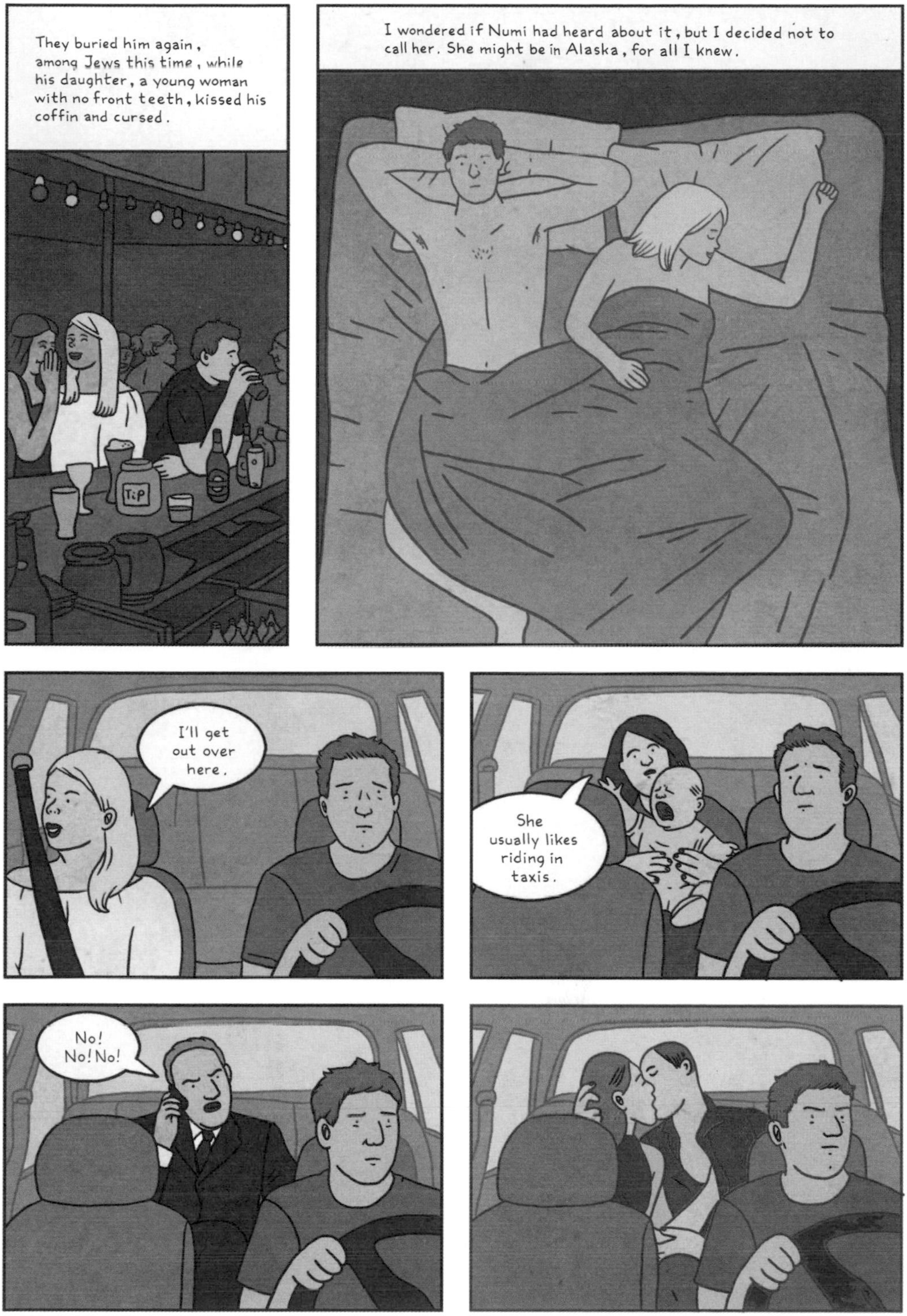
They buried him again, among Jews this time, while his daughter, a young woman with no front teeth, kissed his coffin and cursed.
TIP
I wondered if Numi had heard about it, but I decided not to call her. She might be in Alaska, for all I knew.
I'll get out over here.
She usually likes riding in taxis.
No! No! No!

I developed a theory, as yet unfounded, that my father had been having an affair with Aunt Ruthie.

Despite her eternal animosity towards him—or maybe because of it ... it explains too many things.

I don't have any proof, but that time, long ago, when he kicked me out of his house, he had been so uptight. And Aunt Ruthie had been there, after all.

The way I see it now, if I'd showed up just fifteen minutes earlier I might have caught them in the act.

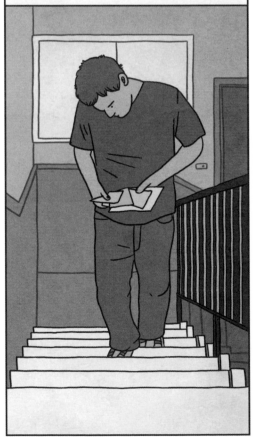

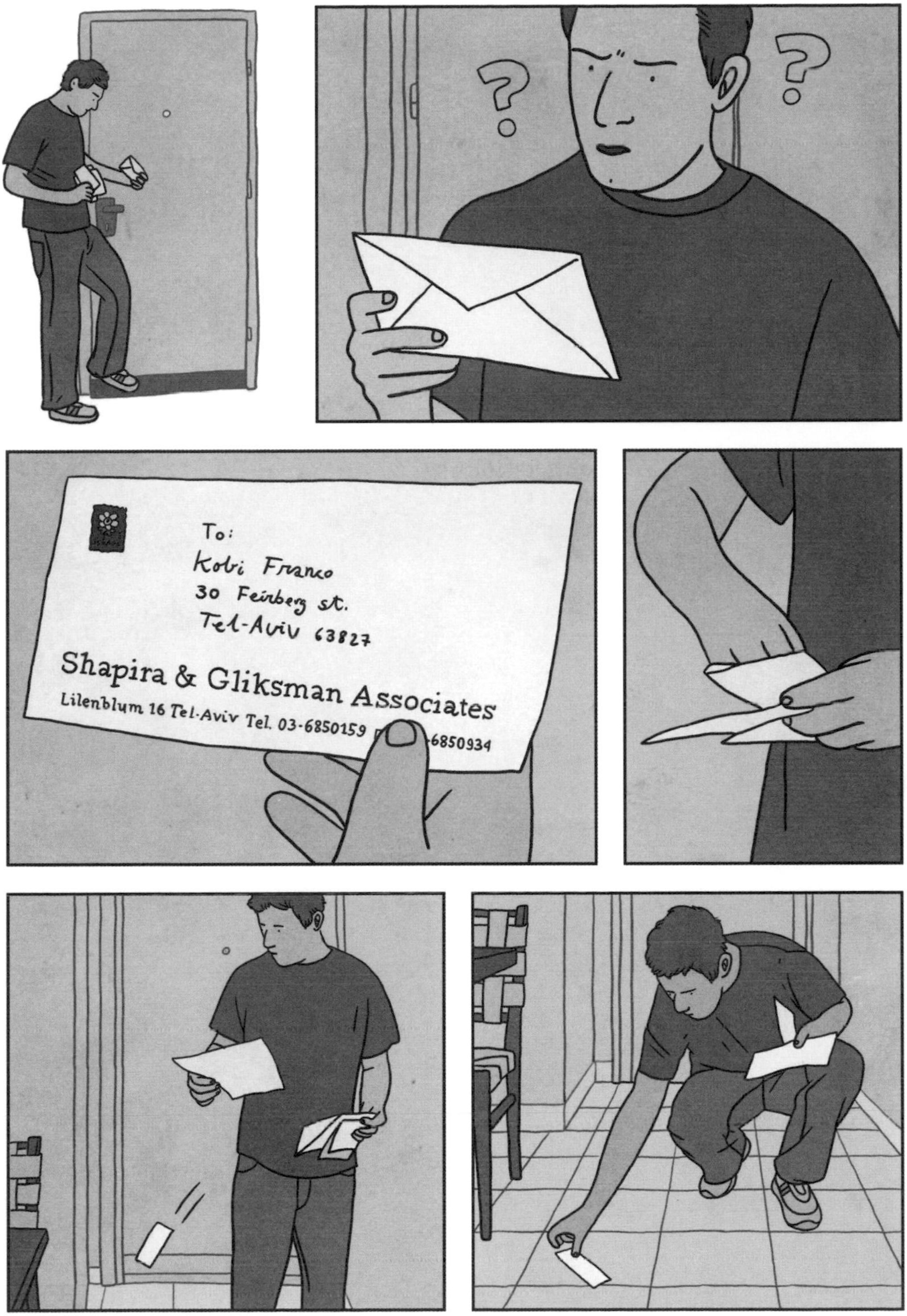
To:
Kobi Franco
30 Feirberg st.
Tel-Aviv 63827
Shapira & Gliksman Associates
Lilenblum 16 Tel-Aviv Tel. 03-6850159

בנק לאומי
bank leumi
FRANCO GABRIEL
ID 059372
ACCOUNT No 506138/79
BRANCH 811
PAY Kobi Franco
176,000xx
One hundred Seventy six thousand shekels
N.I.S
5/6/2002
DATE
G. Franco
SIGNATURE
"1150618879 =10/21131= 454
What the fuck!

Dammit Orly, pick up the phone.
Kobi Franco
10/6/2002
Dear Sir,
On Behalf of my client, Mr. Gabriel Franco, please find enclosed herein your share of the sale of the property on 18 Bialik St, Tel-Aviv.
Sincerely,
Moses Shapira, esq.
Shapira & Gliksman Associates Ltd.
Lilenblum 16 Tel-Aviv Tel. 03-6850159 Fax. 03-6850934

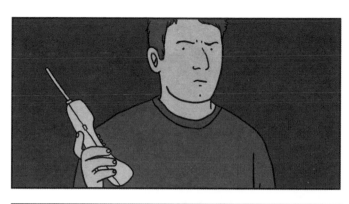

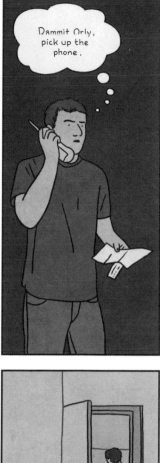

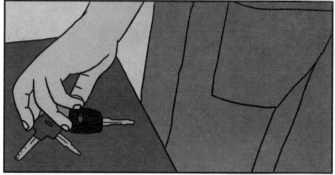

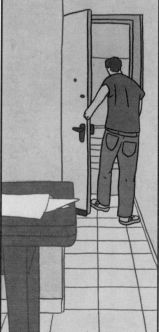

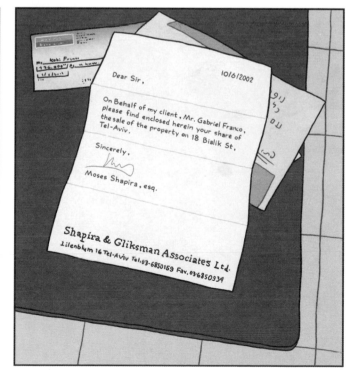

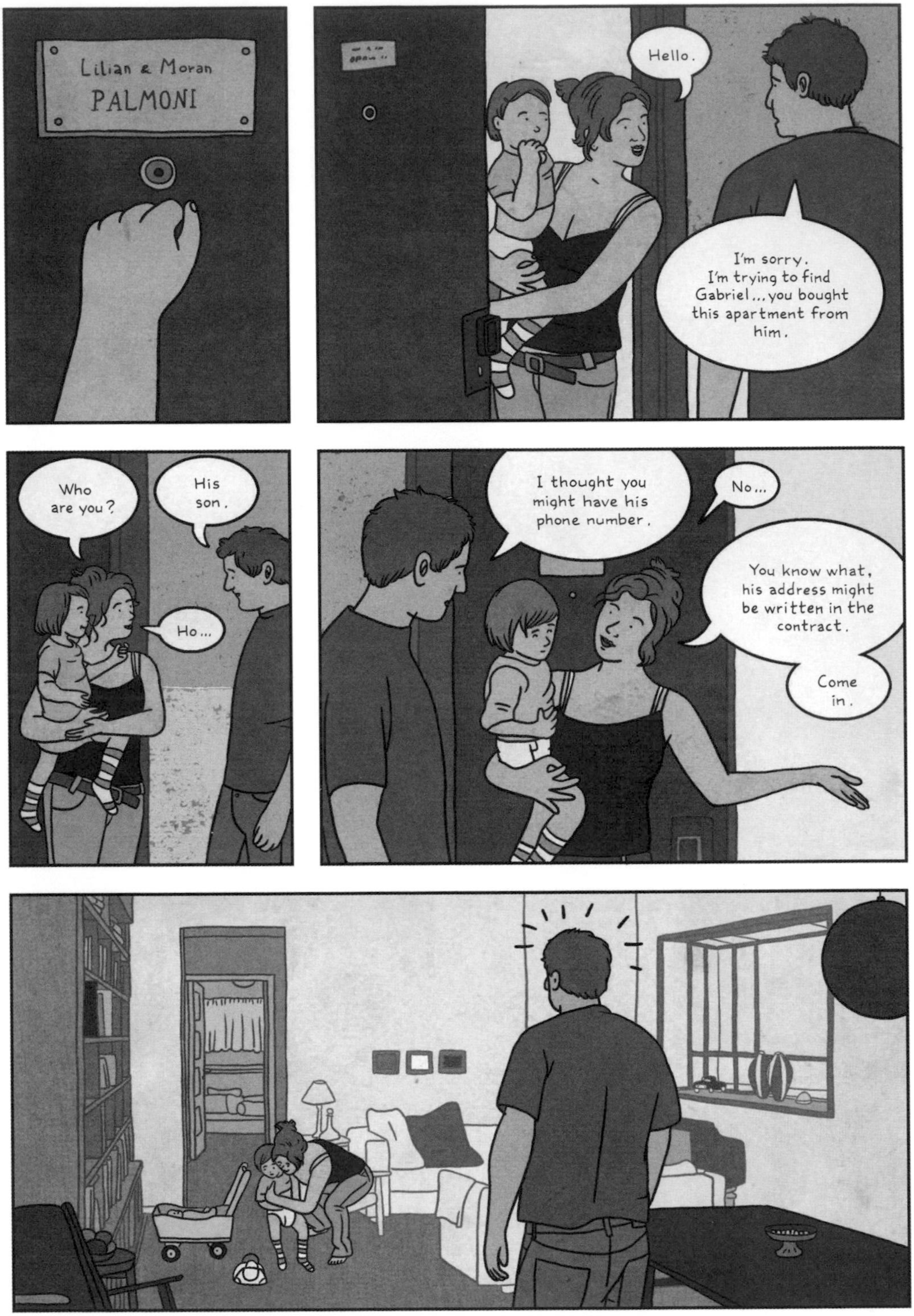
Lilian & Moran
PALMONI
Hello.
I'm sorry. I'm trying to find Gabriel... you bought this apartment from him.
Who are you?
His son.
Ho...
I thought you might have his phone number.
No...
You know what, his address might be written in the contract.
Come in.

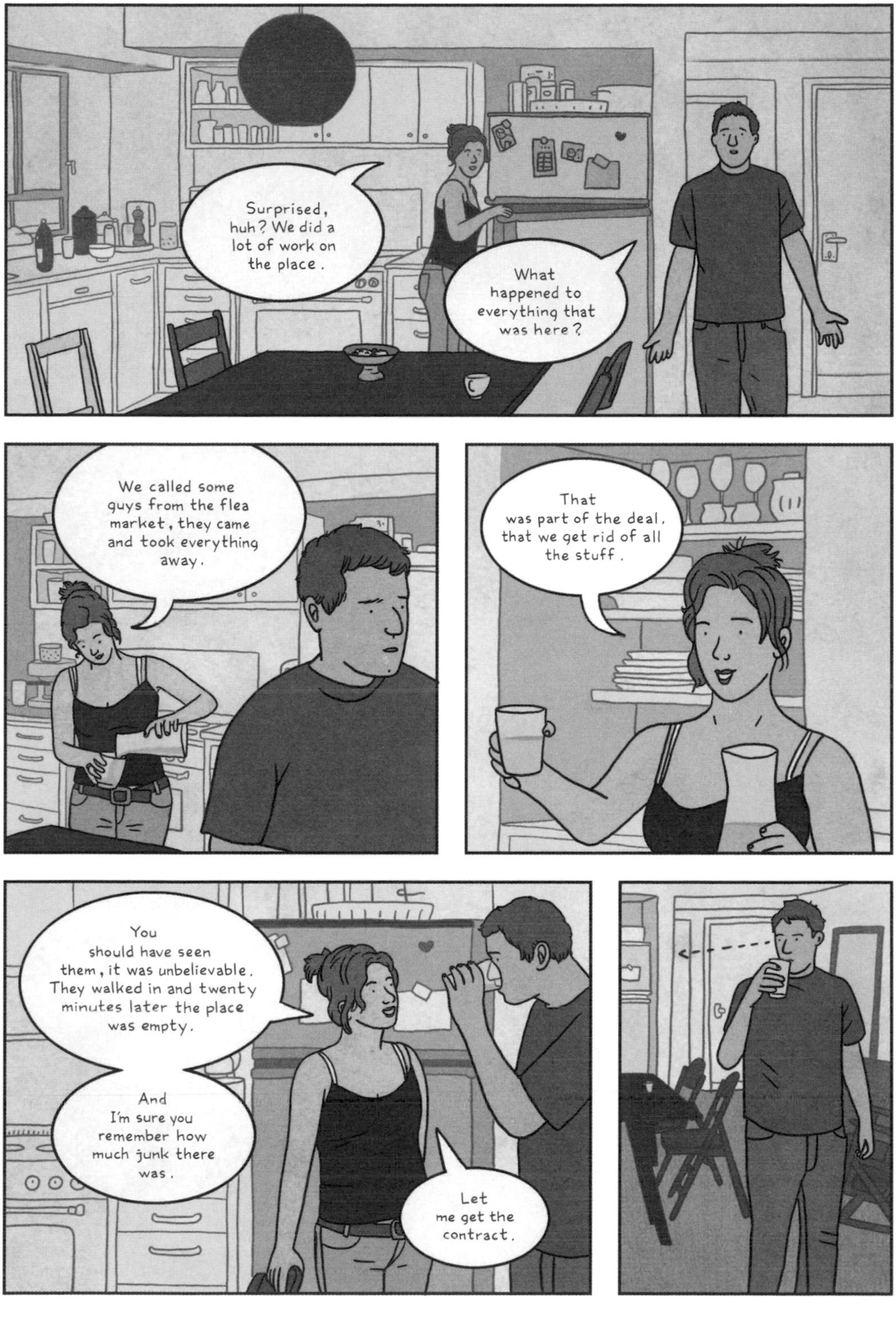
Surprised, huh? We did a lot of work on the place.
What happened to everything that was here?
We called some guys from the flea market, they came and took everything away.
That was part of the deal, that we get rid of all the stuff.
You should have seen them, it was unbelievable. They walked in and twenty minutes later the place was empty.
And I'm sure you remember how much junk there was.
Let me get the contract.

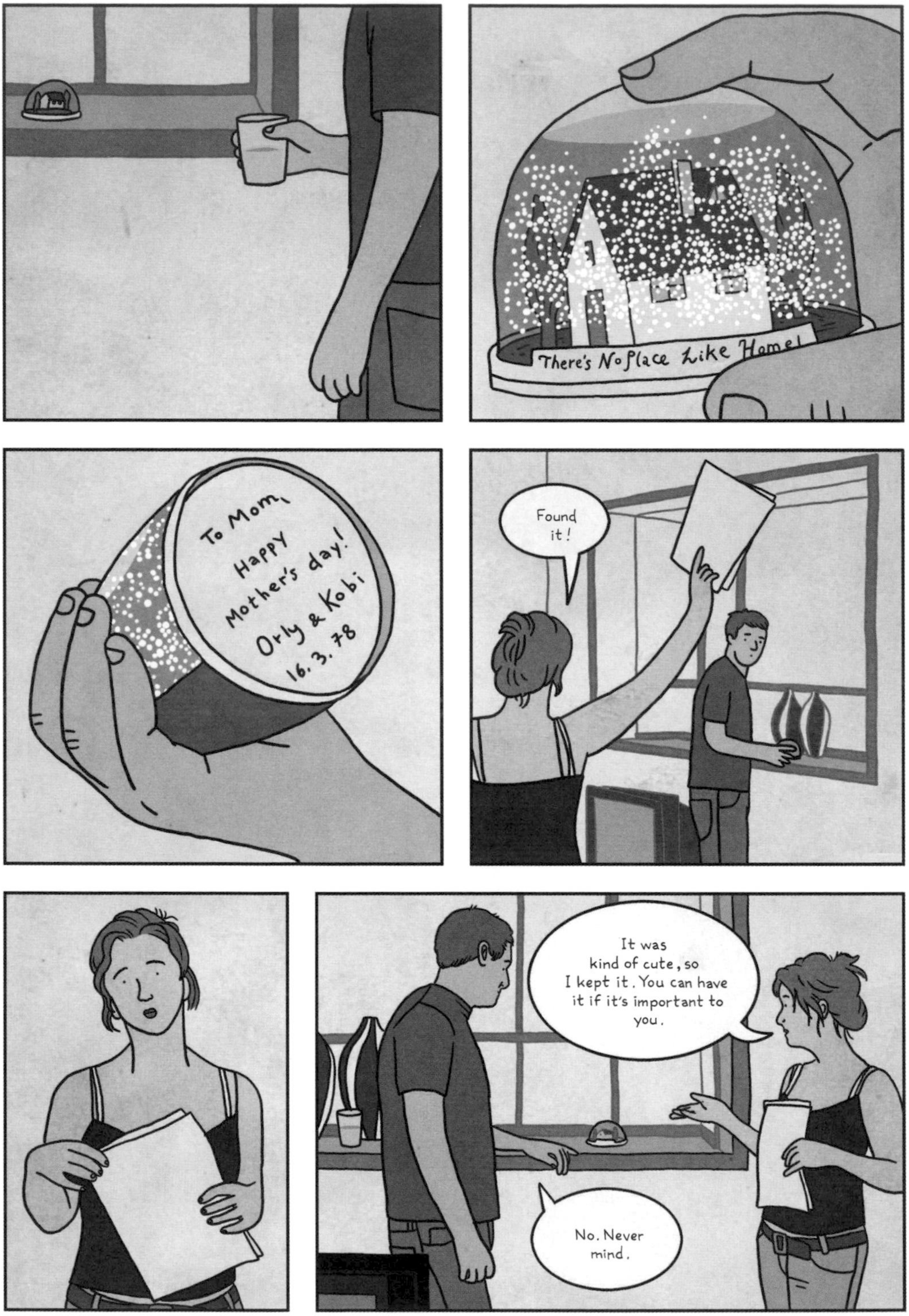
There's No Place Like Home!
To Mom, Happy Mother's day! Orly & Kobi 16.3.78
Found it!
It was kind of cute, so I kept it. You can have it if it's important to you.
No. Never mind.

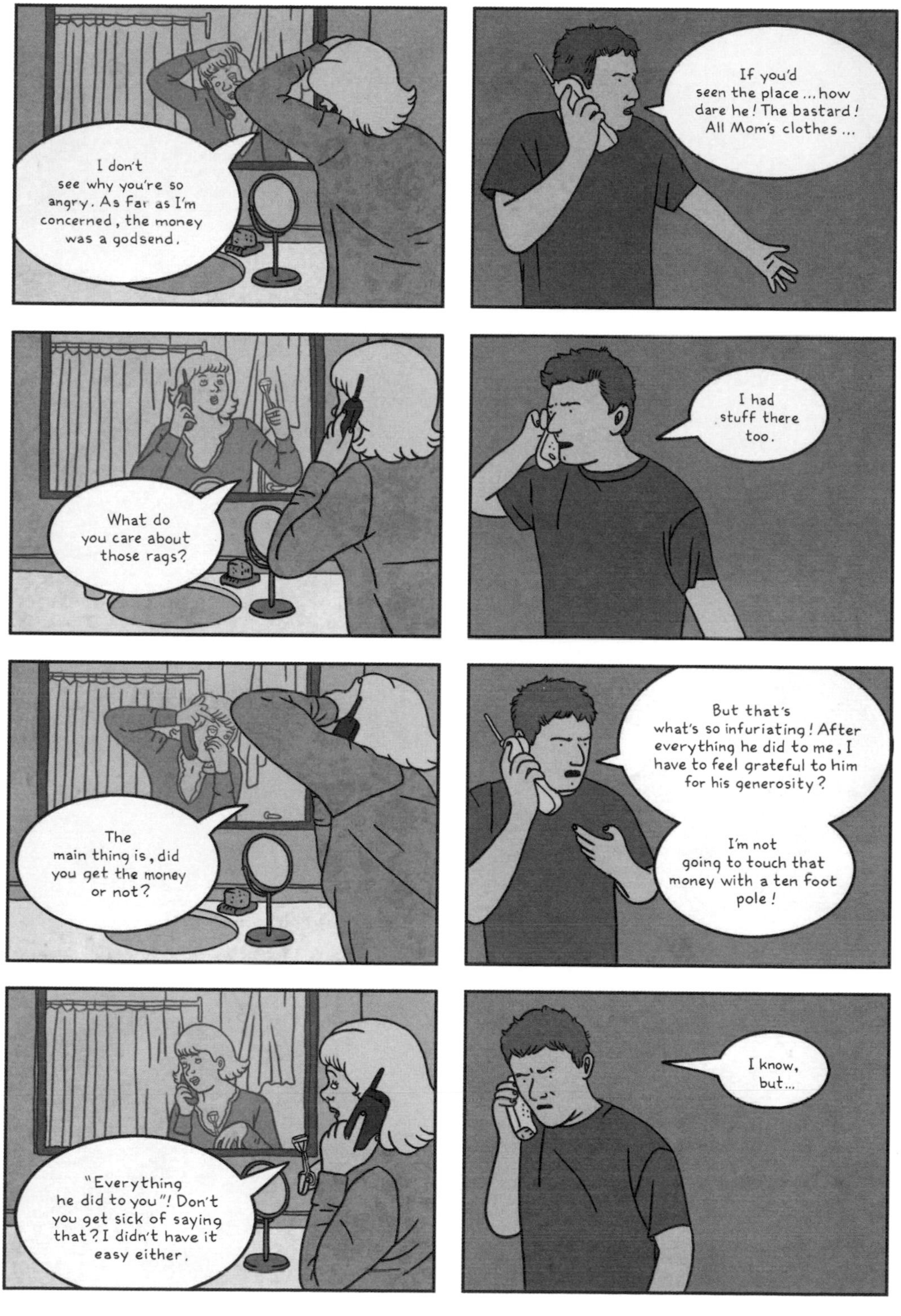
I don't see why you're so angry. As far as I'm concerned, the money was a godsend.
If you'd seen the place ... how dare he! The bastard! All Mom's clothes ...
What do you care about those rags?
I had stuff there too.
The main thing is, did you get the money or not?
But that's what's so infuriating! After everything he did to me, I have to feel grateful to him for his generosity?
I'm not going to touch that money with a ten foot pole!
"Everything he did to you"! Don't you get sick of saying that? I didn't have it easy either.
I know, but...

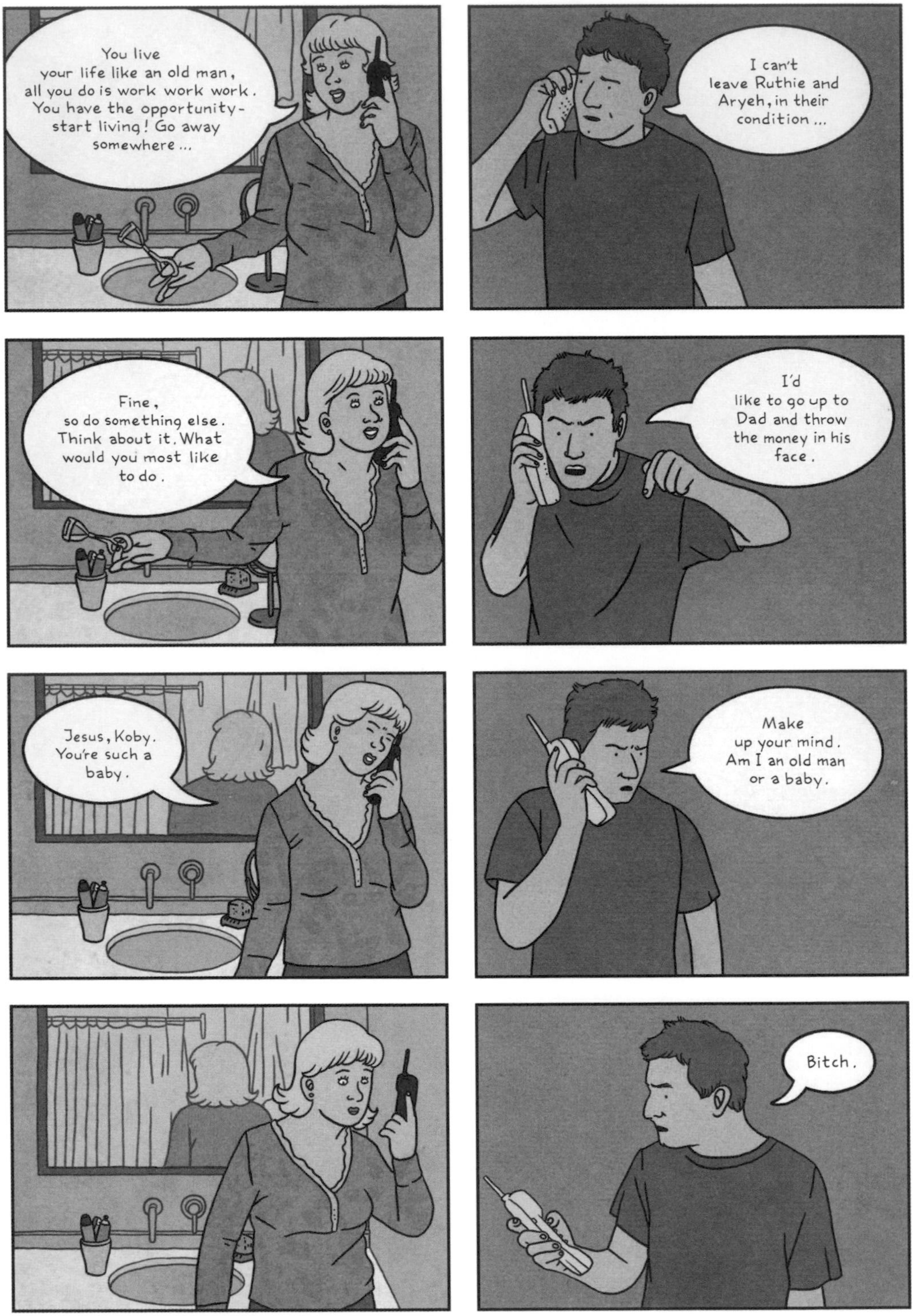
You live your life like an old man, all you do is work work work. You have the opportunity- start living! Go away somewhere ...
I can't leave Ruthie and Aryeh, in their condition ...
Fine, so do something else. Think about it. What would you most like to do.
I'd like to go up to Dad and throw the money in his face.
Jesus, Koby. You're such a baby.
Make up your mind. Am I an old man or a baby.
Bitch.

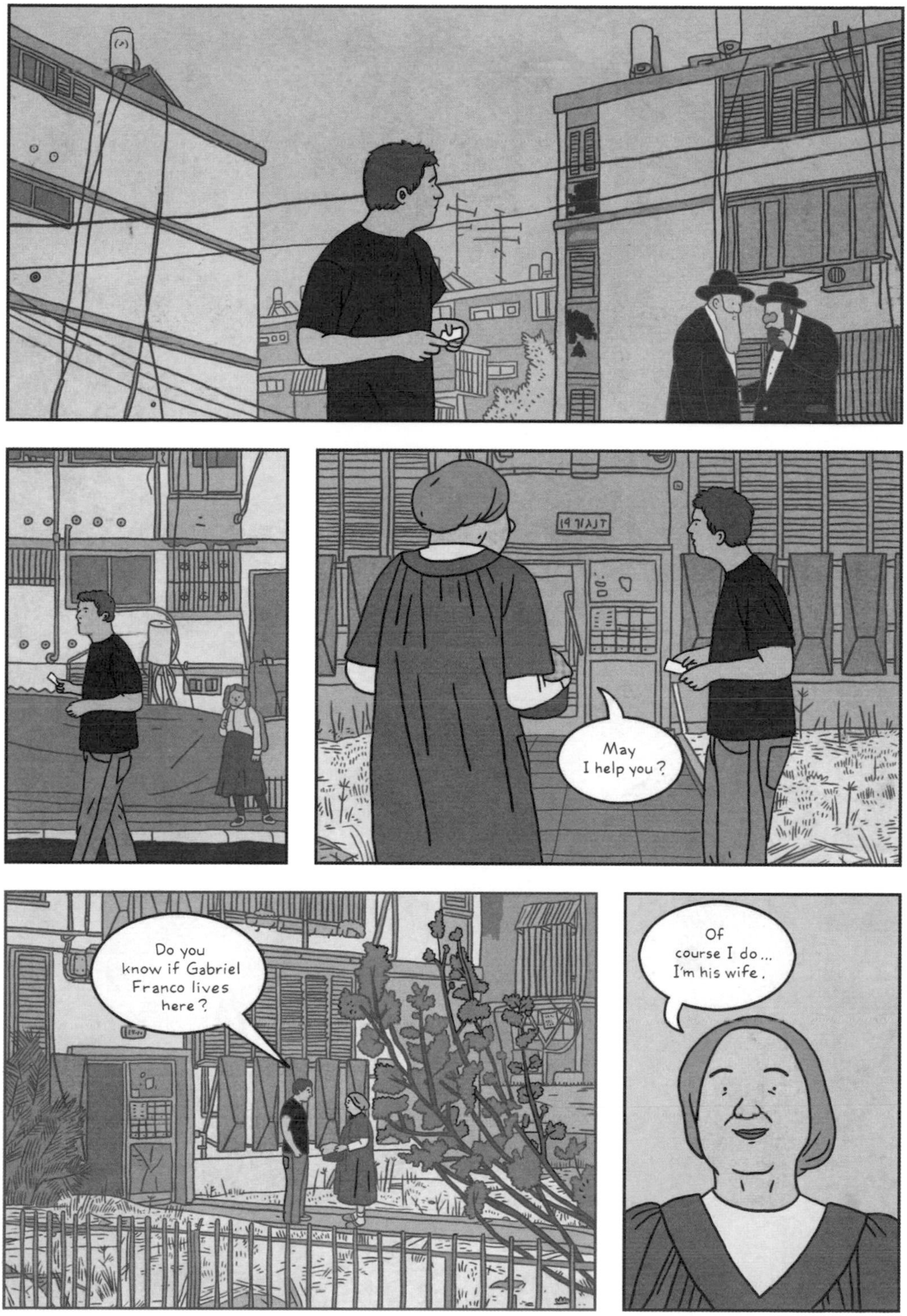
May I help you?
Do you know if Gabriel Franco lives here?
Of course I do... I'm his wife.

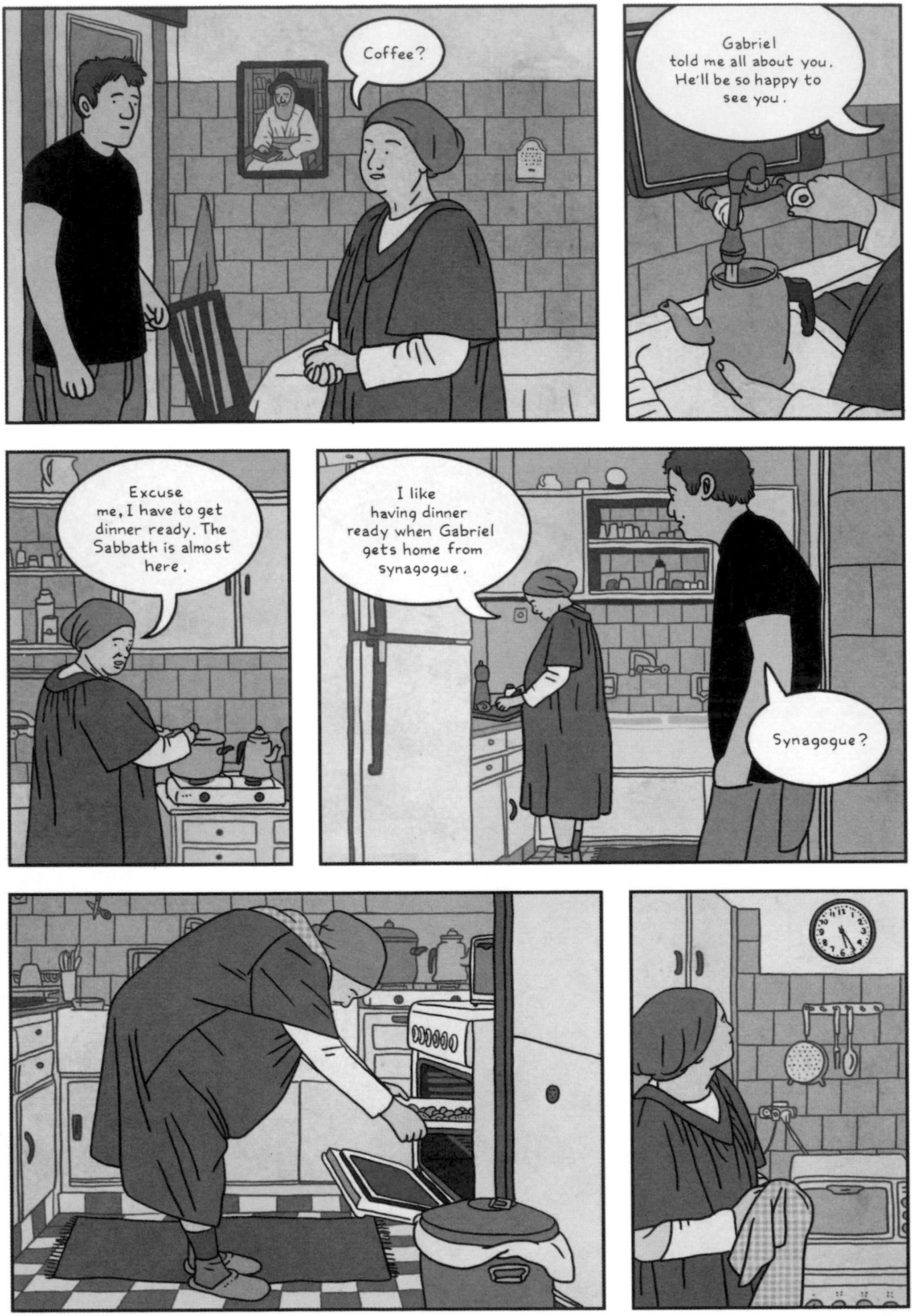
Coffee?
Gabriel told me all about you. He'll be so happy to see you.
Excuse me, I have to get dinner ready. The Sabbath is almost here.
I like having dinner ready when Gabriel gets home from synagogue.
Synagogue?

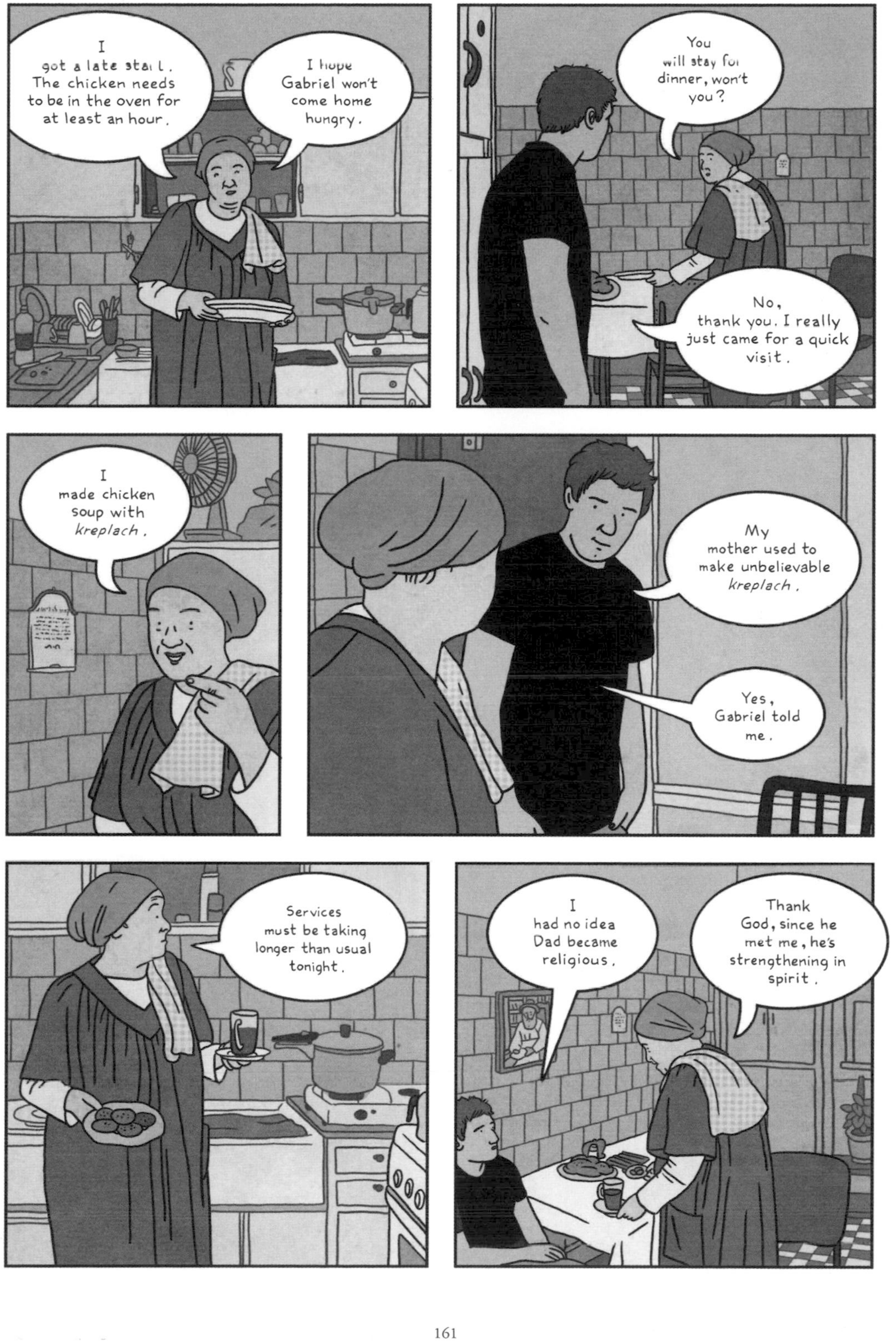
I got a late start. The chicken needs to be in the oven for at least an hour.
I hope Gabriel won't come home hungry.
You will stay for dinner, won't you?
No, thank you. I really just came for a quick visit.
I made chicken soup with *kreplach*.
My mother used to make unbelievable *kreplach*.
Yes, Gabriel told me.
Services must be taking longer than usual tonight.
I had no idea Dad became religious.
Thank God, since he met me, he's strengthening in spirit.

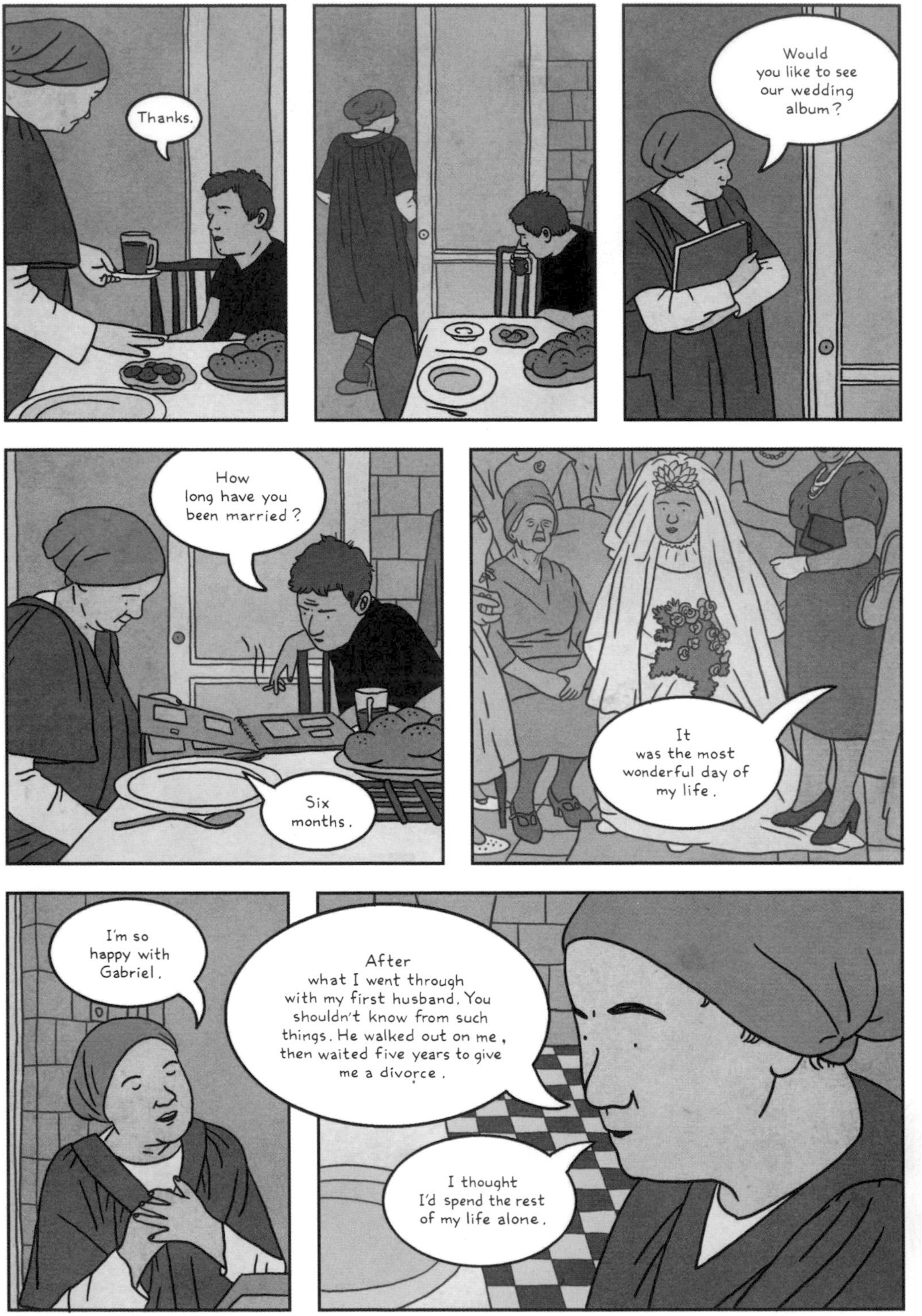
Thanks.
Would you like to see our wedding album?
How long have you been married?
Six months.
It was the most wonderful day of my life.
I'm so happy with Gabriel.
After what I went through with my first husband. You shouldn't know from such things. He walked out on me, then waited five years to give me a divorce.
I thought I'd spend the rest of my life alone.

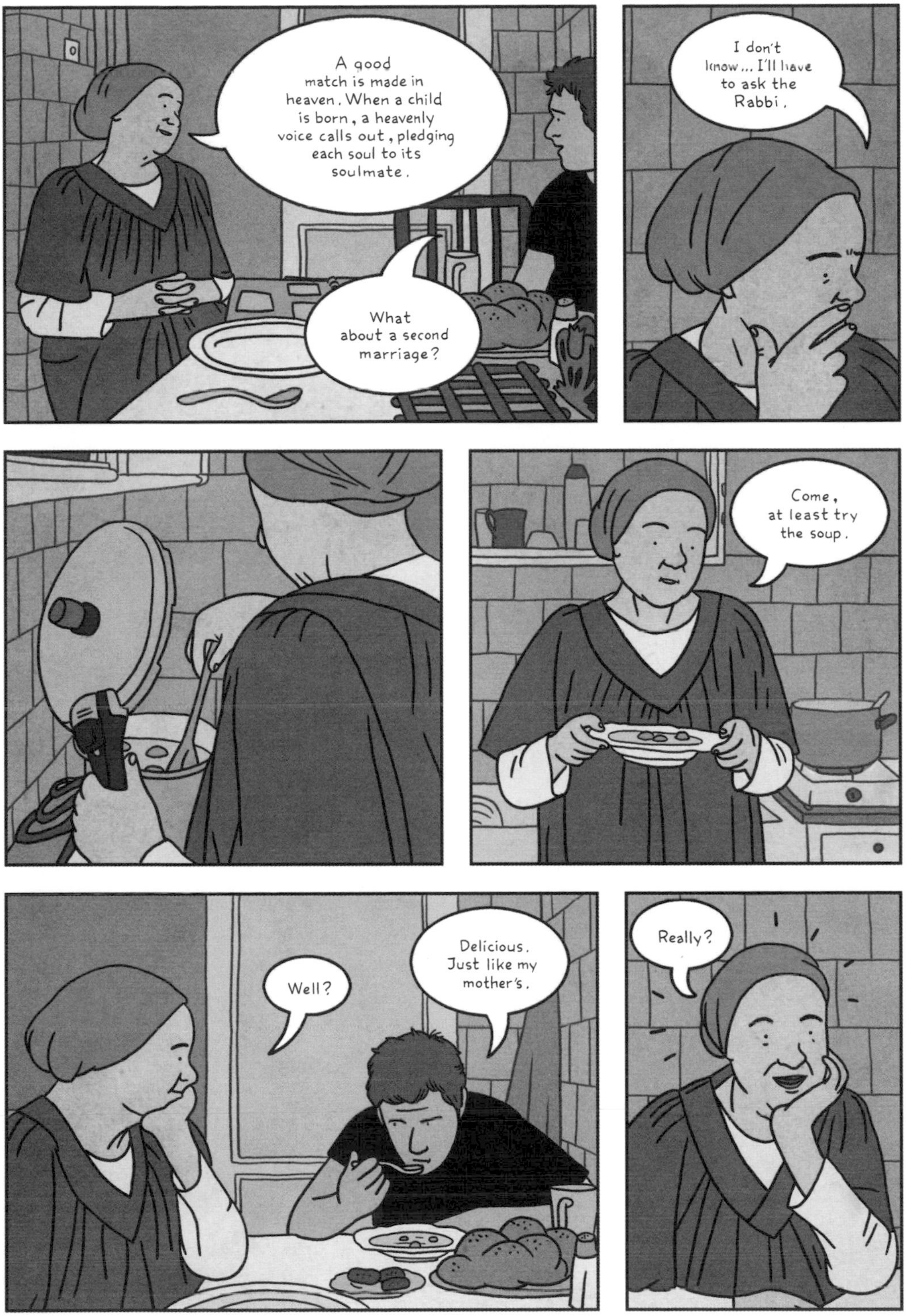
A good match is made in heaven. When a child is born, a heavenly voice calls out, pledging each soul to its soulmate.
What about a second marriage?
I don't know... I'll have to ask the Rabbi.
Come, at least try the soup.
Well?
Delicious. Just like my mother's.
Really?

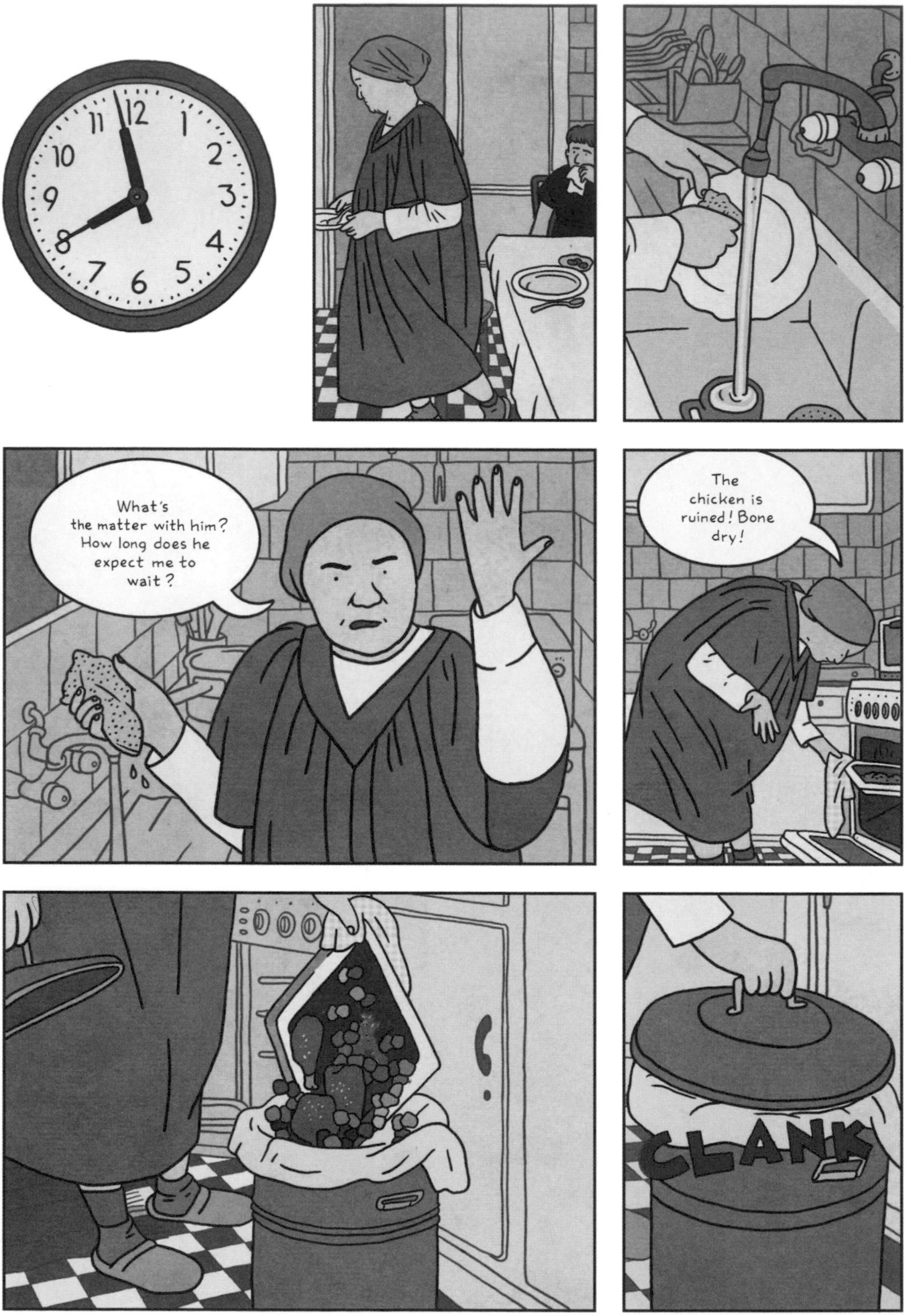
What's the matter with him? How long does he expect me to wait?
The chicken is ruined! Bone dry!
CLANK

One hour later.

I shouldn't have thrown it away. I could have made chicken salad.

I really should go.

Why? Gabriel will be here any minute.

I've waited enough.

It's a shame you missed each other. Do you want to leave him a message?

No. Just tell him I was here.

165

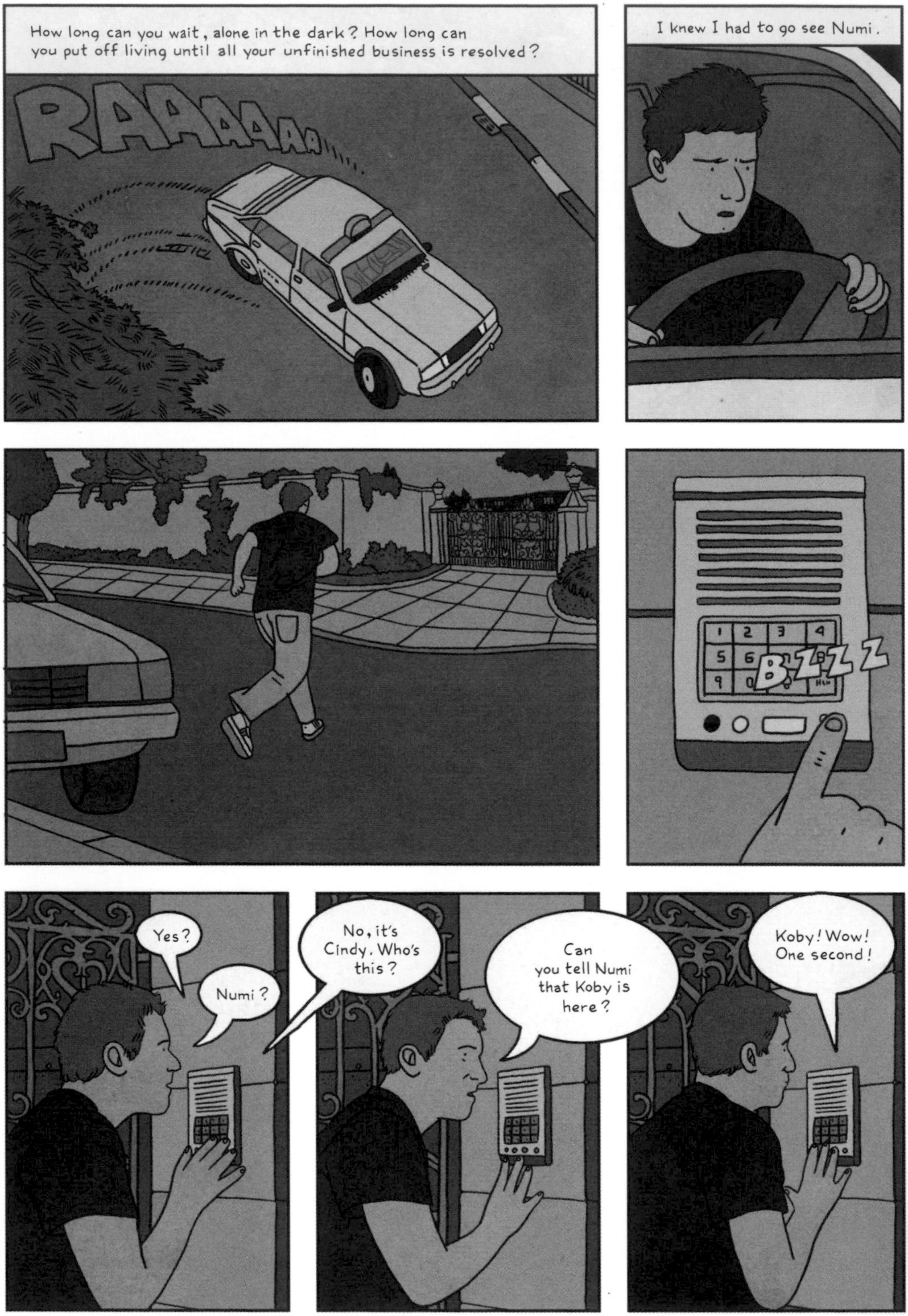
How long can you wait, alone in the dark? How long can you put off living until all your unfinished business is resolved?
RAAAAAA
I knew I had to go see Numi.
BZZZZ
Yes?
Numi?
No, it's Cindy. Who's this?
Can you tell Numi that Koby is here?
Koby! Wow! One second!

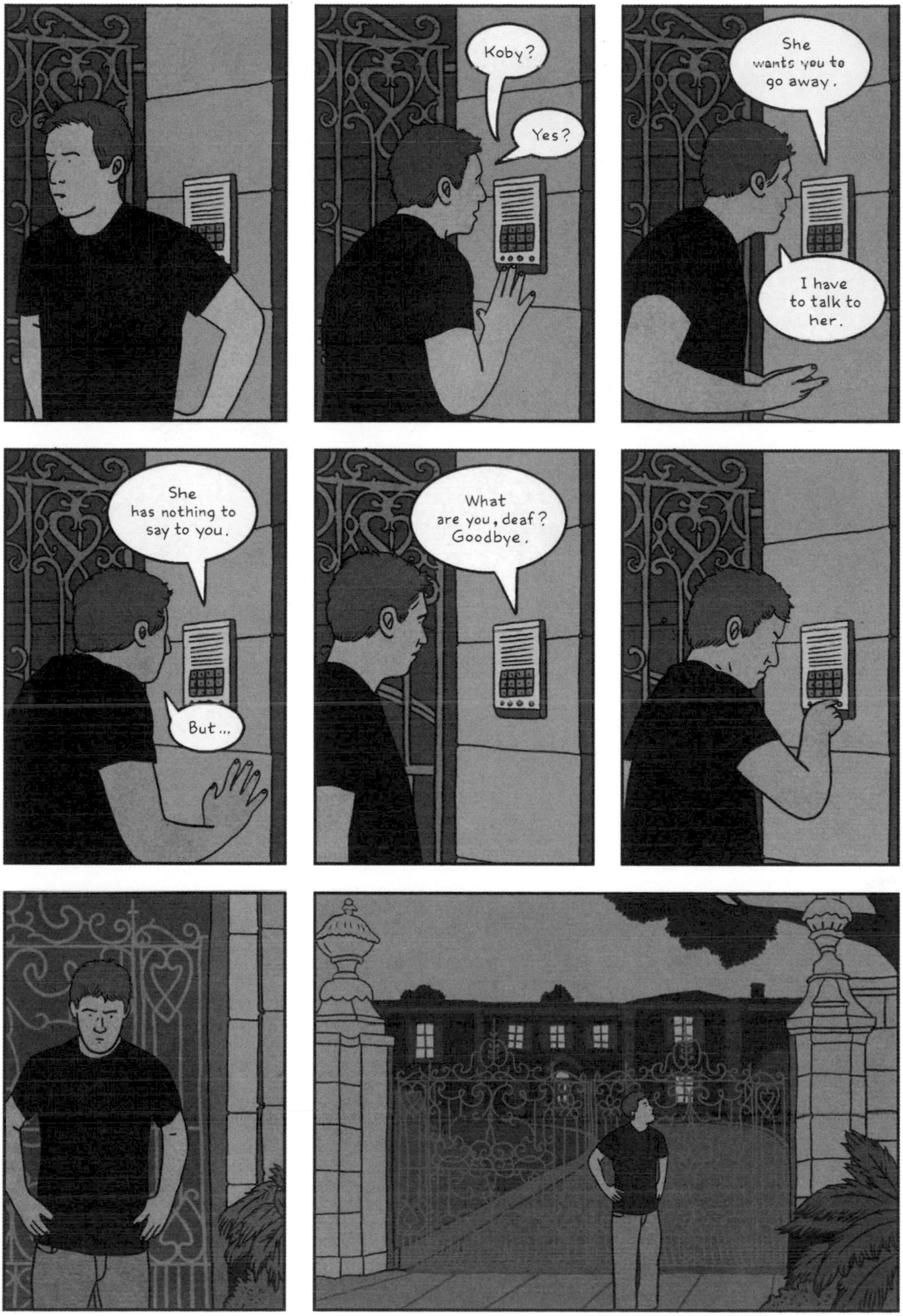
Koby?
Yes?
She wants you to go away.
I have to talk to her.
She has nothing to say to you.
But...
What are you, deaf? Goodbye.

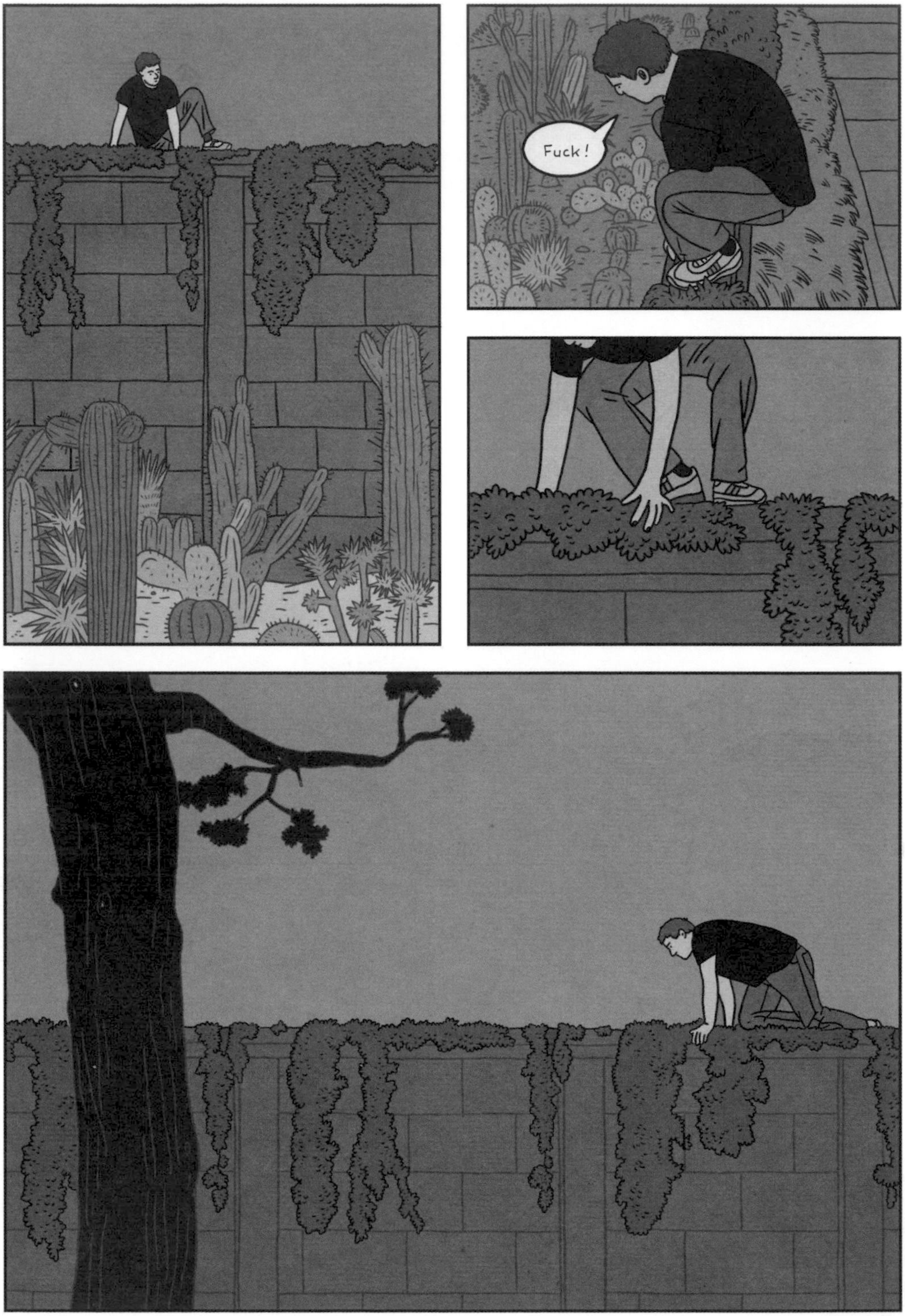
Fuck!

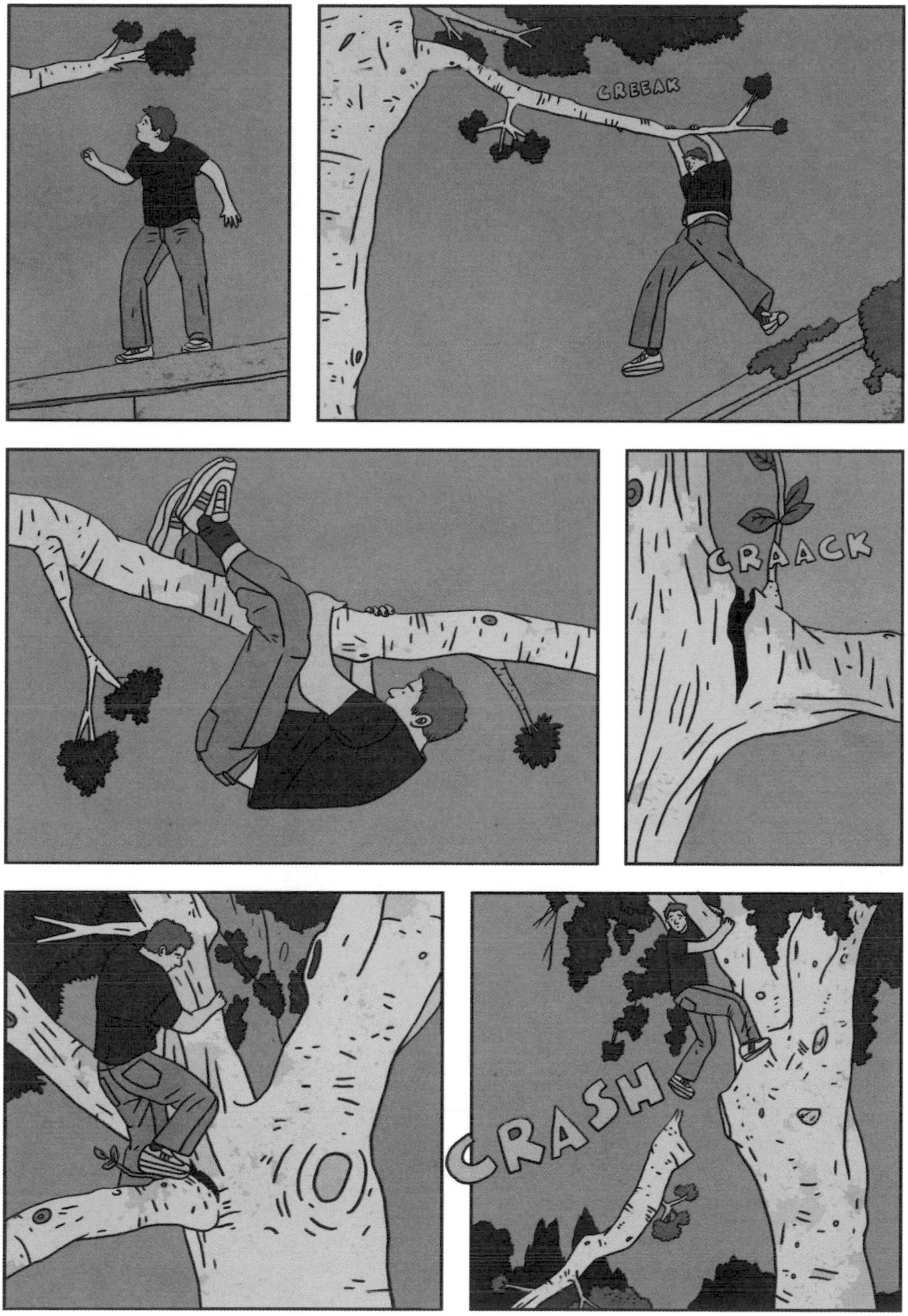
CREEAK
CRAACK
CRASH

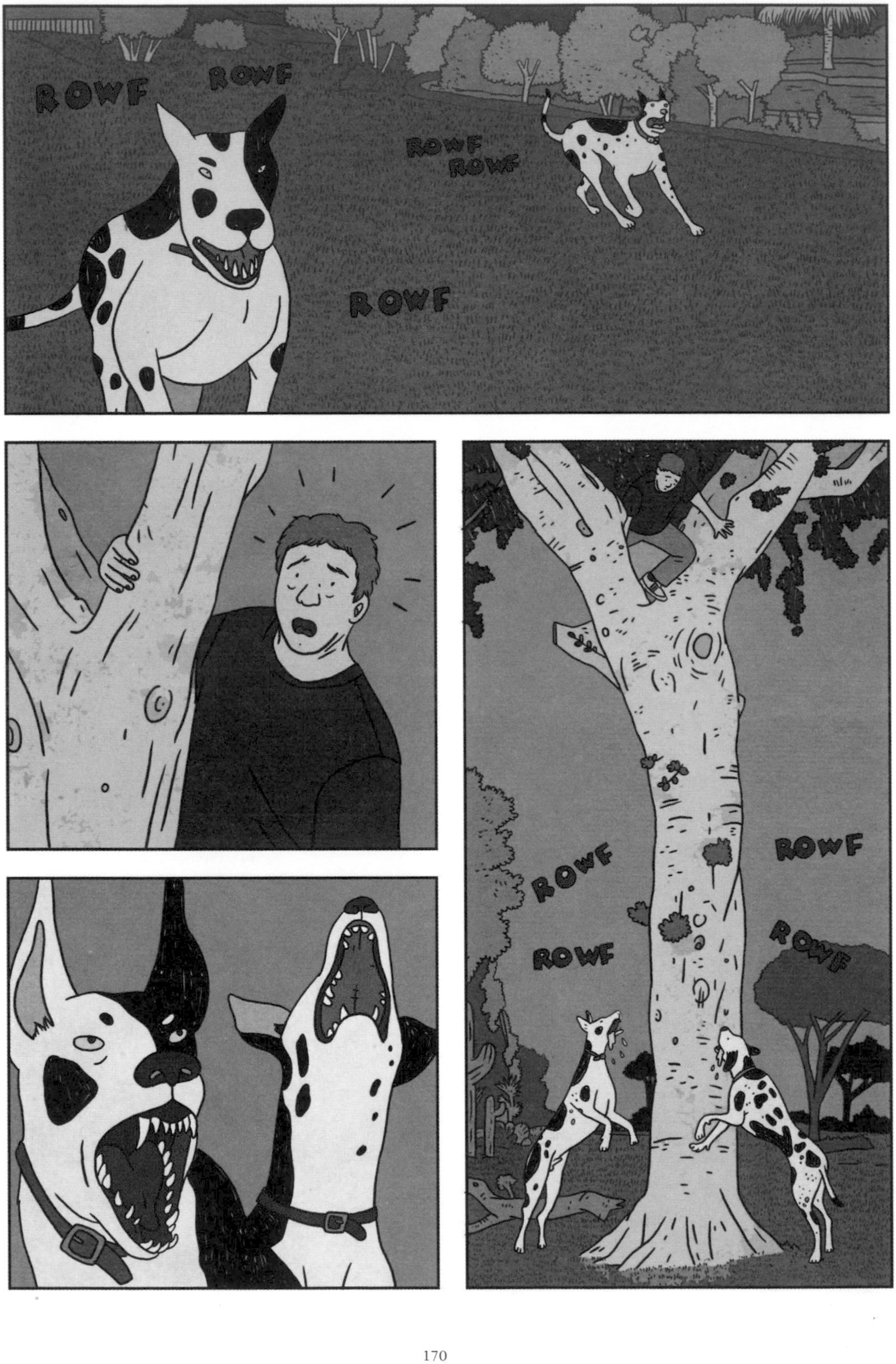
ROWF
ROWF
ROWF
ROWF
ROWF
ROWF
ROWF
ROWF
ROWF

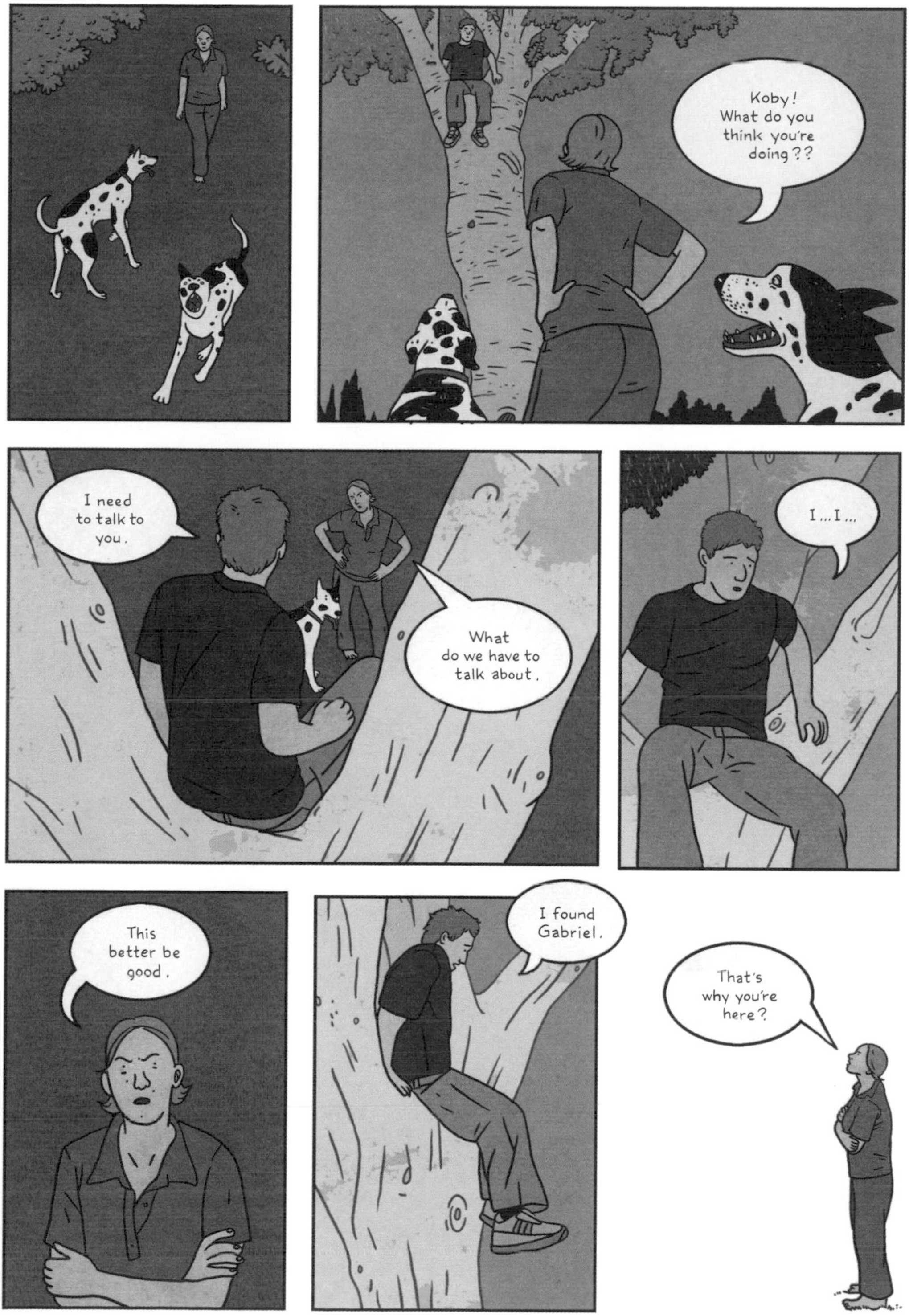
Koby!
What do you think you're doing??
I need to talk to you.
What do we have to talk about.
I... I...
This better be good.
I found Gabriel.
That's why you're here?

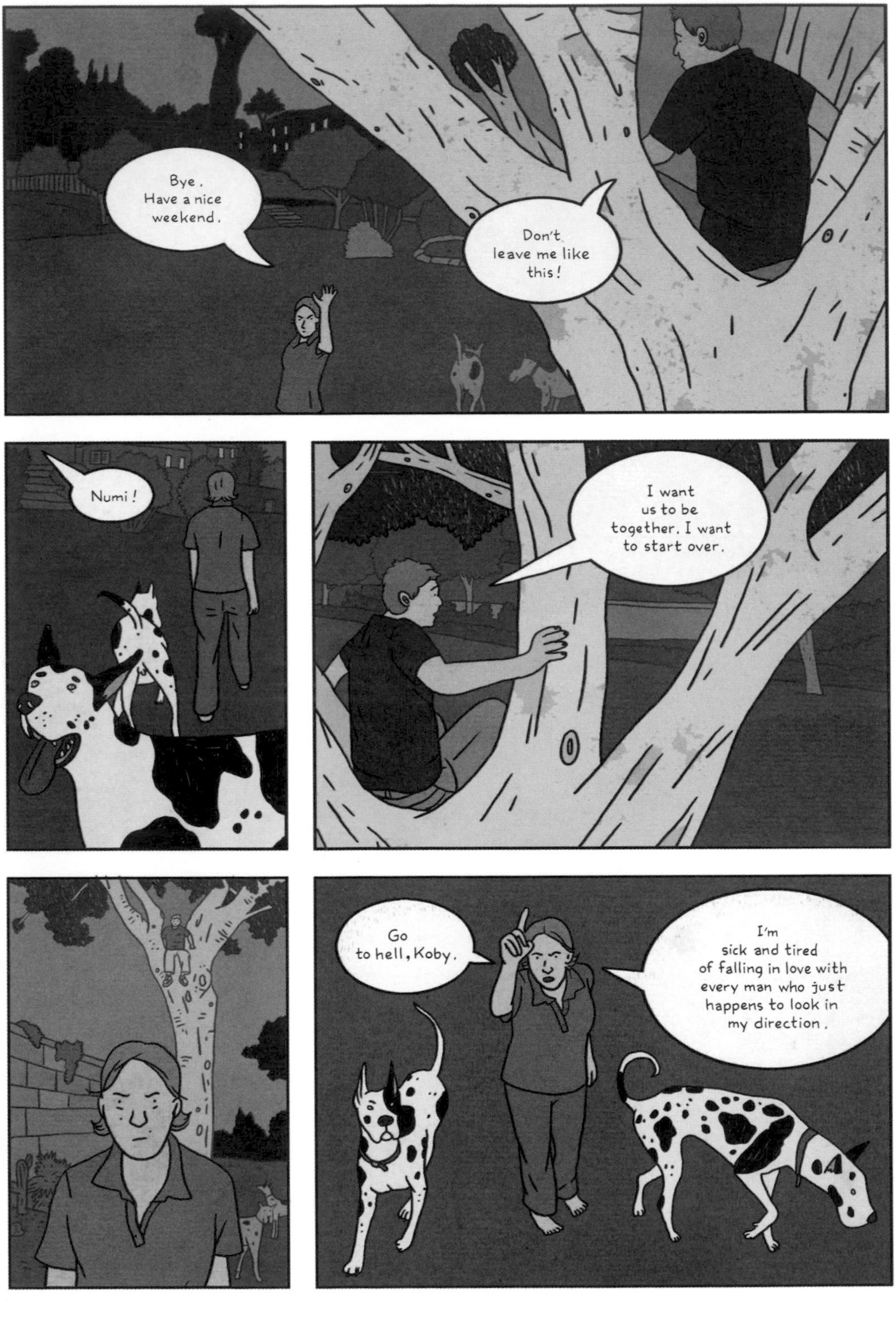

Bye. Have a nice weekend.
Don't leave me like this!
Numi!
I want us to be together. I want to start over.
Go to hell, Koby.
I'm sick and tired of falling in love with every man who just happens to look in my direction.

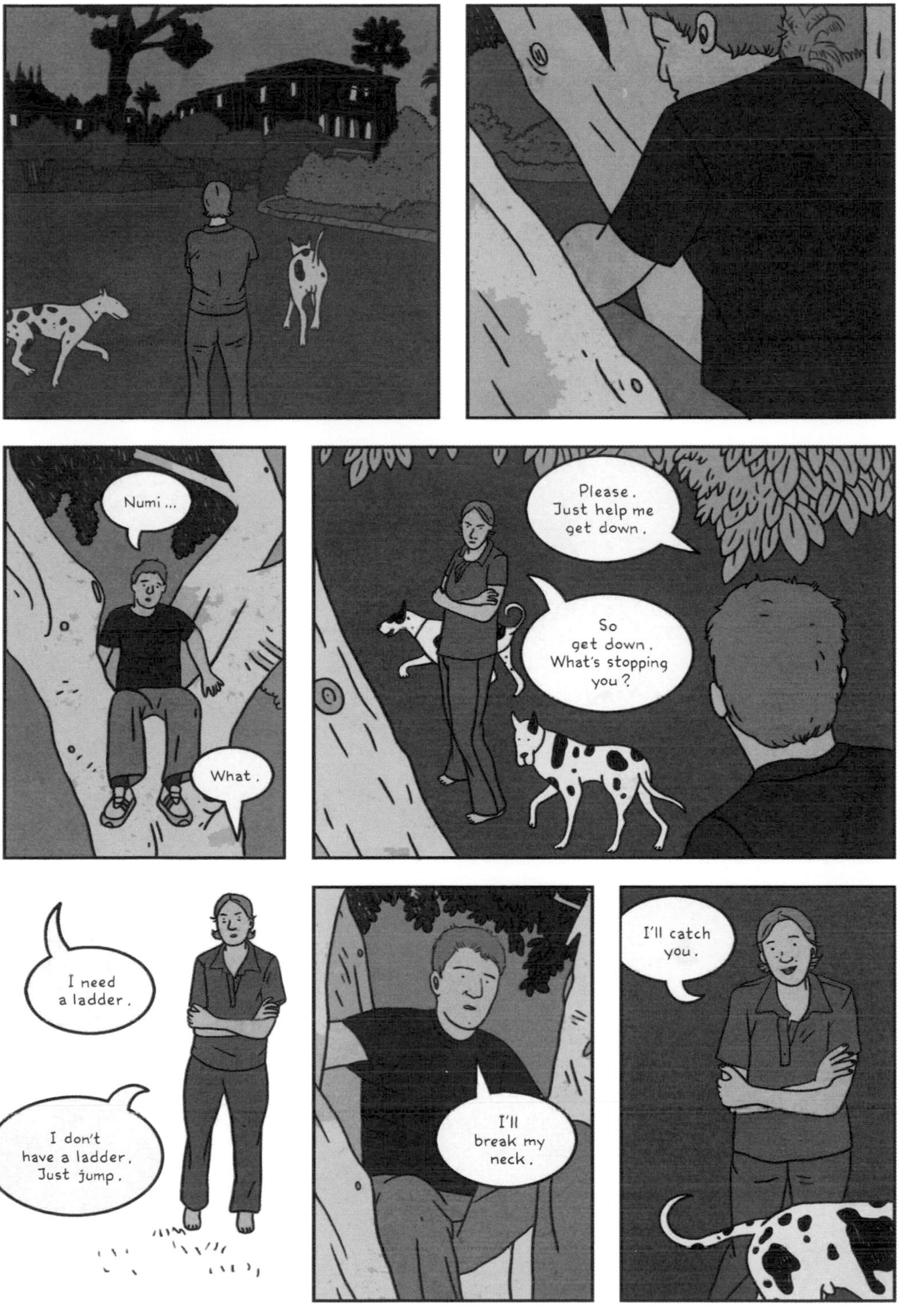
Numi...
What.
Please. Just help me get down.
So get down. What's stopping you?
I need a ladder.
I don't have a ladder. Just jump.
I'll break my neck.
I'll catch you.

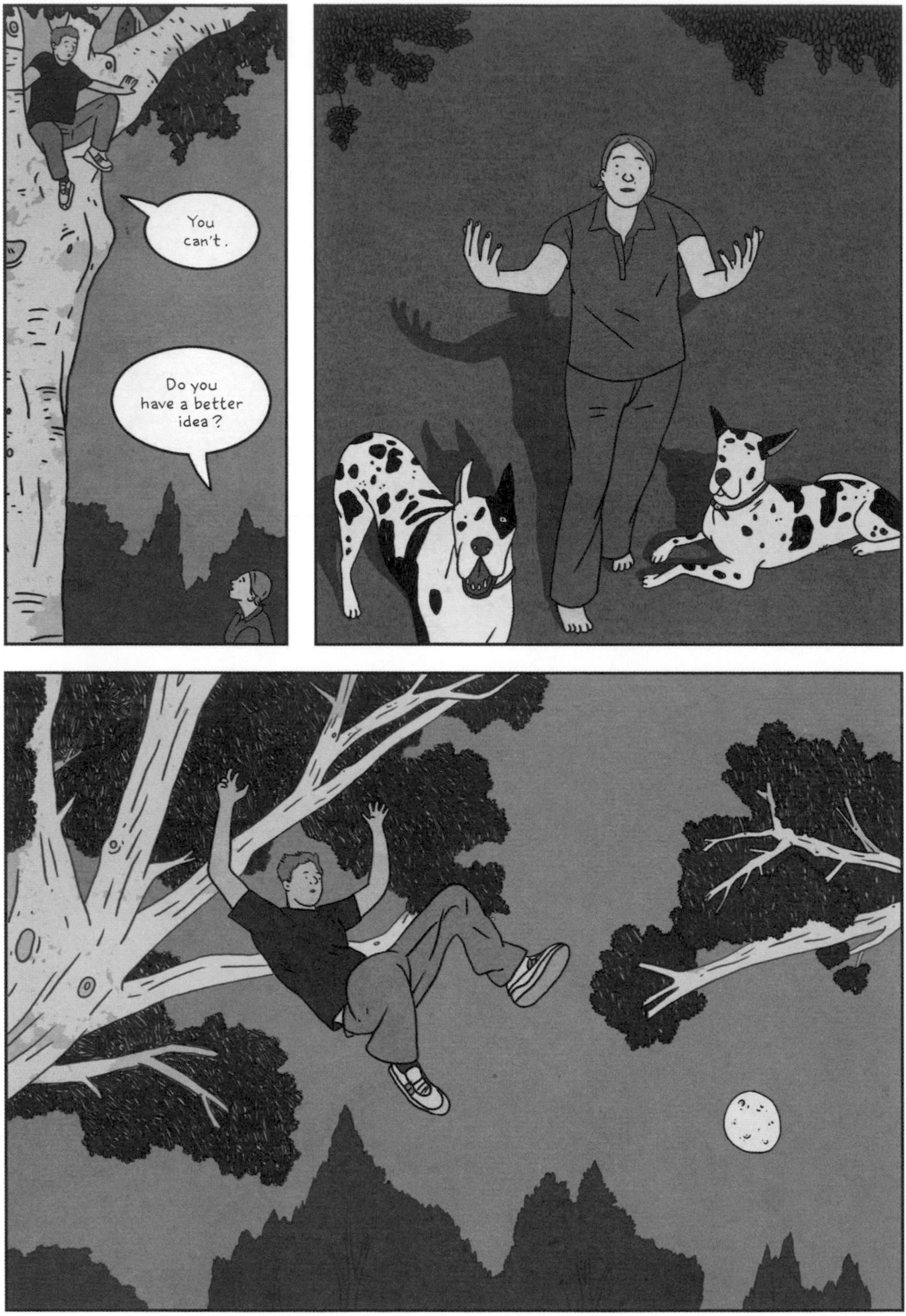
You can't.
Do you have a better idea?

AN INTERVIEW WITH RUTU MODAN

Conducted by Joe Sacco (*Safe Area Gorazde*, *Palestine*, *The Fixer*)
and originally appeared in *The Comics Journal* (TCJ.com); and is used with permission.

I conducted this interview with Rutu Modan (who is currently living in Sheffield, Great Britain with her husband and two children) by e-mail. Full disclosure: I wrote a favorable blurb for Modan's book *Exit Wounds* before being asked to do this interview; I agreed to interview Modan because I believe *Exit Wounds* is a truly remarkable, insightful work of comics that deserves significant attention.—Joe Sacco

JOE: *It seems that you graduated with all sorts of honors from the Bezalel Academy of Art and Design in Jerusalem in 1992. When you were going to school, which way did you see your career going? Were comics only one of a number of artistic interests? I ask, because you've also done a number of children's books, too?*

RUTU: It is very strange for me to think about it now, but I never thought that I was going to be a comics artist or an illustrator. Not even when I went to art school. It is strange because I was writing stories and illustrating them since I was 5. But comics wasn't something that was around me when I grew up. In the '70s and '80s there were maybe two people in Israel doing comics as a profession. There were almost no comics to find, not even *Superman* or *Tintin*. Only here and there you could find a strip in a children's magazine, but it was never an industry or a scene I could relate to and dream I could do too. In my teens, I was more interested in boys and in saving the world (in that order), and I almost stopped drawing, till I suddenly decided to come back to it and apply to Bezalel.

In my family, art was not considered a real profession. I was supposed to be a doctor, maybe a lawyer—an architect would have been an extreme choice. Going to art school was considered a strange, even laughable move—so comics?!!

It was only in my third year that I took a comics class. It was the first one ever at the school. Our teacher, Michel Kishka, was an immigrant from Belgium and in the first lesson he brought us piles of books: *Tintin* and Moebius but also *Raw* magazine, Charles Burns, Crumb. For two hours, he let us just read what he brought. It was a cultural shock. It took me 30 minutes to understand this is exactly what I want to do. It was like falling in love at first sight.

But I also understood that I couldn't be just a comics artist. The Israeli market was (and still is) not developed enough to make a profession out of comics. Since I graduated, I've worked as a magazine and children's book illustrator, as an animator. I did everything connected to drawing combined with text. I still do all these, and enjoy them. I'm not sorry I wasn't just a comics artist from the start. In this way, when doing my comics, I can do just what I want and I never bother about being commercial or communicative. Comics was the "pure art" part of my career and that helped me develop my personal style more freely.

You've worked on a couple of strips for major Israeli dailies. What kind of strips were they?

About the same time I started getting interested in comics, a very lucky thing happened. My friend's ex-boyfriend was appointed editor-in-chief of a new weekly magazine. I was looking for a job as a student, and my friend suggested I do a comic strip and suggested it to this guy.

So I made two or three examples and I went and showed them to him. He had no idea, he was new at this job, he never read comics, and he thought having a comic strip in his newspaper would be something very unique and hip. He hired me immediately. Not even as a freelancer: I actually got a salary. (OK, it was a very small salary, but still it was better than the cleaning job I was doing then.) I started publishing a weekly strip and a full-page or a double-page spread on special occasions. I had complete freedom. Since nobody understood anything about comics, since mainstream comics were considered weird exactly like alternative comics, I just did whatever I wanted, including using very macabre, vulgar humor, including changing the format from time to time when I was bored.

Two years afterwards, when I graduated, I already had a name as a comics artist, and for eight years I moved from one newspaper to another, doing strips.

What sort of strips influenced you?

My influences were kind of accidental, based on comics that I happened to come across. My first strip was influenced by Jules Feiffer; we had a pocket book of his comics when I was a child. My strip featured a new character every week talking about diet, the coming elections, Passover, etc. Then for a while I was influenced by Mark Beyer. I had a strip telling macabre, pointless stories and the drawings were grotesque. Then I discovered Edward Gorey and for a while I was rhyming and drawing in a Victorian style.

In 1994, I started working with Etgar Keret. I wanted to develop from those funny strips and start doing more serious and longer stories, but I did not have the confidence to write myself. I contacted him, he was a young author publishing stories in magazines, and his stories were very visual and strong. I suggested we work together. (In Israel, it is very easy—you always know someone who knows personally anyone.) Luck again: I started working with him and after a few months his own book was published and—Boom!—he was a major star. He could get whatever he wanted from any newspaper's editor. We started publishing short comics stories in a big weekly, a spread or two every other week. Again, no one interfered even though some of the stories were quite strange. It was amazing working with Etgar, he is one of the most brilliant men I ever met. I learned so much about writing from him.

Alas, this wonderful period was finished. Print journalism stopped being the hen that laid golden eggs. Editors started thinking about what sells and I was fired from the newspaper. I didn't care. By this point I was already an established comics artist—whatever that means in Israel (not much, really). Anyway, I was fed up doing a weekly strip. The weeks are passing too quickly when you have a weekly deadline.

How did you get the gig as editor of the Hebrew edition of Mad *magazine? What was that like?*

In 1994, an Israeli publisher decided to publish an Israeli edition of *Mad* magazine. I think that at that period the American *Mad* was over its prime and they started selling rights to foreign countries. The format was supposed to be 75 percent translated American material and 25 percent original local material. I guess the Israeli publisher looked for someone to do the editing job at a low cost. I was offered the job, and I asked Yirmi Pinkus, who was my classmate and a comics artist himself, to do it with me. It was rather fun. We did not have to use up-to-date material. We could, and we did, order whatever we wanted from the *Mad* archive. We ordered material from the '60s, the '50s, some of it great stuff. We also commissioned comics by all the comics artists in Israel whose work we liked and ourselves.

It was a great opportunity to learn about editing, printing, production, marketing, because we did everything ourselves, including translating. Since we liked alternative comics, that was the original material we used. We also hired a graphic designer to do a revision of Mad's design. The American publisher wasn't interested in what we were doing. The only thing we had to do was to send the cover to be approved. We did have one cover censored because one artist drew Alfred E. Neuman as a punk. The American publisher thought he looked like a skinhead and insisted it would hurt the Jewish readers' feelings. It was impossible to explain to them that there are no Nazis in Israel. Apart from that, we did what we wanted. The problem was, people who liked *Mad* magazine hated the Israeli stories, and fans of alternative comics hated the American parts. Nobody bought the magazine. Another attempt to publish comics in Israeli had failed. The magazine was shut down after 14 issues. But at least Yirmi and I had a good time, and this episode led directly to the founding of Actus Tragicus.

Tell us something about Actus Tragicus. When did that get off the ground, what's it about, and what sort of people were/are involved?

After *Mad*, Yirmi and I were looking for a new way to continue publishing our comics. Actually, the failure of *Mad* was a relief. It was clear that doing comics in Israel was not going to be profitable for us, and that, if we were going to lose money anyway, we'd better do exactly what interests us and stop trying to be commercial. (We are both hopeless optimists.) Yirmi had spent a few months in Berlin at the time and met Anke Feuchtenberger, Atak and Henning Wagenbreth, who had a comics collective in East Germany before the collapse of the Wall. That gave us the idea to establish a group and self-publish our comics. Mira Friedmann and Itzik Rennert joined us. They were both already established illustrators when Yirmi and I graduated (we were in the same class) and they both did comics from time to time. Yirmi and I adored their work and were really pleased they agreed to participate. Batia Kolton was a student in the first class I taught. I thought she was a genius. I asked her to join us, too.

The comics we published were in English, since we wanted to try and distribute it abroad as well as in Israel. We figured we had a better chance to survive this way. Israel's comics fans are used to reading comics in English, so we were not going to lose many of them by this move. We were criticized a lot for it in Israel, by the way. Another thing we knew from the start is that the production values should be high. We were influenced by the American alternative scene and European comics. With our first series (small-format, black-and-white booklets) we went to the Angoulême Comics Festival in France. It was amazing. Not that anyone was particularly interested in our booklets, but it was the first time for me to be with so many comics and comics people around me. It was so wonderful to feel that liking comics is not some rare mental disease that I have.

After Angoulême, Actus, which was supposed to be a fun project, became the center of my career for the next years. The idea of working in a group was to share the tedious work of production and distribution. In Israel, we did the distribution ourselves. As the years went by, however, the main thing became the joint creative process. When we start a new project we decide on a format, and each of us starts to create our own story. Every few weeks we meet, show our work, discuss it together, give each other criticism. From abstract idea until coloring. For me this is the best thing I get from Actus. Being a comics artist is such a lonely job. You do everything alone, isolated in your studio, torn between the feeling you are a genius and the feeling you are a worm and your work is worthless. When the comic is finished you don't want to hear any criticism, you only want to hear it is wonderful. How can it help you to know the faults? The comic is printed; it is too late to change anything!

But it is so comforting, so helpful during the process, when you can still fix things up, to have friends whose opinions and good will you trust give you feedback and useful advice, people who are committed to your work almost as much as you are. It is not a favor, because you are committed to their work, too. Even while working on *Exit Wounds*, which wasn't published by Actus, I was consulting with Actus members through the whole process.

We are working on a new project now: a book called *How to Love*, to be printed in December 2007 [Editor's note: Rutu's contribution appears in her recent short story collection, *Jamilti*, as do most of her Actus Tragicus anthology contributions].

You mentioned you taught a class? What sort of class? What's the story behind that?

About a year after graduating, I was offered a job teaching a newspaper illustration course in a design school in Tel Aviv. I thought it would be fun to teach and also it seemed like a good idea to have something stable in such an unstable profession. My first class was one boy and six girls—one of them was Batia Kolton, who is now one of my closest colleagues and friends. I've taught ever since. After a few years, I was asked to teach at the Bezalel Academy in Jerusalem. I was very happy, since it was my art school, and I spent four wonderful years there. I started teaching as a freelancer, but in the last four years I've been one of the staff. During the years, I've taught many different classes. Basic illustration, children's book illustration, magazine illustration, character design...

A few years ago, I started teaching comics. The professor who taught me comics (the first comics course in Israel, I guess) was (and is) still teaching, so it was hard to convince the head of the department that another comics course was needed, but I convinced him by nagging and by suggesting a course called "Alternative Comics." The title impressed him. It sounded very up-to-date to him. This title, and the fact that it was "the second comics course," allowed me to be more free with the syllabus. The other professor was teaching basic comics and he did it wonderfully. I could focus on aspects that interested me like writing for comics or expanding the limits of the medium.

What I like about teaching is that, since I have to explain to my students about their comics and illustrations, I have to think about it myself in a very clear way. They cannot be abstract thoughts. After I explain to them, it becomes clearer to me, too. Another benefit is staying in touch with young people with fresh minds; it helps me stay up-to-date. I learn a lot from my students. It is also nice to get out of my studio once or twice week and meet and talk with people.

Moving to England forced me to take a break from teaching, and I really miss it.

We'll get to Exit Wounds *soon, but has your other recent comics work been based in reality?*

Everything I write is based on or influenced by reality. Where else can you get inspiration? Even when I wrote those weekly funny strips, they were based on life. I once read an article about a new birth method: giving birth in a dolphins' pool. I wrote a strip about giving birth among sharks, where you can choose whether you take the baby home or leave him in the pool.

I was pregnant at the time, terrified by the idea of motherhood.

Reality provides wonderful materials. In fact, it is much more extreme and peculiar than anything I could imagine. On the other hand, I never stick to reality; it is just a starting point for the story. The problem with reality is that it is too chaotic. Too coincidental. Art is supposed to make some order in this chaos we call life. To give it some sense, some meaning. Life, reality, has no meaning, at least not one we can be sure of. I better say it like this: life has no subtext. And a story without subtext is a soap opera. I am not talking about comics-journalism—this is another matter. Journalism has a different duty. I am talking about fiction.

"The Homecoming"—a story I wrote few years ago—was based on a true event that happened at the time. A small airplane arrived from Lebanon and was circling above the shore. The pilot did not want to identify himself. After a few hours, fearing this might be a terrorist who is going to crash on a populated area, the Israeli air force shot the plane down. The body of the pilot fell—without the head—on the table in the office of a high-school principal of a nearby kibbutz. Great story for comics, isn't it? Grotesque, local, airplanes, bombs...but if I used it as it was, it would only be an anecdote. An episode from a far away place. Nothing emotional about it.

I turn this event into the story of an old man who believes the pilot is his son who had been kidnapped in the Lebanon war seven years before. The old man thinks his son managed to steal an airplane and come home. The son had a wife, who now has a new boyfriend. The story is the struggle between the old man and the boyfriend, who would actually prefer that the pilot isn't his girlfriend's lost husband. I left all the background almost as it was—including the headless body—which causes more confusion: is it or isn't it the missing son? So it became a story about how people use facts to [match] their beliefs. When the facts are not compatible with their opinions, people won't change their opinion. They would rather twist reality to fit their beliefs.

For me it is a political story. But the story is also personal. When one loses someone close, it is very difficult to believe he disappeared forever. For years you keep thinking you see him on the street, you're waiting for him to call and come out of his hiding place. The story was about this feeling, as well.

Not all my stories are based on a real event like this one, but they all have some connection to things that happened to me, or problems that I have, which are part of reality, too. Writing a story is a recommended way to deal with your problems.

Exit Wounds is your first book-length comic. If you don't mind my simplifying the plot, it's about a somewhat awkward young woman, Numi, who believes the unidentified victim of a suicide bombing is her elderly lover, Gabriel. She tracks down Gabriel's estranged son, Koby, and he reluctantly gets involved in her effort to prove the body is Gabriel's. This certainly seems like the sort of story that could be based on a real incident. Was it?

The main plot is based on an actual event, a body that was destroyed in a terror attack on a bus. This has happened before, unfortunately, but this time no one claimed the body. It seems it was a body of someone no one missed. A wonderful documentary was done on this event (*No. 17* by David Ofek). The director tried to find the identity of the body. I saw the film and it was so strong. We would like to think that if we disappeared at least someone would notice—a relative, a neighbor, at least the vendor at our local shop. Although I've not experienced a terror attack myself, it was happening a lot around me a few years ago, and it did affect my everyday life and feelings. But sudden, brutal deaths are actually around all of us, anywhere, anytime, not just in Israel. (Every death feels sudden and brutal, even those called "natural.") I tried to describe this in *Exit Wounds*, and not just the dramatic side of it, but also the matter-of-factness of death and the everyday aspect of it.

Another experience contributed to the plot: many years ago I dated a guy, and he did not call me afterwards. After a week, I came to the conclusion this guy must be dead: why else didn't he call me? I could not think of any other reason. Worried, I called him—he was perfectly all right. (Now I can be happy about it.) That gave me the idea of this girl who prefers to believe her lover was killed rather than thinking he abandoned her.

The characters, the love story, everything is invented, but I did use a lot of events, anecdotes that happened to me or people I know. For example, when Koby goes to his father's apartment (his childhood home) after it was sold, the new owner tells him about the flea-market people who emptied the place. I based that on my own experience after my parents had died. I was there when the flea-market people came, so I could identify with Koby's emotions about the experience. Or the relationship between Numi and her mother: that's based on a friend I had in my childhood. Her mother was a very beautiful woman who married a short, bald millionaire, and my friend looked more like her father (though she wasn't bald). Her mother couldn't stand it. She made her life miserable. She forced her to have a nose job when she was 16 and a few years later made her marry her first boyfriend. The mother convinced her daughter that no one would be interested in her besides him. Actually, I had to reduce the abuse from reality for the story. Numi is not really my friend from school. But using her history made it easier to give Numi a feeling of a real person (to me and hopefully to the reader).

Exit Wounds is also a rather grim portrayal of a society almost inured to violence. Suicide attacks are discussed without much emotion or sympathy for the victims. The forensics people make jokes and in one scene a family member who retrieves the body of a loved one is particularly callous.

When the reality around you is so complicated or too frightening, people tend to detach themselves from it. We cannot live our lives fearing what's going to happen next; we have to protect ourselves. Ignoring it is one way. Macabre humor is another. It is like a shield you build around yourself. The problem is this shield becomes part of your personality eventually. You can't take it on and off like a shirt. Koby, who was hurt by his father, by the death of his mother, by living in such a violent country, becomes an untouchable person. He fears getting close to people. As an opposite to him, there is this girl, Numi. Maybe because she is younger, she lets herself be more vulnerable, which is dangerous but also, I believe, rewarding in the end.

What's interesting, too, is Palestinians are never even mentioned. It's as if the attacks have become such a part of life that their context is no longer of interest. Am I on the right track? How much of this jibes with your own experience?

I know it seems strange that the Palestinians are not mentioned in the story. You are right. Israelis prefer not to think about the context of the terror. For most of them the Palestinians are those bad people living far away who try to kill Israelis just for the fun of it. (The common belief is that "they are crazy.") It is too complicated to think of the context (the context depends on who you ask) and depressing, too. At the time of the Oslo agreement, things were different.

Israelis had hope and were more willing to be politically active. There was a feeling that peace was near. Since the Second Intifada and the assassination of Rabin, people lost hope in finding a solution or at least understanding the political situation. So they refer to it as if it were some bad destiny that you just try to live with somehow with as little contact as your fortune allows. This is a very sad and dangerous situation. It is also not so comfortable to think about the context. It is difficult for us (Israelis) to stop seeing ourselves as the innocent victims, a role that we love so much and are such experts at being. (To be just, I will mention that historically we are not completely responsible for becoming such experts in being the ultimate victims.) We would have to see that we have responsibility, and then we would feel that we should—God forbid—do something about it! No, we much prefer to go and have coffee with friends, or do some comics.

Forgetting the context is very human. For example, when a beggar asks for some change many people think—"Why can't he work like I do?"—and keep going, ignoring him. They don't think of the whole economic system that put this man on the street. Having said that, it is strange how much Israelis ignore thinking about the Palestinians and the Palestinian problem. There are huge political forces that make sure to detach Palestinians and Arabs from the Jewish Israeli population. It is amazing that in such a small area, where 20 percent of the population are Arabs (not including the Occupied Territories)—and without any laws (causing] it—there is a complete separation between the societies. Mixed marriages are rare. We live in different cities and areas. You can live your whole life and not have one single acquaintance, not to mention friend, who is Arab.

In *Exit Wounds* I tried to reflect this reality, not explain it or say what I think should be—just to show it. As Susan Sontag once said: "Art should tell truth not opinions."

Despite its dark atmosphere and black humor, there is a real sweet streak in Exit Wounds. *The character Numi has a real warmth and innocence about her. I'm curious, by the way, why you made her so tall—her nickname is "the giraffe"—and gangly.*

I knew from the start that my heroine would be different from the average female character in comic books, i.e. extremely beautiful and sexy. Have you noticed that the male hero is always falling in love with the prettiest girl in the comic or the book or the film? The plain girl has to settle on the role of the best friend of the heroine. (The exact rule is: if a man is writing the story, the most beautiful girl is the main female hero; if a woman is writing the story, the most beautiful girl is the friend or the sister of the female hero.) In real life, I see that men are open to a much wider variety of women. There are many reasons we can fall in love with a person.

I tried not to use the clichés of an unattractive girl which are that she is fat, freckled and wears eyeglasses. I made her tall because tall girls are from their early teens being mocked about it and tend to feel awkward with their bodies. By making her taller, it made it something less thinkable that they could have a love affair. And besides, how else would you be able to believe she is capable of catching Koby when he falls?

It seems to me that, at its heart, Exit Wounds *is about how humans connect and, more commonly, how they don't. Do you think people everywhere and in all situations have this problem or is this something that is more prevalent in a society hardened by so much violence?*

I think it's the same everywhere. It is the basic conflict between our desire to be in touch with other people and our desire or capacity to think only about ourselves. Life is difficult everywhere. We all have problems and we think our problems are the most important. We suffer most of all and other people should notice it—the world should notice it! If our lives are tougher, we become less compassionate about other people. It is easier to be nicer to others when you are happy and content. That is true of nations, too, not just of people. Israelis and Palestinians, for example. Each of them thinks they are more miserable and the other should pay for it.

In *Exit Wounds*, I tried to suggest that if we drop the victim role, if we try to stop calculating who did what to whom first, stop waiting for closure, for "justice to be done" (which means we are the just and the others are wrong), if we would be able to do that we might find a way to live happily ever after. It is difficult. We might break our neck or our heart trying, but it is our only hope.

I've noticed that you've done some recent work for the New York Times *website. How did that come about?*

The New York Times got an advance proof of the book from D+Q. Maira Kalman, who had an illustrated column on the *New York Times* website, had just started a six-month break from her column and they suggested I replace her. My column, "Mixed Emotions", was more an illustrated text than comics. I wrote stories about my family, which is quite crazy and funny. (Aren't all families like that?) Family is my favorite subject. It is like a laboratory of human emotions and relationships, concentrated and intense. The worst and the best of human beings reflects in the family. [Editor's Note: In 2008, Rutu's strip "The Murder of the Terminal Patient," was also selected by the *New York Times Magazine* to appear in its "Funny Pages" section. "Mixed Emotions" appeared online at the New York Times in 2007. Drawn & Quarterly has plans to publish both stories sometime in the future.]

Are you beginning to feel that your career is moving to a new level?

Exit Wounds was a big step for me. It reached a much bigger audience than I have ever had. I got attention that my short stories could never achieve. It now allows me to do more writing and more books. But what has made it a big step or a "new level" has been doing the book itself. Writing a long story, drawing a full novel—I thought I could never do it. And the most satisfying thing was to find out I really like to do it. It was a dream for so many years: to write a graphic novel. You know, sometimes when you get your dream you find out you don't really want it any more. But in this case, I really had a great time. I worked like a madwoman, sometimes 14-16 hours a day, and still I was waking each morning with a smile, eager to start the working day.

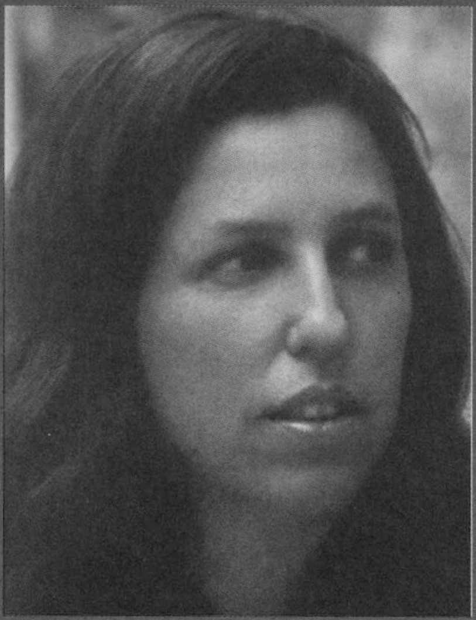
Photo by Ephrat Beloosesky

Rutu Modan was born in Tel-Aviv in 1966. She graduated cum laude from the Bezalel Academy of Art and Design in Jerusalem. After graduating, she began regularly writing and illustrating comic strips and stories for Israel's leading daily newspapers, as well as co-editing the Israeli edition of *MAD* magazine. She is a co-founder of Actus Tragicus, an alternative comic artists collective and independent publishing house. She collaborated with Israeli author Etgar Keret on her first graphic novel, *Nobody Said it Was Going to Be Fun*, an Israeli bestseller.

Modan contributes to magazines and books around the world, including *The New York Times*, *New Yorker* and *Le Monde*, and others; she has had two comics appear in the *New York Times*, "Mixed Emotions" appeared as a comics blog and "The Murder of the Terminal Patient" on the pages of the *New York Times Magazine*. *Exit Wounds* was Modan's first full-length English graphic novel and is the winner of the Eisner Award for Best Graphic Album–New, and was nominated for the Quill Award and the Ignatz Award, and lauded by *Entertainment Weekly* and numerous international publications and websites as the best comic of the year. Modan is the recipient of four Best Illustrated Children's Book Awards from the Israel Museum in Jerusalem, the Young Artist of the Year by the Israel Ministry of Culture, the International Board on Books for Young People in Basel, Switzerland Honor List for Children's book Illustration, and is a chosen artist of the Israel Cultural Excellence Foundation since 2005.

Modan currently lives in Sheffield with her family.